Better
Buildings
for the
Aged

Better Buildings for the Aged

JOSEPH DOUGLAS WEISS, A.I.A.

Hopkinson and Blake, Publishers, New York, N.Y.

Joan Steen Wilentz, Editor
Lura LaBarge, Technical Consultant
William J. Meyerriecks, Designer
Arnold Roston, Art Consultant
Harvey Satenstein, Production Consultant
Ralph J. De Jong, Project Coordinator

ACKNOWLEDGMENTS   Grateful acknowledgment is due many persons whose writings, opinions, and work in the field of caring for the aged influenced and helped the author. Special thanks are extended to:

Mrs. Kallia Bokser, housing specialist for the Citizens Committee on the Aging, Community Council of Greater New York; Mrs. Alice Brophy, Director of the Mayor's Office on the Aging, New York, N. Y.; Jack M. Brown, President of the Jewish Home and Hospital for the Aged, New York, N. Y.; Mrs. Jean W. Carey, Staff Assistant for the Aging, Department of Public Affairs, Community Service Society of New York; Dr. Michael M. Dasco, Professor of Rehabilitation Medicine, New York University Medical Center; Mother M. Bernadette De Lourdes, O. Carm., Carmelite Sisters for the Aged and Infirm, St. Joseph's Manor, Trumbull, Conn.; Dr. Wilma Donohue, Co-chairman of the Division of Gerontology, University of Michigan, Ann Arbor, Mich.; Dr. Alvin I. Goldfarb, consultant on the aged for the New York State Department of Mental Hygiene; James S. Hays, philanthropist and leader in civic affairs; Richard Hill, Jr., Special Assistant on Housing for the Aging, New York State Housing and Finance Agency; George E. Kassabaum, President of the American Institute of Architects; Lawrence Larson, Executive Vice President of Isabella Home, New York, N. Y.; Miss Marie C. McGuire, Commissioner of the Public Housing Administration, Washington, D.C.; Miss Ollie Randall, consultant on the aging for the Ford Foundation; Caspar W. Rittenberg, participant in many programs dealing with problems of the aged; Herbert Shore, Executive Director of the Golden Acres Home for the Aged, Dallas, Tex.; Mrs. Alan V. Tishman, participant in many programs dealing with problems of the aged; David Turteltaub, consultant on the aged for the Council of Jewish Federation and Welfare Funds, New York, N. Y.; Mitchell M. Waife, Executive Director of the Jewish Home and Hospital for the Aged, New York, N. Y.; Morris Zelditch, consultant on housing and institutions for the aged, New York, N, Y.; Dr. Frederick Zeman, Chief of Medical Services of the Jewish Home and Hospital for the Aged, New York, N. Y.

ARCHITECTS REPRESENTED

American

Alan L. Aaron, A.I.A., Lynbrook, N.Y.

Clark R. Ackley, A.I.A., Lansing, Mich.

Ames-Torkelson and Associates, Madison, Wis.

The Architects Collaborative Inc., Cambridge, Mass.

Bellante and Clauss, Philadelphia, Pa.

Joseph Blumenkranz and Associates, New York, N.Y.

Brewer, Skewes & Godbold, Clarksdale, Miss.

Brown & Slemmons, Topeka, Kan.

Coder Taylor Associates, Kenilworth, Ill.

Cohen, Haft & Associates, Silver Spring, Md.

Forrest Coile and Associates, Newport News, Va.

Daniel Comm Associates, Chicago, Ill.

Cross and Adreon, Washington, D.C.

Daverman Associates, Grand Rapids, Mich.

Dietz, Prince & Fischrupp, Mobile, Ala.

Duncombe/Roland/Miller, Santa Rosa, Calif.

Durham-Anderson-Freed, Seattle, Wash.

Eason Anthony McKinnie and Cox, Memphis, Tenn.

Edward Coe Embury, A.I.A., New York, N.Y. and
    G. E. Diekema & Associates, Kalamazoo, Mich.

Eggers and Higgins, New York, N.Y.

Enloe, West & Granade, Inc., Atlanta, Ga.

J. Herschel Fisher-Donald E. Jarvis, Dallas, Tex.

Fletcher-Thompson Inc., Bridgeport, Conn.

Freedman and Clements, Jacksonville, Fla.

Goleman & Rolfe, Houston, Tex.

John Graham and Company, Seattle, Wash.

Gruzen & Partners, New York, N.Y.

Hellmuth, Obata & Kassabaum, Inc., St. Louis, Mo.

Hucker & Pargé, Amarillo, Tex.

Ireland & Associates, Columbus, O.

William D. Jones & Marmon & Mok, San Antonio, Tex.

Kaltenbach Associates and Rennie, Elgin, Ill.

Larson, Playter, Smith, Eau Claire, Wis.

Leonhard and Askew, Bismarck, N.D.

James H. Livingston Associates, Ann Arbor, Mich.

Losch & Haeuser, Milwaukee, Wis.

Manske and Dieckmann, St. Louis, Mo.

Mayne, Oseroff, Van Besien & Associates,
    Arlington, Va.

Mills, Petticord & Mills, Washington, D.C.

Mittelbusher & Tourtelot, Chicago, Ill.

Moon and Iwatsu, Englewood, N.J.

Neumann, Taylor and Schonwald, New York, N.Y.

Neville, Sharp & Simon, Inc., Kansas City, Mo.

Pearce & Pearce, Inc., St. Louis, Mo.

Eleanore Pettersen, A.I.A., Saddle River, N.J.

Mark F. Pfaller Associates, Inc., Milwaukee, Wis.

Gordon Powers, A.I.A., New York, N.Y.

Ratcliff, Slama, Cadwalader, Berkeley, Calif.

Sanzenbacher, Miller, Brigham & Scott, Toledo, O.

Sappenfield-Wiegman-Hall-Associates, Asheville, N.C.

Sargent-Webster-Crenshaw & Folley, Syracuse, N.Y.

Savage & ver Ploeg, West Des Moines, Ia.

W. Thomas Schaardt, A.I.A., Bellmore, N.Y.

Sleight Associates, San Francisco, Calif.

S. C. Smiley & Associates, Minneapolis, Minn.

Smith and Williams, South Pasadena, Calif.

Charles Edward Stade & Associates, Park Ridge, Ill.

Stevens & Wilkinson and Abreu & Robeson, Inc.,
   Atlanta, Ga.

Steward-Skinner Associates, Miami, Fla.

Stewart-Robison-Laffan, Davenport, Ia.

Strange, Inslee & Senefeld, Los Angeles, Calif.

Tibbals, Crumley, Musson, Columbus, O.

Kenneth H. Walijarvi, A.I.A., St. Paul, Minn.

Joseph Douglas Weiss and Associates, New York, N.Y.

E. Todd Wheeler and The Perkins & Will Partnership, Chicago, Ill.

Foreign

Peter Barefoot and Associates, London, England

Anders Tengbom, Stockholm, Sweden

Giorgio Zennaro, Venice, Italy

Guy Bisson, Paris, France

Carl Nyrén, Stockholm, Sweden

Paul Chemetov & Jean Deroche, Paris, France

Wilfried Beck-Erlang, Stuttgart, Germany

Greenspoon Freedlander Plachta & Kryton,
   Montreal, Canada

Marani, Rounthwaite & Dick, Toronto, Canada

Contents

Foreword

Herbert Shore

*Past President,
American Association of
Homes for the Aging*

Housing for America's elderly has just now begun to receive the attention it needs and deserves. Though a start has been made, much work needs to be done in providing a great variety of living arrangements. There are many issues that have been identified—such as integrated or segregated age group housing, high rise or single story, urban or rural, under proprietary or voluntary auspices, free standing or part of a campus or complex of aged facilities services, etc.

We are indeed indebted to Joseph Douglas Weiss for his contributions to this volume. Mr. Weiss is not only a capable and imaginative architect who has designed superior facilities for the elderly, but he combines a distinct social philosophy and practical foundation and approach.

This volume serves several important functions in reviewing the steps to be taken in the proper development of a project. His advice is sound. To the extent that feasibility and need are established and responsible parties are involved and participating there will be a better building that is assured success.

The second part of this book illustrates the broad variety of design and approaches possible. In discussing the particular projects we are able to get a clear understanding and direction of the relationship of the purpose of the project to the way in which this was achieved in the actual delivery of service. There are highlights of design features, site problems, sponsorship, cost. All of this is a veritable gold mine of information that provides guidelines for all future undertakings.

We are embarking on a new era in housing for the elderly. As we enter a period where we will have increasing numbers of older people, in better health, with better education and more adequate financial resources, we have the opportunity to provide a milieu for creative and satisfying living. The history of serving the aging has shown us that the initial need was to provide facilities to care for the indigent and the ill. The community response was a crash program to provide nursing homes and congregate facilities that met the treatment needs. Now, fortunately, we are at the turning point where we can devote our efforts and attention to the prevention of deterioration and breakdown of the elderly.

Newer findings in the social sciences are beginning to teach us the necessity for understanding the use of space, territorial imperatives and privacy. Design embodies more than creature comforts and storage functions but meets subtler needs for satisfying interpersonal relationships. Increasing governmental programs now make it possible for groups to embark on bold new programs of housing for the elderly.

This volume is more than a how-to-do-it manual—more than another collection of already created structures—because it attempts to extract for analysis the major factors that contribute to successful planning, financing, and satisfying living.

Introduction

Joseph Douglas Weiss

This book presents 77 contemporary housing and health facilities for the aged, reflecting social attitudes and architectural concepts current in the United States, Canada, and Europe. Each project serves a special need within a particular environment, for example: a low-income housing project in a midwestern city, a geriatric hospital in Italy, a church-sponsored community for the elderly in Florida, a high-rise apartment house and infirmary in New York.

These approaches are as diverse as the elderly themselves. Individuals over 60 vary as widely as teenagers or middle-aged persons. Those who enjoy reasonably good health do not think of themselves as old. Some, completely self-sufficient, guard their independence proudly. Others have always been dependent—both emotionally and physically—on family, friends, or doctors. Those with greater financial resources have different problems in finding housing and health care than those less privileged. To these differences must be added the normal divergencies of personality, education, upbringing, life styles. If they share anything, it is the feeling that they deserve a choice.

In 1900 the average American could expect to live 47 years, but by 1965 life expectancy rose to 70 years. Each year the proportion of aged in the population grows larger. While the total United States population increased by 18 per cent from 1950 to 1960, those over age 65 increased by 35 per cent and those over 85 increased by 61 per cent.

At present about 12 per cent of the population consists of persons over 60; 10 per cent is over 65. In some countries these proportions are even higher. In England some 12 per cent of the population is over 65, in France 13 per cent, and in Sweden 14 per cent.

The United States now has 7.3 million people over 75 years old, compared with 900,000 in 1900. And those 7.3 million may be expected to grow by 225,000 a year, according to the Administration of Aging of the Social and Rehabilitation Service.

Following is a breakdown of the U.S. figures by age and sex:

	U.S. Population in Millions (1966 figures)		
	Total	Men	Women
Over 60	26.4	11.8	14.6
Over 65	18.5	8.0	10.5
Over 85	1.1	0.4	0.7

Clearly, women dominate each of these population groups, a reversal of the situation at the turn of the century. In 1900 the ratio of women over 60 to men over 60 was 98 to 100, but by 1965 women outnumbered men 129 to 100. By the year 2000, moreover, it is expected that the ratio of women to men in the 60-plus age group will be 148 to 100. At present there are about four times as many widows as widowers. The majority of residents of nursing homes are women, and the older the residents the greater is the likelihood. In some old age homes the ratio is 75 women to 25 men, and the author knows of several where the residents are almost all women.

Statistics like these must be borne in mind when planning or expanding residential or health facilities for the aged. They are the hard facts to which may be added the following characteristics of the life of the elderly:

• A decline in health. Although many people in their nineties enjoy good health and live happy, independent, and active lives, generally people over 60 are in poorer health, are poorer surgical risks, stay in hospitals longer, and need more recovery time, nursing and medical care. A large number of the elderly may have one or more chronic diseases, such as diabetes or heart conditions, but are still able to lead relatively normal, unimpeded lives. An average of 68 per cent of residents of nursing homes (in some old age homes, 80 per cent) are said to be suffering some degree of mental impairment, but the majority of them can function well under most circumstances.

• Insecurity and uprootedness. The loss of a spouse or separation from children who have married and moved away often contribute to insecurity or fear among the elderly. Such feelings may exacerbate physical problems in those whose health is deteriorating. The loss of family contacts may leave even a healthy person without resources for coping with the practical details of living. (In a study of totally ambulatory aged persons having suffered such losses, for example, the Scottish Housing Authority Commission found that 12 per cent could not prepare meals, 15 per cent could not clean house, 16 per cent could not shop, and 27 per cent could not wash clothes.)

Older people, of course, do not like to be uprooted. Only when they feel insecure, abandoned, or ailing will they accept or seek some degree of sheltered care, and still they tend to postpone it. Any form of communal living interferes with individual personal freedom. Even scheduled meal times and ordinary house rules may irk an old person who has been accustomed to independence all his life.

As people get older they lose friends and generally do not make new ones. This attrition among both friends and family deepens the fear of illness and the awareness of death's inevitability. In these circumstances changes in the neighborhood or the death of a friendly news vendor, mailman, or local shopkeeper may contribute to the older person's depression and feeling of isolation.

• A decline in income. The financial situation of the elderly in today's society is complex and it shifts with continuing changes in social welfare legislation. Almost always, however, retirement means a drop in income for the head of the household (although it does not necessarily mean a lowered standard of living since expenditures may also drop). Generally, the retirement years are not "fat," as the following income data for 1963 show:

Income	Percentage of Couples with Head of Household over 65	Percentage of Persons Living Alone
$5,000 or more	25%	5%
Under $5,000	75%	95%
Under $3,000	52%	89%
Under $1,000	7%	35%

That three-fourths of couples and 95 per cent of single persons have incomes under $5,000 is not too surprising, considering that retirement at 65 is now common, if not mandatory, in many fields of employment. In 1900 only 35 per cent of men retired at 65. By 1950 the figure was 55 per cent, and by 1965 it increased to 70 per cent. Of the 28 per cent still in the labor force at age 65, men outnumber women two to one.

The percentage may seem low, but in actual numbers there are almost a million couples (940,000) with incomes over $5,000. More than a third of these, 350,000, have incomes over $10,000. These are the people most likely to move to attractive retirement areas in the south or southwest, or who can afford the more luxurious cooperative apartments, communities for the elderly, and nursing homes. (Examples of all are shown in this book.)

The aggregate income of persons 65 or over is more than $40 billion a year. The following table shows how they spend their money:

	Percentage of Income
Housing and housekeeping	29.1
Food	26.1
Transportation	11.7
Medical services	10.2
Clothing	7.2
Recreation	6.5
Home furnishings and equipment	4.0
Personal care	2.7
Alcohol, tobacco	2.5

Housing is the major item in the elderly person's budget. Indeed the combination of housing, food, and medical services constitutes two-thirds of his total expenses. Formerly it was expected that those too poor to buy these necessities would rely on the philanthropy of church, county home, or hospital ward. Today the picture is changing rapidly. Social Security insurance, old-age pensions, and Medicare and Medicaid laws have provided more dignified and independent ways of meeting expenses and indicate to what extent housing and caring for the aged has become the public concern. Lawrence Larson, director of the Isabella Home in New York City, put it this way: "Everyone in this nursing home is a paying resident. Those who have money pay from their own funds, and those who do not have money pay from funds the government provides for them."

With the growth in public responsibility, social scientists, public officials, civic-minded individuals, and the general public have become increasingly concerned with facilities for the aged. It is obvious that many different sorts of facilities have to be made available, but how many, and what kind? Is the need for residences greater than that for nursing homes or combined nursing-residential buildings? Where should facilities be located? What number of occupants is ideal? Should the aged be segregated? Would they be happier in mixed-age communities than in "retirement ghettos?"

Just as there is no typical elderly person, there is no single answer to each of these questions. Some older people are spry; they want to play golf and live with a mixed-age group. Some are annoyed by children and seek quiet surroundings. In a group of housing developments totalling about 3,000 dwelling units, the writer found that the aged tenants, distributed over many buildings, after a while asked to be moved into one separate building in each development. This was also true in suburban developments of rental apartments. Evidently, some elderly people want to escape from noise, from children running underfoot, from bicycles, roller skates, and boisterous teenagers carrying blaring radios. They want to see life going on and have children around, but at their option and from safer and more serene surroundings.

The key is freedom of choice for those who want and are able to choose. An affluent society can afford such variety. Some Scandinavian societies provide it already. A description of the range of facilities available to the builder and planner follows, together with a discussion of relevant architectural, financial, and administrative details.

TYPES OF FACILITIES

Hospitals for the Aged

Hospitals devoted solely to the care of elderly persons during short- or long-term illness are rare in the United States but quite common in Europe. These geriatric institutions are completely medically oriented (some in Europe also include surgery departments) and place little emphasis on personal social needs and organized activities. Patients are admitted when ill and discharged when cured or able to return home. The physical requirements of these institutions are those of a hospital, except for modifications for the special use of the elderly. A good example is the Ospedale Guistinian in Venice (p. 164).

Extended Care Institutions With Medical Services

These institutions provide care for elderly convalescents after hospitalization. They may be independent buildings or buildings annexed to existing hospitals or nursing homes. The requirements and services for the patients' floors are similar to those of a nursing home. Licensing and accreditation laws define the necessary medical services and hospital associations.

Nursing Homes with Medical Services

Sometimes called "skilled" nursing homes, these facilities provide varying levels of health care for ailing long-term aged residents. The greatest shortage today is in this type of facility, which attempts to provide appropriate health services for residents who range from ambulatory and fairly active to completely bed-ridden. The average age of occupants is now about 83. (Some homes in Kansas report an entrance age of 80 and an average age of 87.)

Old-Age Homes With Infirmaries

This type of institution also cares for long-term residents but can absorb more of those who are relatively well and able to move about on their own. The requirements are essentially the same as those of nursing homes, but a larger proportion of single rooms is needed. Ideally, the buildings should be near businesses, entertainment, churches, and community activities in which the ambulatory residents may take part.

Some flexibility is possible in the floor layout of those parts of the building used by ambulatory or domiciliary residents. Since nursing care is minimal in these areas the number of beds per nursing station may exceed the 40 which is considered the maximum for the infirmary type of nursing home. However, the history of these institutions has convinced the writer that it is a mistake not to plan these buildings to be convertible to full-service nursing homes with 40 or fewer beds per nursing station. Eventually, increasing age and community need will reduce the number of well residents, and more accommodations for the ailing will be needed.

Residential Facilities With Some Organized Services and Care

This type of housing may take several forms: for example, a garden apartment development with a central community facilities building, or a high-rise building in a metropolitan area. Quaker Gardens in Stanton, California (p. 52) and The Four Seasons Home in Columbus, Indiana (p. 94) are examples of garden apartment projects; the Isabella House in New York (p. 120) and the Admiral in Chicago (p. 90) are high-rise buildings.

Isabella House is unique in having separate entrances and elevators for the apartment residents and for the sick who are patients in the nursing home part of the building. Residents have their own independent efficiency or 1-bedroom apartments with kitchenettes where they may prepare breakfast or snacks. They take their main meals in a central dining room. On all floors there is a community living room to encourage socializing, and a community laundry room with lounging space and a good view. Among other communal facilities are an auditorium, a tea shop, and a bar. Nurses are on call in case of emergencies and a physicians' suite in the lobby assures that doctors are also available. (Residents may also call their own doctors.)

The nursing home part of the building consists of a medical clinic floor (to which doctors may refer residents), and three infirmary floors. Should a resident need long-term care he can apply for admittance to the nursing home in the building or to any other home of his choice.

The building has been designed in such a way that four floors currently used for residential purposes can be converted to infirmary floors with only minor alterations. All wiring and piping is built in.

Projects like this have the same physical requirements as any building for the aged. All protective and safety features must be built in as unobtrusively as possible. These buildings offer residents independent living conditions with some sheltered care, plus the availability of an infirmary type of nursing home. This combination of facilities, all under one roof, is one that elderly persons find most reassuring.

Close in concept to the type of facility just described is the "intermediate service" project, a number of which have been built in large cities such as Philadelphia and New York. The design of these buildings emphasizes a full range of services, providing to elderly residents the needed assurance that present and future needs will be met. Intermediate service projects, usually sponsored by existing non-profit nursing homes, provide independent apartments with built in services like those described above. Instead of an infirmary on the premises, however, there is usually an agreement that if a tenant becomes ill the facilities of the sponsoring home are available to him.

For examples of residential facilities with some organized services and care but no infirmary see the Public Housing Project for Senior Citizens in Kansas City, Missouri (p. 68), or Lurie Terrace in Ann Arbor, Michigan (p. 80).

Housing for the Independent Elderly
Apartment buildings or residential units catering to an elderly clientele, but offering no health care or community activities, appeal to some independent and self-sufficient elderly persons.

Retirement Communities
In many parts of the country entire communities have been built for an elderly or retired population. Most of these "Golden Aged Havens," "Retirement Villages," or "Rest Communities," in places like California,

Arizona, or the East Coast, are scarcely 10 years old. Many are eminently successful. Whether or not they will remain so depends on what happens when the resident population gets older and new residents have to be found to replace those who die or who leave for health reasons. While the clientele is comparatively well-to-do, the maintenance and day-to-day problems of home ownership may cause complicated situations. Experienced, well-staffed organizations with adequate social services are needed to cope with this problem.

OWNERSHIP OF HOUSING AND HEALTH FACILITIES

The sponsors of housing and health facilities for the aged may be local, state, or Federal agencies, or non-profit or commercial organizations in the community. Following the terminology used for hospitals, the words "proprietary" and "private" refer to profit-making enterprises, "voluntary" and "non-proprietary" to non-profit enterprises. The latter enjoy some degree of tax exemption. A third category of ownership, the "limited profit corporation," enjoys a lesser degree of tax exemption.

Federal, state and county institutions for the indigent aged are still in existence, but they are changing. The dismal "County Home" of the past is giving way to attractive modern facilities. (See the Menard County Home, p. 173, or the Steuben County Nursing Home, p. 174.)

The elderly in middle or higher income groups are generally cared for in the so-called private pavilions of church-sponsored or other special group-sponsored nursing homes. They are also candidates for the residential facilities planned by non-profit organizations. The intermediate service projects found in big cities serve this group.

Private industry provides all types of housing such as cooperatives, rental housing, retirement villages, proprietary nursing or rest homes, and combinations of these.

SOURCES OF FUNDS

For Construction of Nursing Homes

In most states non-profit nursing homes for the aged must provide their own financing from philanthropic sources. Until very recently this was the traditional (and only) way to obtain capital for building. Now the Federal government will insure 20-year loans for capital investment through the Federal Housing Authority (F.H.A.). Unfortunately, these are at interest and amortization rates which few institutions can afford. Special legislation enables some states to provide long-term mortgage funds at a low rate (about 4 per cent) to cover the complete cost of land, buildings, and equipment. In addition, Federal funds for the construction of non-profit nursing homes are available as a one-time gift under the Hill-Harris Act. These gifts, in limited amounts which vary from state to state, cover only a part of the building cost. (New York State has a financing law covering almost the whole cost of both proprietary and voluntary nursing homes and "health related facilities"—conglomerate living accommodations for the aged.)

Proprietary nursing homes can borrow under the F.H.A. insured-loan program, but they cannot receive Hill-Harris gifts.

For Construction of Residence Facilities

Sponsors of non-profit or limited-profit housing for the elderly can borrow from Federal sources, such as branches of the Housing and Urban Development Department or of the Department of Agriculture (for farm housing). Though the legislation on financing of housing facilities is complicated—with conditions varying according to rent limitations, types of services, and plans—combinations of various legislative provisions can provide funds for almost any situation. In any case, information should be sought directly from the Federal agencies involved.

As in the case of nursing homes, a number of states provide loans to non-profit or limited-profit sponsors of housing for the aged. These loans, backed by bond issues from State Housing Authorities, are available for "cooperative" housing (where residents buy their apartments) and also "congregate" housing (where residents may be assigned to multiple-bed rooms).

In addition to their support of housing projects specifically planned for the aged, most states require that publicly assisted general housing programs set aside some percentage of the total number of dwelling units for the exclusive use of aged tenants.

Hotels converted for housing the aging have been successful in metropolitan areas. They often have the advantage of a good downtown central location. Before conversion is attempted, the local building codes must be checked for restrictive regulations. Federal financing for renovations is available.

Single or row house developments and garden apartments can all be financed through a variety of Federal programs either with insured mortgages or direct loans.

Of course, private funds from banking institutions, insurance companies, and pension funds are always available for any type of building, and many projects—from private houses to retirement villages—are financed in this manner. The usual reasons for seeking private financing are that the borrower is not subject to as many government rules and regulations, he can usually avoid lengthy delays in the processing of permits and loan applications, and he has a greater freedom of action.

For Operating Expenses

The tenant in a residence for the aged may pay rent for his apartment or he may participate in a cooperative or condominium plan. Some plans are of special interest to the more affluent aged. For example, a prospective tenant may buy a dwelling unit with a one-time payment. At the same time he obligates himself to pay a monthly sum for upkeep, medical expenses, services, and food. (Usually hospital expenses are not included.) If the tenant dies, ownership, or part of it, reverts to the sponsoring corporation; the tenant cannot dispose of it by will.

In the case of the intermediate service projects the tenant leases his apartment for the year, his monthly payment covering the rent, meals in the dining room, electricity, linens, cleaning, and health services. If these projects are sponsored by non-profit groups, such as church organizations or labor unions, they may be wholly or partly exempt from real estate taxes. This exemption, combined with lower interest rates, results in a saving of about 18 per cent of the rent in metropolitan areas, an important consideration for the elderly.

Many states today provide reimbursement of the costs of care to indigent patients in nursing homes—even rent in apartments. The bulk of this reimbursement comes from the Federal government through Social Security, Medicare, and Medicaid payments. Some states augment these amounts with welfare funds to bring the reimbursements close, if not equal, to the total cost.

Public housing, using government construction funds and benefiting from subsidies and tax exemptions, charges minimal rents but tenancy is limited to the lowest income groups. Non-profit housing mortgaged with the aid of state or Federal agencies, and helped by some tax exemption, limits tenant incomes, but rents must reflect costs. "Limited-dividend housing," with Federal or state support, is available for middle-income tenants, but again, rents must reflect costs. Cooperative housing sponsored by non-profit groups and financed through Federal or state mortgages must also be self-supporting. The recently passed rent-supplement law cuts across income lines and enables tenants with low incomes to live in middle-income apartments. Federal subsidies supply the rent differential.

PLANNING AND IMPLEMENTATION With the population over 60 increasing twice as fast as that below 60, we need every kind of accommodation for the aged. But some types of facilities are in greater demand than others or are better suited to special areas. Rural, suburban, and urban regions each present different problems. Deciding what kind of facility to build will depend on the quality and availability of social service agencies, medical services, and hospitals. It will also depend on economic and social factors: what sources of funds may be tapped, how abundant are they, how concerned are the local citizens, what per cent of the population is elderly, and how much support can be mustered by the sponsoring organization.

The most pressing needs of the elderly are connected with health care. While hospitals are as indispensable for them as for the population as a whole in the case of acute illness or emergency, the real need of the elderly is for skilled voluntary and proprietary nursing homes. From a practical point of view, the nursing home is far less expensive than a hospital. Most recent estimates put building costs for high standard hospitals in the New York City area (not including cost of land and furnishings) at approximately $45,000 per bed. This compares with approximately $25,000 per bed in high standard nursing homes. Daily maintenance amounts to $90 per patient in hospitals, only $27 a day for nursing home residents.

In spite of these obvious economies, Federal government financing has neglected the skilled nursing home. Available loans are too expensive and outright gifts under the Hill-Harris Act, in most states, are not enough to go around. A low-interest or no-interest long-term loan system to cover capital expenditures, or larger outright gifts, are needed to fill the demand for nursing homes.

How to Start a Project

No matter what kind of facility it plans to build, a non-profit organization should follow certain steps to avoid difficulty. One of the major pitfalls confronting a non-profit organization is the voluntary nature of the organization itself. A group of public-spirited citizens imbued with a social conscience is not enough to insure success. It takes organization and experience.

By comparison, the individual or corporation setting out to build a nursing home or housing for profit has a decided advantage. The routines are well known: a site must be found, finances arranged, permission and approvals obtained, and lawyers and architects consulted. As for such problems as zoning restrictions, building codes, fire and health laws, and local, state, and Federal regulations, a business enterprise is generally better organized to cut red tape and save time than a group of well-meaning volunteers.

These observations are not meant to discourage the non-profit group, but merely to indicate how essential it is to lay the groundwork carefully. Here are some important steps to be followed in starting a project, with allowance for local variations.

1) Organize a group of interested and dedicated citizens. The group may represent a particular church or group of churches, a fraternal order, a labor union, or any combination of non-profit organizations. It is important to have good leadership in the group and more than one individual with the devotion, time, energy, and perseverance to follow through on any decision. (Sponsorship by an established advisory body,

such as the board of trustees of a hospital or an existing nursing home, is often advisable because of its stability and experience.)

2) Establish a realistic aim of what the group wants to accomplish—housing for the elderly, extended care facilities, a nursing home, or any combination of these—based, of course, on an intelligent and thorough examination of community needs.

3) Contact the local, state, and Federal agencies in the area for information regarding procedure, limitation, and financing possibilities. The information should be as specific as possible so the group can compare the advantages of dealing with one agency against another, and can decide which state or Federal financing program would be most useful.

4) Choose a site. If there is suitable land on the grounds of a hospital or nursing home, this may be ideal. Bear in mind that all facilities for the aged should be on level ground in a quiet peaceful neighborhood. Housing or sheltered care facilities should also be near shopping areas in well-balanced neighborhoods. Nursing homes with health facilities should be near hospitals. There should be easy access to public transportation and enough space to allow for parking areas and future expansion. A level, well-planned garden is a great asset.

The elderly want to be part of the community, actively or passively. If they themselves cannot walk, shop, or play, they want to see others doing these things. They do not want to be put out to pasture, out of sight and out of mind.

5) Consult an architect as to the general feasibility of the site. Subsoil conditions and the availability of water, sewer, and other utilities must be checked and foundation complications noted. The use of the site must meet local zoning laws. There may be objections to special housing for the elderly or to a nursing home in an area zoned for "residences." One of the best arguments for the cause of the aged is that they do not load the school population. The site must also be approved by the government agency to which the sponsor applies for financial assistance.

6) Select an attorney. No structure is built in today's society without filling out innumerable forms in compliance with the rules and regulations of a host of local, state, and Federal agencies. A good attorney will have prior experience with these details. He eventually has to organize the non-profit sponsoring corporation, and sometimes he must also establish a separate operating corporation. He must file the appropriate papers governing the corporate structure and establishing its tax-exemption status.

7) Check whether the state requires a certification of need for a nursing home. If such a requirement exists, the permit should be applied for before any commitment is made for the acquisition of land.

8) Prepare a building program. This should state clearly the aims to be achieved and the services to be rendered. The program should include cost analyses of the capital investment for land, building, furnishings, and equipment. Estimates of income and operating expenses should be prepared. The analyses should also include costs during construction (interest, taxes, fees, salaries) and initial expenses (gradual occupancy, renting, promotion, printing, and setting up staff organization).

In some forms of government financing, these related costs are included in the mortgage. All other costs such as purchase and appraisal cost of land, professional fees, test borings, surveys, promotional and renting expenses, vacancy factors, and reserve capital ought to be included in a mortgage in order to relieve the non-profit sponsor of unexpected risks. Some Federal and state government agencies will advance "seed money" to enable non-profit sponsors to pay organization expenses and professional fees. Early application for seed money is essential, as the procedure is lengthy.

Note: Up to this point, some of the obligations and professional work may be on a conditional or optional basis, but at this stage definite steps have to be taken concerning land ownership, architectural fees, and attorney's fees. At some point before final commitments are made—usually at the time the site is approved by the financing government agency—the agency should give the sponsors a written declaration of intention that the project will be accepted subject to approval of final plans.

9) Submit plans for approval. At this stage the architect should have completed a schematic plan of the building and site development. This must be filed with and approved by all agencies involved. A preliminary or "design development" plan follows, with the same approval requirements, and after this the final working drawings and specifications are prepared.

During this period, the attorney must have the corporate structure ready for authoritative action. Closing of the mortgage and the award of the actual building contract can now take place based on plans approved by the appropriate local, state, and Federal authorities, and financing agency.

Some agencies, or some provisions of the law, allow negotiated contracts for construction. In this case, the sponsor can select a contractor and negotiate the contract sum or a guaranteed maximum, within which the contractor's profit and overhead is expressed as a percentage of the cost. Other agencies insist on competitive bidding.

Payments are issued or approved by the governmental agency periodically as they become due during construction. Any contract made by the sponsor in connection with this type of project should be based on payments and approvals as received from the financing agency.

Experience teaches that "it always costs more, and it always takes longer." Any sizeable project usually takes a minimum of three to five years from concept to completion. Building costs escalate about 3½ to 7 per cent per year. It is very difficult to estimate the cost of any project in advance.

All government agencies are helpful. The general public does not realize the number of highly qualified, socially conscious and hard-working people employed in government service. Before contacting them, the sponsors should outline a definite program. Otherwise the advice they receive may be too general to be useful.

Many helpful booklets are published by government agencies explaining how to organize and finance building projects. When action is imminent, however, nothing can take the place of personal contact.

Information can also be obtained from many national and local social service organizations such as the National Council on Aging and from foundations, charitable organizations, community service agencies, study groups, and universities. (The Division of Gerontology of the University of Michigan is a good example.)

Generally the best source to contact about housing problems is the nearest U.S. Housing and Urban Development Department office; for health facilities, the nearest office of the U.S. Department of Health, Education and Welfare (H.E.W.), and the corresponding state organizations.

GENERAL DESIGN CONSIDERATIONS IN PLANNING A SKILLED NURSING HOME

Design data on housing is available in many publications. Since the most specialized building type for the aged is a skilled nursing home we treat it in detail in this and following sections.

A nursing home for the aged should be planned primarily for the benefit of the patients. Efficiency, economy, and administrative convenience are powerful goals, but they should never be emphasized to the detriment of the patient's well-being, personal dignity, or privacy.

How to house patients and provide adequate space for staff and supporting activities is a challenge to the architect. In general he can make a real contribution to the well-being of the patients by providing a cheerful atmosphere; small intimate interiors rather than large institutional spaces, fine vistas, bright colors, and uncluttered communal rooms. It takes approximately 550 square feet of space per patient to provide these accommodations, but this figure varies widely with the standards of care and the funds available.

Single or Double Rooms?
The issue that is most commonly raised in nursing home layouts is whether patients should be housed in single or double rooms. Directors, nurses and social workers usually favor single rooms. Doctors also like single rooms for ambulatory patients, but accept multiple-occupancy rooms for the bedfast sick. Elderly patients generally prefer single rooms.

They have lived independently all their lives and don't want to have to adjust to a strange roommate.

A single room means privacy and a degree of independence, two things which mean a lot to an institutionalized person. Very few will willingly go into a double room, unless they feel insecure alone, or unless the roommate is a good friend or relative.

For higher standards, nursing homes should have about 90 per cent of residents in single rooms, and only the very sick 10 per cent in multiple occupancy rooms. If enough nursing personnel are available, an institution composed entirely of single rooms would be ideal.

But, because it is desirable to avoid the excessively long corridors needed for a floor with only single rooms, the current practice of high-standard nursing homes is to house two-thirds of the residents in single rooms, and one-third in double rooms. With this division a good patients' floor with 40 beds can be designed within an area of 14,500 square feet.

Clusters

Various opinions on patient care influence the basic design of nursing homes. Some medical men feel that patients should be divided into small groups of 10 to 12 patients according to their condition and compatability, and that their rooms be clustered around a common living-dining room. Others feel that these cluster groups should consist of six to eight patients in rooms joined by balconies and a common living room. These groups would then share with other groups the use of occupational therapy and rehabilitation rooms, medical facilities, lounges, and dining rooms.

These arrangements take more space and sometimes result in longer walking distances for nurses and the loss of visibility of corridors from the nursing station. But they do offer the advantage of keeping a group of patients together and thus creating a small homogeneous community within a large institution. Much current research is devoted to the "ecology of aging," "proxemics," and patient care. These studies, while not conclusive, have influenced design concepts. The bibliography refers to several publications on this subject.

Minimum and Maximum Sizes

The size of a nursing home should be at least 50 beds in order to support an economic administrative unit with adequate medical services. More than 250 patients tends to create an impersonal institutional atmosphere. There are exceptions to this; a number of nursing homes render fine service to as many as 500 patients.

Larger nursing homes separate their patients according to their physical and mental condition, usually in five categories: patients requiring minimal care, average care, maximum care, infirmary care, and protective care. The last classification is a unit which cares for the confused, incontinent, or mentally impaired patients. As people live longer this will be a growing problem, and the unit should be planned to house an eventual 20 per cent of the patient population. While a number of medical and psychiatric methods are effective, this type of patient often responds favorably to group activities. Several small separate rooms are needed, each large enough to seat a dozen or more people in a circle. Admission policy will influence the need for a protective care unit.

Preliminary Data

Before accurate figures are available, the planner of a high quality nursing home may assume that the ratio of staff and employees to beds in a nursing home is approximately 1 to 1, (25 per cent male; 75 per cent female).

Also, the planner may consider the following figures as a convenient rule of thumb in estimating necessary floor space:

	Sq. Ft. of Space Per Bed
Food preparation and storage including	
employees' dining areas	20
for Kosher food	27+
Dining area	15 - 20
(In general 20 to 25 per cent of patients eat in their rooms, another 20 to 25 per cent eat in dining rooms on their floor, 50 to 75 per cent are able to go to a central dining room.)	
General areas	50
(Public Health regulations call for a minimum of 50 square feet of space to be allowed per bed for 75 per cent of the total beds for recreation, occupational activities, and patient dining; however it is very difficult to stay within this figure and provide all the space a well-programmed institution needs.)	
Rehabilitation medicine room	5
Occupational therapy room	6
Storage areas for general storage	15
for patients' trunks	4

Recommended ceiling height minimums:

Boiler room	12 feet and over	General areas	8 feet
Kitchen	10 feet and over	Patients' rooms	8 feet
Central laundry	11 feet and over		

The following is a checklist of the services needed in a skilled nursing home with high standards.

Patient Floors

There should be no more than 40 patients to a nursing station.

One single room on each floor near the nursing station should be an isolation room; it must have a connecting bathroom equipped with a bed-pan washer, lavatory and toilet.

Nursing Station

This should be located with a view of the elevator and, if possible, all residents' corridors. The farthest patient's room door should not be more than 100 feet away. The nursing station should have counters, chart spaces, a nurse's call system, and an adjoining workroom and toilet. Complete visibility from the nurses' station is sometimes difficult to achieve; mirrors and closed-circuit television may have to be used.

Rooms

Singles should be a minimum of 11 feet wide with a minimum area of 100 square feet (in some codes, 125).

Double rooms should be a minimum of 12 feet wide with a minimum area of 160 square feet (in some codes, 200).

Multiple rooms should have a minimum area per bed of 80 square feet. Beds should be free-standing and 3 feet apart. Each patient needs a closet 3 feet wide by 2 feet deep, plus a dresser and a chair.

Doors

Room doors should be at least 3 feet 8 inches wide and open inward. Doors to toilets and baths, or to other rooms used by patients, should be 3 feet wide. All toilet doors should open out. Avoid door interferences; avoid saddles. Use swing-clear hospital hinges. Never use double-acting doors.

Toilets

For each room a connecting washroom with toilet is best. A washroom between two rooms and connected to each is next best. If toilet facilities are grouped for common use, allow one toilet for each eight patients. Each room must have a lavatory. The best location of the toilet fixture in the washroom is opposite the door and centered on the door opening. An emergency call button to the nurses' station should be no more than 26 inches from the floor.

Every nursing floor requires a training toilet, minimum 5 feet by 6 feet.

Bathing

In general, patients are not allowed to take baths without supervision, hence there are usually no private baths. Common bathing facilities should be provided: one shower or tub for each 10 patients. Since the ratio of sexes changes, two groups of bathing facilities should be provided, but each shower or bathtub should be placed in a separate enclosed compartment. Tubs should be free on three sides; the rim height is 20½ to 27 inches (this is not standard); showers should be at least 4 feet by 4 feet minimum. Allow space for dressing, for a chair, and for an attendant in all compartments.

Grab Bars
These should be installed at all toilets, tubs, and showers. Use heavy-duty bars, through-bolted, precisely placed for easy, safe reach. Bars should have 2⅝ inches clear space from wall.

Mirrors and Shelves
Mirrors should be low enough for wheelchair users, high enough for a standing man. All shelves should be stainless steel or plastic.

Hardware
Round knobs cannot be used by arthritics; use lever handles or elliptical shapes.

Utility Rooms
These should be centrally located. The minimum size for the clean utility room should be 8 feet by 11 feet. The same size is adequate for the soiled utility room, but some rooms may be eliminated or reduced in size under some codes.

Laundry Chute
If a chute is used, it should be centrally located and equipped with an interlocking system so it can be opened on only one floor at a time.

Treatment Room
This should be near the nurses' station with a minimum width of 9 feet, and minimum area of 100 square feet.

Stretcher Closet
This should be 2 feet 8 inches wide and 7 feet deep.

Wheelchair Storage
Generally not more than 5 chairs are stored on a 40-bed floor, but each type of patients' floor is different.

Linen Closet
The best system is a tiered, movable-rack storage; the entire rack is changed as needed. This requires a closet with a door opening 7 feet wide (open on complete width). The closet should be 4 feet deep.

Janitor's Closet
Minimum dimensions should be 4 feet by 6 feet (cleaning machinery is getting bigger).

Nourishment Station

This is a ready-made cabinet, containing a counter, sink, refrigerator, crushed-ice maker, two electric burners, and upper and lower cabinet space. It provides light snacks, drinks, and refreshments. The width is 4 feet to 6 feet. Allow a minimum of two feet of space in front of the unit.

Day Room, Sitting Room

Allow a minimum of 18 square feet for 75 per cent of the number of patients on the floor.

Dining Space

If there is a dining space on each floor allow a minimum of 18 square feet per patient on floor. If there is a central dining room, allow a minimum of 18 square feet of dining space for 50 per cent of the patients, but on each floor plan a dining space for 25 per cent of the patients. It is not practical to use the day room space for dining as well.

Food Service

The present tendency is to have a dining room on each floor or for each group of patients on a nursing station, thus avoiding a large institutional dining room.

Food is served either "family style," in which it is sent from the kitchen in bulk containers to floor pantries, or by "tray service," in which all food is placed on trays in the kitchen and sent by specially heated and cooled carts to the various floors. These carts can be plugged into electric outlets on each floor to keep food hot and cold. Many types of food carts are used, some with pre-heated palettes instead of direct heating elements.

Generally, a cart will hold about 20 trays. Each tray may be marked for special diets by the dietician. A vertical conveyor system can be used for more efficient service. If this is used, it is advisable to use an up, a down, and a reversible conveyor. When these systems are used, no pantry is needed on any floor except in kosher food service.

Corridors

These must be 8 feet wide; 10 feet in front of elevators. They should have a stair or exit at each end, with no room door at a dead end. Some codes allow a 30-foot dead end. There should be handrails on both sides. Electric outlets should be provided for floor cleaning and polishing equipment, for heating portable food carts, and for portable X-ray equipment. Provide fire extinguisher and fire-alarm equipment. Night lights and emergency lights are also needed in case of power failure. Some building codes require smoke-barrier doors in lengthy corridors.

Drinking Fountain

There should be one fountain on each nursing station floor, with two heights of faucets for standing and wheelchair use.

Public Telephone

Telephones, placed in alcoves 4 feet wide by 3 feet deep, should be accessible to wheelchair and ambulatory patients.

Special Provisions

Oxygen piped to some rooms or to each room is an increasing requirement. Air-suction piping is required in some institutions. Public-address systems, audio-visual nurse's call, communication and monitoring system, and television wiring and master antenna systems are now commonly used. If air-conditioning is installed, individual room temperature control is essential. Sprinkler protection is necessary in storage rooms and other spaces where local regulations call for it. Some codes require 100 per cent sprinkler protection. Telephone connections in rooms are optional.

The Patient's Room

The long-term patient's room is his home. Mere efficiency of physical layout is not enough; the room should have a spacious feeling and an uncluttered, cheerful atmosphere with places for pictures, vases, and mementos. There should be a minimum of 4 feet 6 inches between the outside wall or radiator to the bed, and at least 3 feet clear between any bed and wall and, if possible, beyond any door swing. There should be ample room to pull out dresser drawers and open closet or washroom doors without interfering with the door. Every patient will need space for a dresser and a comfortable armchair. In multiple rooms bed enclosure curtains should be provided.

Windows

All windows should be equipped with a safety stop, to limit the opening to less than 10 inches. A casement or hopper window extending beyond the inside sill line should not be used. Low sills are desirable and so are large window areas, but glare must be controlled by Venetian blinds or other type of adjustable shades.

Flooring and Levels

Non-slip flooring without door saddles should be used and carefully maintained. Carpeting has been tried successfully, even though it makes "walkers" somewhat difficult to use. Floors should be level. If ramps must be used, they should have handrails and not exceed a 1 foot rise in 12 feet.

Elevators

Elevators must be self-leveling and each car should contain a telephone and a folding seat. Old people move more slowly, so automatic door closers must be correspondingly adjusted; also the stops at each floor will be longer. Cars should be a minimum of 5 feet, 4 inches wide by 8 feet deep, and the door opening 3 feet 10 inches wide. The number of elevators required is usually spelled out in codes.

Exits from Rooms

If patients' rooms are on the ground floor, exits to the garden from patients' rooms should be planned with caution. Such exits are difficult to control and patients may wander away.

Heat and Hot Water

Any hot-water line supplying fixtures used by patients must be controlled to a maximum temperature of 110 degrees F. Heat in rooms should be individually controlled and designed for a minimum of 75 degrees F. Air-conditioning has to be separately controlled in each patient's room.

Lighting

Old people need high illumination levels without glare. At beds, direct and indirect lighting fixtures should be used so that the patient can read by direct light, sitting up or lying down in bed. The indirect light should be controllable both from the bed and from a switch at the door. All convenience outlets should be a minimum of 18 inches above the floor. An outlet for the doctor's examination light should be provided at the bed or as part of the bedlight fixture.

Sound Protection

In any area where noise originates, such as a pantry, utility room, the nurses' station, and corridors, acoustical ceilings are recommended. Use quiet toilets, flushers, and fans. Avoid loud paging systems. Place radios and television sets away from walls between patients' rooms.

Medical Department

This should include a waiting room; an office for a medical secretary and records; doctors' rooms; medical library; examination rooms with toilets and dressing rooms; rooms for the chief nurse, staff directors of nurses and nurses' training; dental, optometry, podiatry, E.K.G. facilities; and an X-ray department with equipment rooms, a dressing room, a film-viewing room and a darkroom. There should also be space for laboratories, a pharmacy, a central sterilization and supply unit, bulk-drug supplies, and oxygen storage.

Group Medical Activity Space

This includes occupational therapy, rehabilitation medicine, and special therapy rooms such as for hearing and speech defects. In some cases, a sheltered workshop is needed. In a sheltered workshop residents perform light work such as stuffing envelopes on a contract basis which provides them with some income and helps build morale.

Recreation and Personal-Service Spaces

An auditorium with a projection room and a stage, a chapel, library, sundries store, beauty and barber shops, and coffee shop or snack bar come under this category. Outdoor garden and recreation areas are important and should be provided.

One or more lounges separated from the entrance lobby are desirable, preferably with a view of a garden or a busy street. A family room, where residents can meet their children or grandchildren, also is desirable.

Administration
In addition to the director's room, there will be a need for a waiting room, general office space with an information window opening onto the waiting room and the entrance lobby, a vault, an office machine room, space for record storage, social service rooms, and a board or meeting room.

Service Spaces
The list includes the boiler room; emergency generator, air-conditioning compressor, and fan room; incinerator room; maintenance and supply shops for steam-fitter, plumber, and electrician; a paint shop; a furniture-repair shop; space for electric and telephone gear; and a meter room. Also, the housekeeper's office and storage spaces; linen storage; central laundry with institutional equipment and sometimes laundromat-type units; paper-goods storage; kitchen; space for food storage, refrigeration, food preparation, dishwashing, cart-washing, cart storage and garbage refrigeration.

Cafeterias for staff and employee dining are also needed, as well as locker rooms, showers and restrooms for nurses, medical staff, male and female employees. Also needed are spaces for the residents' trunk storage; a morgue; a loading and delivery deck; a checker's office; a personnel entrance, and an ambulance entrance.

Note on Wheelchairs
Wheelchairs are able to pass through a three foot opening in a straight line. A person seated in a wheelchair is able to reach an object 4 feet high and 1½ feet to the side. The damage done by wheelchairs, attachments, and cleaning devices to door bucks and walls is approximately 14 to 16 inches above the floor. Some institutions erect a guard rail at this height in the corridors. Stainless steel corner guards should be placed at all important outside corners in corridors.

SOME FINAL OBSERVATIONS

Architects and social planners can learn from existing designs, but new ideas must be tried in anticipation of changes which will affect the aging population in the years to come. For one, the number of women among the elderly will increase; for another, pressure from younger population groups and from technological advances will accelerate the trend toward mandatory and earlier retirement. The architect's imagination is further challenged by the varied need, wishes and resources of the aged.

Differences in interest or hobbies among residents must be taken into consideration. Residents of an elderly community like Sun City, Arizona, apparently are not as interested in attending lectures or concerts as they are in playing cards or golf. In New York City, on the other hand, university-level classes are led and eagerly attended by elderly persons.

Society must attack the problem of housing and care for the aged not only by studying how best to meet the current needs of the elderly, but by preparing the middle-aged working population for retirement. The new science of "social gerontology" is developing around this problem.

For some persons, retirement may be a disturbing emotional experience. Sudden freedom from the routine of work and purposeful activity can be dull and depressing. A man may feel stripped of his feeling of achievement unless he has other outlets for energy and self fulfillment. If people could be prepared to cultivate broader cultural and recreational interests, they might need a very different kind of retirement housing and environment than exists today.

Serious studies in the United States and in Europe would indicate what kinds of accommodations will have to be provided. Such studies might best be undertaken by elderly persons themselves, to avoid the pre-conceived notions held by many young researchers in the field of social planning.

The future development of housing and health care for the aging is closely connected with the availability of organized services right in the community. The noted geriatrician Dr. Frederick Zeman of the Jewish Home and Hospital for Aged in New York City says that "medical solutions cure only half of a person." Community recreational, social, and health services can provide elderly people with an opportunity for constructive use of their free time, greater feelings of security, and the knowledge that friendly help is available in case of need, making housing problems much simpler. With such services there will be less need for sheltered care or other types of conglomerate living arrangement and institutionalization.

Community service should provide medical care, home nurses, the loan of medical equipment such as wheelchairs, bedpans, and rubber sheets, and the delivery of medicine. It should include meal distribution by "meals on wheels," eating clubs, or pick-up, take-home meals, and it can provide help in housekeeping, washing, cooking, dressing, and personal hygiene. Social visiting services and emergency telephone contacts should also be part of the program.

All these could be provided from activity centers. Indeed, many of these services are available to the elderly in some Scandinavian countries. In the United States they are being tested in some areas.

The growing field of the "boarding-out" approach should also be investigated. Welfare and social service agencies place an elderly person with a young family and pay his board; in turn, the children of the family acquire a grandparent who has time to enjoy life with them. This arrangement is meeting with success in many communities. Both the younger family and the elderly boarder benefit from the arrangement.

It is a fundamental principle that the elderly should live independent lives in their homes or apartments as long as possible. Such dwelling units can, of course, be part of a new housing project. If organized services are incorporated into such a project, a sophisticated balance must be achieved lest the elderly develop an unhealthy dependency which would virtually institutionalize them.

Society must make available educational, recreational, social, and cultural opportunities to prevent or forestall the decline to passivity and dependence. There should be sufficient preventive medical measures as well as a full range of health facilities, especially geriatric hospitals and after-care accommodations. The aging must have the means of living decently when in good health and have a feeling of security for the future. They should be assured that there are adequate facilities and intelligent, accessible help in the event of illness.

All this is attainable within the means of American society and can be considered a right of our aging men and women. We are far from catching up with this goal and old people do not have the time to wait.

Residential Facilities

The buildings described in this section are designed primarily for elderly persons in reasonably good health. In some cases a small infirmary or even a modest-sized nursing facility is included on the premises, but the number of dwelling units dominates the number of nursing facility beds. Within this category of housing for the elderly there are some projects which offer very independent living conditions, such as separate houses or garden apartments with full kitchens, and others which provide a hotel-like atmosphere which offer some degree of sheltered care. The projects are arranged in order from low to high-rise buildings, the latter more often including the larger nursing care units.

NOTE: Cost figures were supplied by the architect and refer to the year of construction. Unless otherwise noted the total figure reflects basic construction cost plus electrical, mechanical, and plumbing charges and the cost of any built-in or stationary fixtures. The total also includes the architectural and engineering fees. It does not include the cost of land, site development, landscaping, or movable furnishings.

AN EXPLANATION OF ABBREVIATIONS

AB	assisted bath	OT	occupational therapy
ACT	activity room	P	pantry (serving)
AD	admission	PH	pharmacy
APT	apartment	PT	physical therapy
AUD	auditorium	R	receptionist
B	bath	REC	recreation
BALC	balcony	RM	room
BLDG	building	S	staff
BP	bedpans	SD	staff dining
BR	bedroom	SERV	service
BRB	barber shop	SERV ENT	service entrance
C	closet	SEW	sewing
CENT	central	SL	sleeping area
CL	clean linen	SOC SERV	social service
CONF	conference	SP BR	special bedroom
CONS	consultation	SUN	sun room or solarium
CU	clean utility	SUP	supply
D	dining	ST	storage
DAY	day room	T	toilet
DL	dirty linen	TH	therapy
DU	dirty utility	TR	treatment
E	employee's	TV	television
ED	employee's dining	U	utility
EFF	efficiency apartment	V	vault
ENT	entrance	VEST	vestibule
EQ		VOL	volunteer
EQUIP	equipment	W	women's
EX	examination	WA	waiting room
FLEX	flexible	WL	women's lockers
GCW	garbage can wash	WS	wheelchair storage
GEN	general		
HT	hydrotherapy		
INCIN	incinerator		
INFO	information		
ISO	isolation		
J	janitor		
K	kitchen		
L	linen		
LAB	laboratory		
LAU	laundry		
LAV	lavatory		
LGE	lounge		
LIB	library		
LIV	living room or area		
M	men's		
MAINT	maintenance		
MD	doctor		
MEC	mechanical		
MED	medicine preparation		
ML	men's lockers		
N	nurse		
NL	nurses' lockers		
NS	nurses' station		
NT	nurses' toilet		
O	office		
OBS	observation room		

MT. SAN ANTONIO GARDEN COTTAGES
Claremont, California

ARCHITECT
Smith and Williams
South Pasadena, California

PURPOSE
Residential

CAPACITY
60 dwelling units

COST
$990,718

SPONSOR
Congregational Homes, Inc.

Life for the elderly in this southern California community simulates living in a small suburb with tree-lined streets and 1-story cottages—with one exception. There are no automobiles. By restricting internal transportation to electric carts only, not only did the architects eliminate noise and hazards, but they were also able to place the 1- and 2-person units pleasantly on the 9-acre site, avoiding the rigid per-pendicularity of streets and avenues.

Each of the homes is designed for the convenience of convalescent or wheelchair patients. All bedrooms are equipped with swinging or sliding doors so that a single bed may be moved out onto the adjacent patio.

The homes are constructed of redwood plywood, exposed wood beams, and sloping plaster ceilings. Floors are concrete slab on grade. Outside storage units for patio and barbecue equipment are connected to the house by a canopy. Each cottage is furnished with draperies and carpeting.

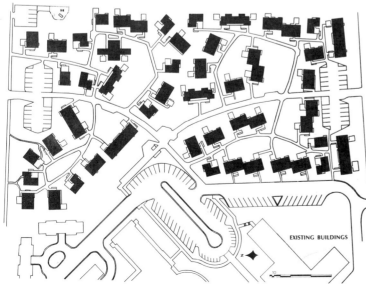

EXISTING BUILDINGS

SITE PLAN

continued

1

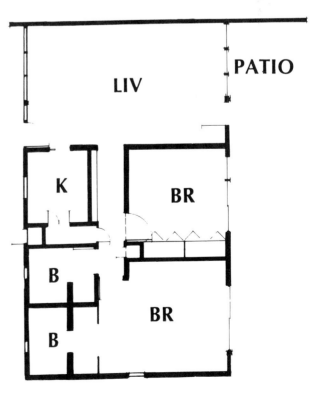

1 Patio and interiors (above) relate to
floor plan shown

TYPICAL TWO BEDROOM UNIT

PATIO

LIV

K

BR

B

B

BR

LUTHERAN SENIOR CITY
Columbus, Ohio

ARCHITECT
Tibbals, Crumley, Musson
Columbus, Ohio

PURPOSE
Residential with infirmary

CAPACITY
310 residents
24-bed nursing facility

COST
$2,251,024

SPONSOR
Lutheran Welfare League of Central Ohio

A dozen or so long houses—looking like modern versions of the Indian longhouse prototype—form the basic building units of a residential and nursing development sponsored by the Lutheran congregations in the Columbus area. The residential buildings, each with 10 or more single rooms, are arranged in groups of two or three around landscaped courtyards. A number of rooms facing the courts have sliding doors opening outside. In addition to the individual dwelling units, each courtyard-and-building complex contains three sitting rooms, one of which is equipped with a kitchenette.

At the center of the rectangular site is a community building housing offices, the main lounge and chapel, beauty and barber shops, dining, recreation and crafts rooms, and a library. To reach the main building residents can use an enclosed ramp, which, since it affords a view of all the courtyards, has become a favorite promenade place.

The site is on a bluff which drops down to a meadow bordered by a stream. The drop is sufficient to permit

View of chapel with stream in foreground

a lower level of rooms which face the stream and provide a handsome view of the city beyond. Several 2-person suites located at this level are available for well residents who prefer a more removed location.

In addition to the residential and community facilities, the development also contains a 24-bed nursing section and adjacent to it, an area which can readily be converted from single units for well persons to 2-bed rooms for the sick.

The construction is typical of

residential buildings in the area. Exterior walls are brick and block. Roofs are wood, finished in asphalt shingles. (The roof of the main building uses laminated wood trusses with an insulating board deck; elsewhere light wood trusses are used.)

Interior walls are dry-wall with small areas of exposed brick. Most floors are tiled; carpeting is used in some areas.

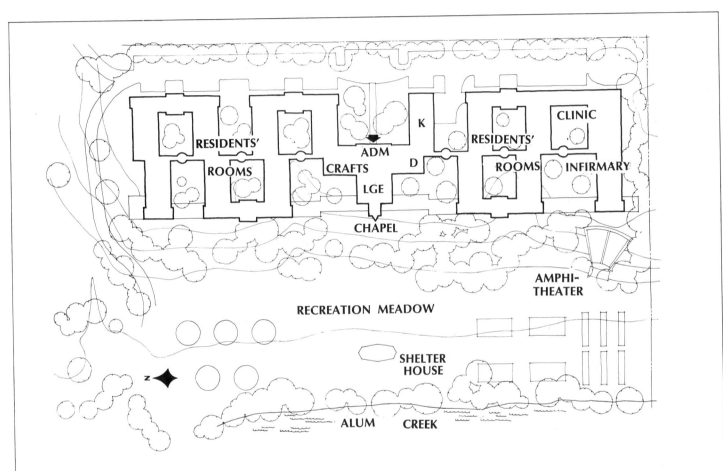

SITE PLAN

continued

1

2

1 Main entrance
2 Sitting room entrance
3 Lounge and chapel

3

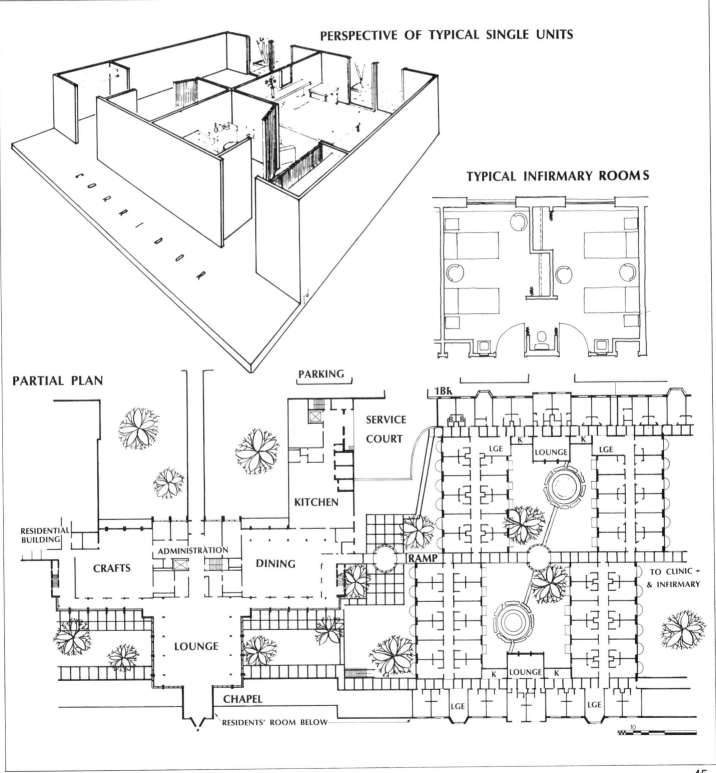

PERSPECTIVE OF TYPICAL SINGLE UNITS

C O R R I D O R

TYPICAL INFIRMARY ROOMS

PARTIAL PLAN

PARKING

SERVICE
COURT

KITCHEN

RESIDENTIAL
BUILDING

ADMINISTRATION

CRAFTS

DINING

1Bk

B B

LGE   LOUNGE   LGE

RAMP

TO CLINIC +
& INFIRMARY

LOUNGE

CHAPEL

RESIDENTS' ROOM BELOW

K   LOUNGE   K

LGE   LGE

45

ROHLFF'S MANOR
Napa, California

ARCHITECT
Sleight Associates
San Francisco, California

PURPOSE
Residential

CAPACITY
100 dwelling units

COST
$1,022,000 (including landscaping; excluding fees)

SPONSOR
Lutheran Church

This garden apartment community in central California was planned for elderly persons of limited income. Rents for the efficiency, 1- and 2-bedroom units range from $78 to $105 a month. The church-sponsored project, financed by federal funds through the Housing and Urban Development Department, is an example of what can be done with a limited budget by keeping the design simple and paying careful attention to details.

To begin with the architects chose a site near shops and public transportation. Local building requirements allowed a density of only six units per acre, so a large 17-acre tract was acquired. The 1-story buildings were then arranged in clusters around landscaped courtyards and lanes.

These sub-complexes have the added social value of allowing residents to identify with small groups as well as with the entire complex. Roadways on the site are owned by the project. Thus curbs could be eliminated and through-traffic discouraged. Utilities have been placed underground and even garbage cans sunk to eliminate any unsightliness.

1 Covered arbor and court
2 Front yards
3 Rear yards

SITE PLAN

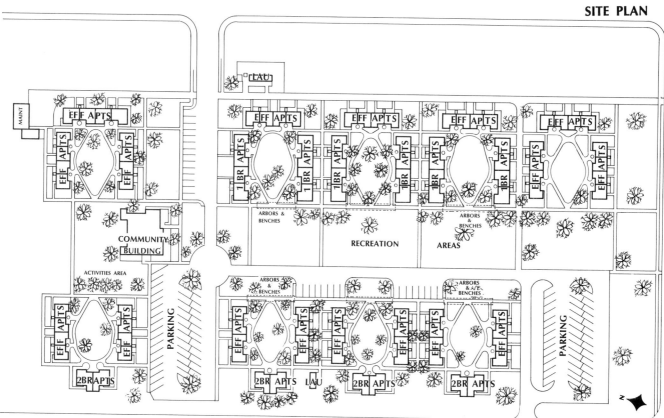

The majority of buildings are E-shapes, each containing four units. The larger 2-bedroom units are paired in smaller buildings along the shorter sides of the landscaped courts. The buildings are insulated and all apartments have kitchens. Bathrooms have wide-rim tubs and grab bars. All doors are three feet wide to accommodate wheelchairs.

In addition to the residential units, there is also a community building on the property containing a library, meeting hall, craft room, and offices. There are two laundry buildings, a maintenance building, and parking areas.

Residential construction materials were used throughout. Floors are concrete slab on grade covered with carpeting or tile. Walls are wood stud with stucco exteriors and dry-wall interiors. Roof construction utilizes prefabricated trusses and cedar shakes. Windows are sliding aluminum. Interior finishing included laminated-plastic-faced cabinets and countertops in kitchens and bathrooms. (This will eliminate re-painting and thus reduce maintenance costs.) Heating is electric.

TYPICAL FLOOR PLAN

ELEVATION

2   3

BLANTON GARDENS
Dallas, Texas

ARCHITECT
Fisher & Jarvis
Dallas, Texas

PURPOSE
Residential

CAPACITY
105 dwelling units

COST
$1,830,930

SPONSOR
C. C. Young Memorial Home (non-profit)

Blanton Gardens is a group of five modern 1-story buildings adjoining a large public park and White Rock Lake in Dallas. It was built to expand the facilities of the C. C. Young Memorial Home across town, a residential and infirmary facility with accommodations for 52 women. The idea for the home dates back to 1919 when a Methodist minister, the Rev. C. C. Young, resigned his pastorate to raise money for "elderly orphans." The new complex, named after one of the best known trustees of the home, can accommodate 128 men and women.

Four of the new buildings are residential, primarily consisting of single bedroom and patio units with central dining areas, lounges, and solariums. Half of one building is devoted to apartments with kitchens for married couples. Covered walkways provide convenient passage from building to building. The fifth building, for communal activities, houses a chapel, a snack bar operated by the residents, recreational facilities, library, beauty shop, barber shop, and physical and occupational therapy rooms. These facilities are open to other elderly

1

2

3

members of the community in addition to residents. Weaving and ceramics are among the activities offered.

The buildings are of reinforced concrete and steel construction with 10-inch masonry cavity walls. The roof structure uses laminated wood beams and steel bulb tees to carry a composition roof deck which also serves as the ceiling. Roofing is built-up asphalt and exposed shale.

1 Aerial view

2 Dining room in residential building with garden court beyond

3 Lounge with double fireplace in residential building

RESIDENTIAL UNIT WITH ONE BEDROOM APTS

COMMUNITY ACTIVITY CENTER

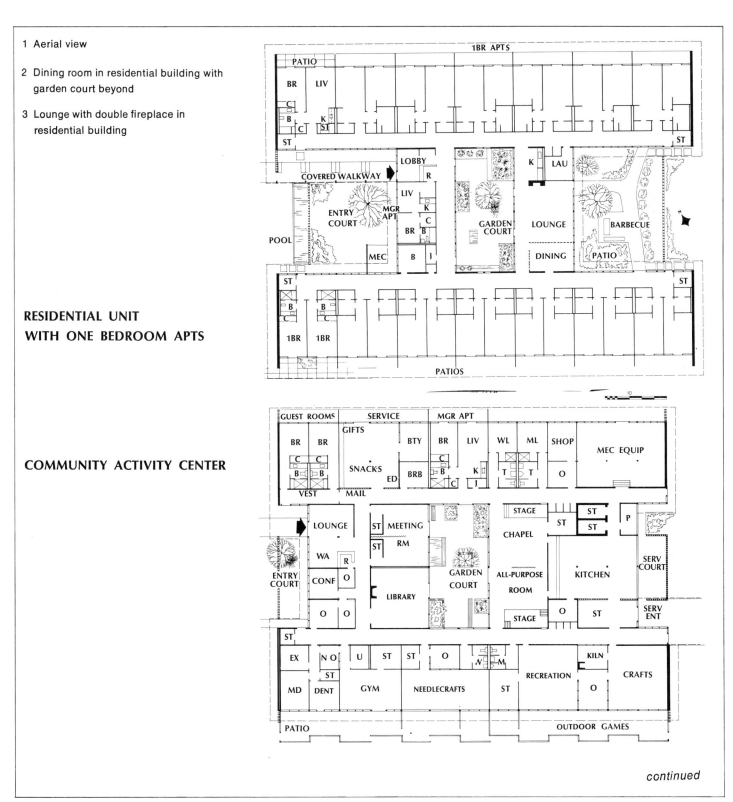

continued

1 Residence entry

2 Weaving in needlecrafts room

3 Chapel (part of all-purpose room)

4 Snack bar

GOLDEN AGE GARDEN COMMUNITY
Valley Stream, New York

ARCHITECT
W. Thomas Schaardt, A.I.A.
Bellmore, New York

PURPOSE
Residential

CAPACITY
120 dwelling units

COST
$1,516,930

SPONSOR
Town of Hempstead Housing Authority

Asked by the local housing authority to design a low-income residential development for the elderly, a Long Island architect conceived of a series of 2-story peaked roof buildings occupying a square block near a major shopping center. The buildings blend with the suburban environment and reflect the architect's belief in the importance of a series of interwoven spaces for an elderly population.

The individual in his own apartment represents the most private space. The six or eight persons or couples in the building form the next grouping, which, together with those in adjacent buildings, constitute a small neighborhood within the complex itself. Solariums and laundry rooms in each building, fountains and pools, walks and seating areas throughout the site, and finally a community building for the development as a whole, are further ways of creating spatial environments where residents can meet and mingle. The community building houses a gallery for the display of arts and crafts, offices, and a variety of social and recreational rooms. Concerts and plays can be given in a small amphitheater in front of this building.

The location of the development near a shopping center insures that the residents need not feel isolated and even offers the potential of part-time employment. Also within walking distance are churches, other business offices or plants, recreational facilities, and transportation systems.

The buildings incorporate several design features of importance to the elderly. There is an emergency alarm system in every unit to alert other dwellers if a resident is in distress. Electric switches and outlets have been placed at convenient heights, and bathrooms are equipped with grab bars and provided with non-skid tubs.

The wood-framed buildings have masonry exterior bearing walls, aluminum double-hung windows and asphalt shingled roofs.

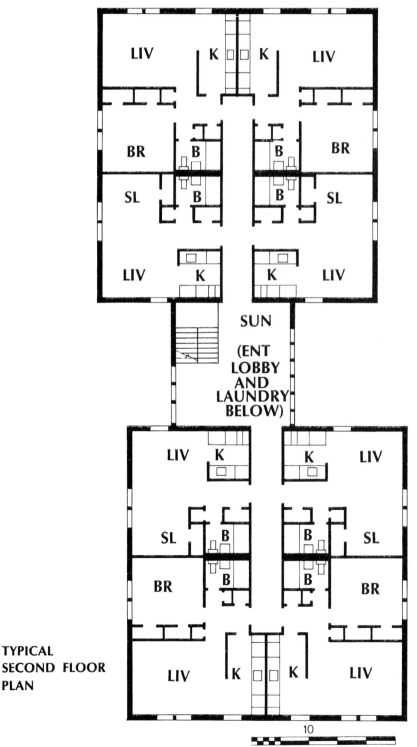

TYPICAL SECOND FLOOR PLAN

10

QUAKER GARDENS
Stanton, California

ARCHITECT
Strange, Inslee & Senefeld
Los Angeles, California

PURPOSE
Residential with infirmary

CAPACITY
171 dwelling units
18-bed infirmary

COST
$2,908,304

SPONSOR
The Friends Churches of California

A retirement community primarily for the healthy has been built by the Friends Churches of California on a 7-acre site 25 miles south of Los Angeles. In an area whose climate and tourist attractions have already attracted a number of the elderly, the architects have designed a building complex that includes residences and communal structures, an infirmary, chapel, and outdoor facilities to accommodate approximately 200 persons.

Single units, suites, and semi-suites are available in two 3-story buildings.

Each of these units has either a patio or deck and includes wall-to-wall carpeting and floor-to-ceiling draperies. Sun-retardant screens, soundproofing, and individual heating and cooling controls are also provided. Residents furnish their own rooms and pay a monthly fee to cover the cost of maid service, meals, linens, telephone, utilities, and a comprehensive medical and surgical program. A utility room on each floor is available for personal laundry services, and there is a locked storage space in the basement for each unit.

1

1 Covered walkway from a residential building to the central dining and lounge building

2 The chapel. Small entrance at right leads to a private meditation chapel

2

One wing in the residential area has been reserved for tenants who are not ill but who may need assistance in dressing. Occasionally they may want meals brought in instead of taking them in the central dining room. Even these residents are encouraged to be independent and active, however. A large main lounge and several smaller lounges with snack bars have been provided as well as arts, crafts, hobby and game rooms, and a library. Outdoor activities include shuffleboard courts and bowling and putting greens. There are also walks and sitting areas by fountains, pools, and gardens. Residents are encouraged to make personal use of a small meditation chapel. The larger chapel is used for religious and cultural programs.

An infirmary on the grounds and two County hospitals are at the disposal of residents needing medical attention. All rooms in the complex are equipped with a 24-hour intercom system should an emergency arise. Other safety or convenience features incorporated are grips and grab bars in bathrooms, forearm rests in toilets, non-skid floors, night lights, and comfortably placed wall outlets. Doors are wide enough to accommodate wheelchairs, and thresholds, stairs, and ramps have been eliminated to reduce accidents. Other amenities include a beauty and barber shop, and a canteen and playground where grandparents can treat children to a soda or give them a place to play. The adult dining room in the communal building has a number of alcoves for small family or private parties.

continued

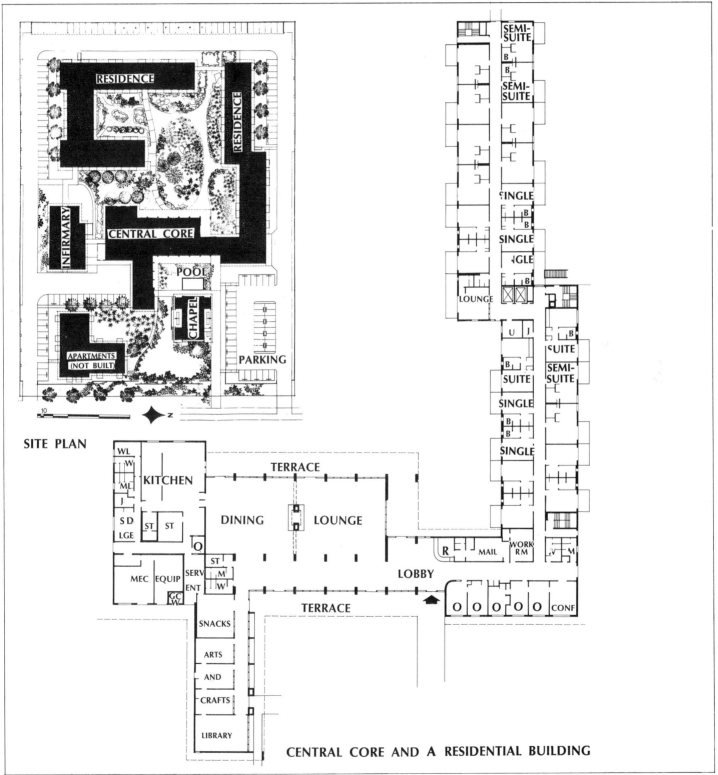

SITE PLAN

CENTRAL CORE AND A RESIDENTIAL BUILDING

QUAKER GARDENS

The 1- and 3-story buildings that make up the complex are concrete with masonry exteriors. Built-up roofing covers poured gypsum roof decks. Interior walls are high density thin set plastic over gypsum board on metal studs. Floors are carpeted concrete. A large covered patio and a reflecting pool surrounded by sub-tropical plantings dramatize the entranceway.

1

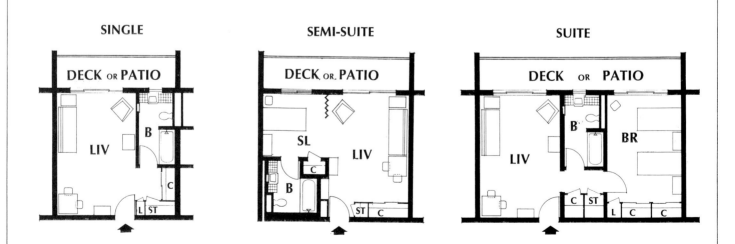

SINGLE   SEMI-SUITE   SUITE

2

1 Main lounge in communal building with
dining room in background

2 Shuffleboard courts next to a residential
building

OUR LADY OF THE SNOWS
Belleville, Illinois

ARCHITECT
Hellmuth, Obata & Kassabaum, Inc.
St. Louis, Missouri

PURPOSE
Residential

CAPACITY
150 dwelling units

COST
$4,800,000

SPONSOR
The Oblate Fathers

The apartment community of Our Lady of the Snows was designed with a well and independent elderly population in mind. The clean lines of the buildings accented by the use of masonry or board-formed concrete, and the interior layouts with their emphasis on private, semi-private, and public spaces, provide a variety of activities and social settings for the residents, all within a modern frame.

The community's 150 dwelling units (24 of which may be divided into smaller apartments) are housed in a series of 1-story buildings and one 5-story building on an 11-acre site just outside Belleville, Illinois. The property is part of The Shrine of Our Lady of the Snows.

The individual apartments in the low-rise units open onto a series of enclosed corridors. These connect the buildings of the complex and provide views of the public facilities such as the dining and recreational areas, the chapel, a meeting hall, and a country store. Small lounges off the corridors can be used for informal

1 Chapel
2 Chapel connected to public buildings at left. Dining hall is at right
3 Board-formed concrete is used above the entrance to the 5-story building
4 Residential units with 5-story building in background

gatherings and leisure activities.

Residents are offered a choice of efficiency apartments or 1- and 2-bedroom units. One 2-bedroom layout includes two baths: This is the unit which can be converted to smaller apartments should the need arise. The apartments have conveniently placed outlets and controls, and there are at least two intercom locations in each so that help may be summoned in the case of an emergency.

The basement and first floor of the

5-story building use board-formed concrete; the four upper stories are masonry bearing walls with concrete slab floors. The low-rise units and public buildings are steel frame with masonry walls. The windows have bronze glass for light control.

2

3

4

continued

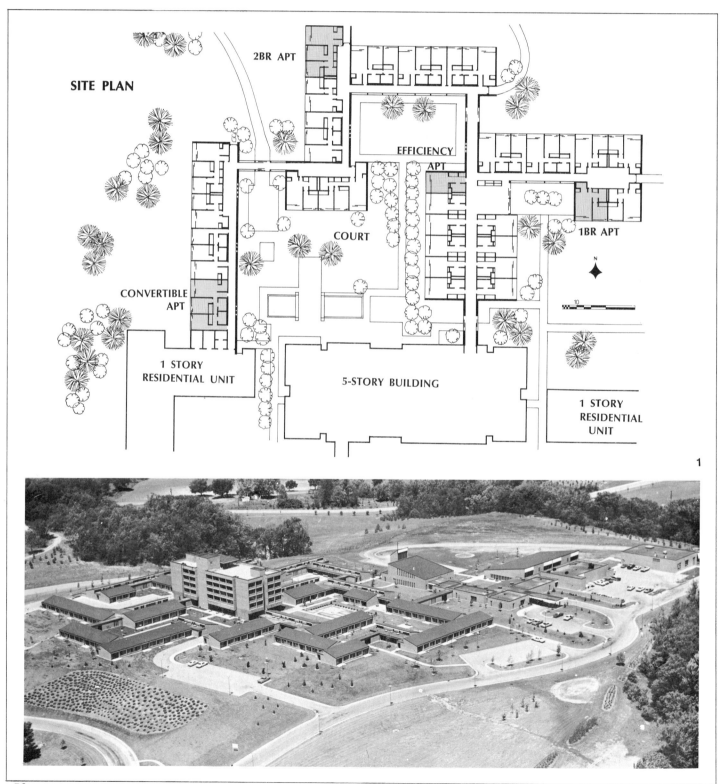

SITE PLAN

2BR APT

EFFICIENCY
APT

COURT

1BR APT

N

10

CONVERTIBLE
APT

1 STORY
RESIDENTIAL UNIT

5-STORY BUILDING

1 STORY
RESIDENTIAL
UNIT

1

  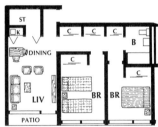 

EFFICIENCY APT **ONE BEDROOM APT** **TWO BEDROOM APT** **CONVERTIBLE APT**

1 Aerial view
2 Courtyard
3 Pool with fountain by 5-story building
4 Enclosed connecting corridor
5 Lobby
6 Chapel interior

RETIREMENT HOME FOR THE ACTORS FUND OF AMERICA
Englewood, New Jersey

ARCHITECT
Moon and Iwatsu
Englewood, New Jersey

PURPOSE
Residential with infirmary

CAPACITY
40 residents
3-bed infirmary

COST
$699,400

SPONSOR
The Actors Fund of America

The architects engaged to design this home for retired actors were given a free hand. No requirements or special provisions were laid down except to replace an existing antiquated structure. So the designers visited the home. They talked and dined with the actors then in residence and got a feeling for their way of life.

The design that resulted from this personal research called for a group of 1- and 2-story buildings with a residential and club-like atmosphere. Residents have considerable degrees of

privacy but can share group facilities as well.

The central service unit approached via a covered walkway at right angles to the entrance driveway houses a large lounge and library. The side of the lounge facing the drive opens into an orangery and terrace. Beyond the lounge on the opposite side of the building are the dining room, kitchen, storerooms, and offices.

The basement below the central unit contains recreational facilities, a

1

2

1 Covered walkway leading from entrance drive to central service building with lounge and orangery

2 Orangery

3 Side view of covered walk from passageway leading to one of the residential buildings

4 The main lounge

laundry, the employees' dining room, the heating plant, and other building service facilities. A second floor is used for the manager's apartment and employees' bedrooms.

The residents are housed in four 1-story buildings which flank the central service facility. The buildings are interconnected by enclosed passageways. In back of one pair of units is a small 3-bed infirmary which includes a day room and occupational therapy facilities.

In keeping with the home's location, a 6-acre knolled site in an old suburban neighborhood, the architects used traditional materials, brick with wood trim, for all buildings.

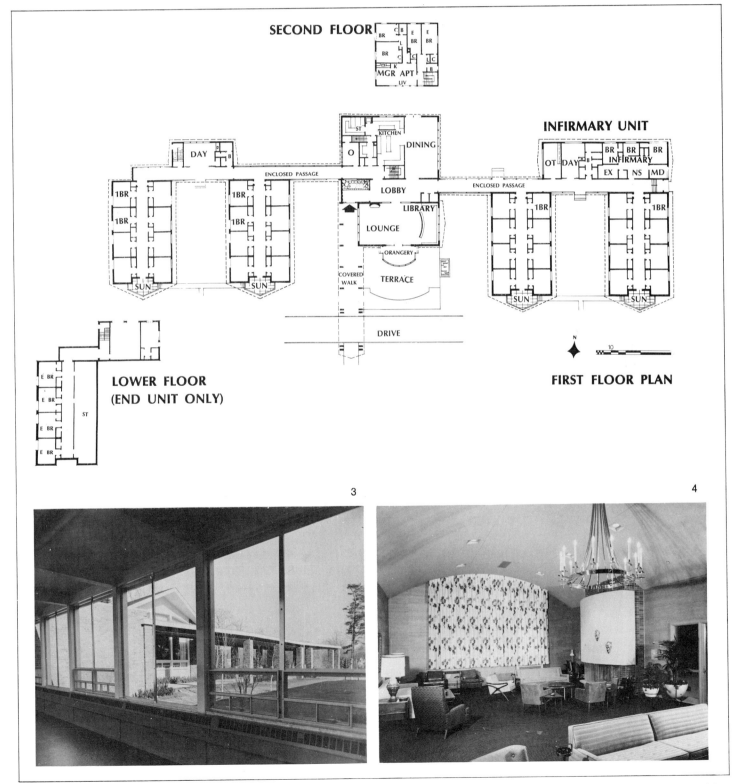

SECOND FLOOR

INFIRMARY UNIT

LOWER FLOOR
(END UNIT ONLY)

FIRST FLOOR PLAN

3

4

PROJECT NC 7-6
Asheville, North Carolina

ARCHITECT
Sappenfield-Wiegman-Hall-Associates
Asheville, North Carolina

PURPOSE
Residential

CAPACITY
119 dwelling units

COST
$1,872,740 (excluding fees)

SPONSOR
Housing Authority of Asheville

Planned as part of an urban renewal project, these garden and high-rise apartments for the elderly are being built on a site where six large but run-down houses had stood. A number of old trees were salvageable and these together with a municipal park just north of the site will create a pleasant backdrop for the modern buildings.

The idea of building both a high-rise and several low-rise buildings placed casually on the site was deliberate: The architect wanted to offer tenants a variety of living arrangements disposed in spatially interesting ways.

The apartments are efficiencies or 1-bedroom units. Five of the low-rise buildings, containing a total of 42 units, are scheduled to be built first, to be followed by another quintet at the west end of the site. The high-rise building will have 119 units in all, with the ground and first floors used for the resident manager's apartment and for Housing Authority offices. A separate maintenance building is also planned.

The high-rise building will use standard concrete frame with 2-way slab. Exterior walls are to be brick veneer. Partitions will be gypsum wallboard on metal studs. Interior finishes will include vinyl asbestos tile floors in living areas; ceramic tile in baths; and acoustical plaster on concrete slab ceilings.

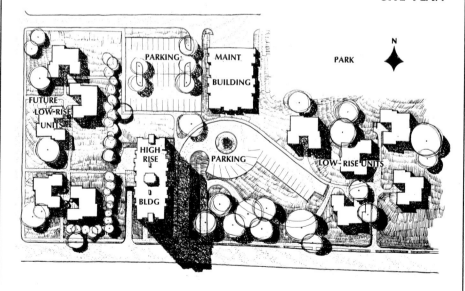

SITE PLAN

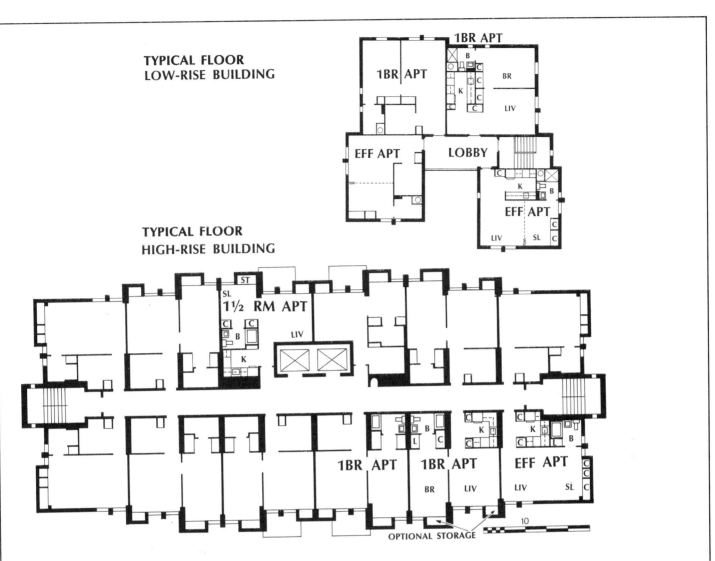

TYPICAL FLOOR LOW-RISE BUILDING

1BR APT

1BR APT

B
C
BR
K
C
LIV
C

EFF APT

LOBBY

C
K
B
EFF APT
LIV
SL
C

TYPICAL FLOOR HIGH-RISE BUILDING

ST
SL
1½ RM APT
C
C
B
LIV
K

1BR APT
BR

C
B
L
C
K
C
1BR APT
LIV

C
K
B
EFF APT
LIV
SL
C

10

OPTIONAL STORAGE

63

MORNINGSIDE MANOR
San Antonio, Texas

ARCHITECT
Marmon and Mok and
William D. Jones and Associates
San Antonio, Texas

PURPOSE
Residential with infirmary

CAPACITY
100 residents
10 bed infirmary

COST
$952,893

SPONSOR
Methodist Church

The emphasis is on light and air in this residence in southern Texas. Architects started with a pentagonal form for the core of the building, placing suites, single, and double bedrooms in wings radiating from the core sides. Three wings have been built so far, and a fourth is planned. The main entrance, approached under a projecting canopy, is on the fifth side of the pentagon. In the center is an enclosed courtyard with pools and plantings.

Core facilities grouped around the court include the dining and recreation rooms, an auditorium, beauty shop, and offices. There is a laundry for the convenience of the residents and several large storage rooms for furniture and trunks, an important consideration for older people.

A considerable drop in elevation across the 28-acre site made it possible to add a partial lower floor 12 feet below the main level. The 10-bed infirmary is included at this level.

The building is of reinforced concrete with a structural steel roof. Exterior walls are finished in brick, structural clay tile, and stucco.

Wood trim, acoustical plaster ceilings, and plastered partitions are used throughout to create a sense of warmth and avoid an institutional feeling. In addition, room entrances in the residential wings have been offset from the corridor to avoid monotony or a feeling of oppressive length.

1

2

3

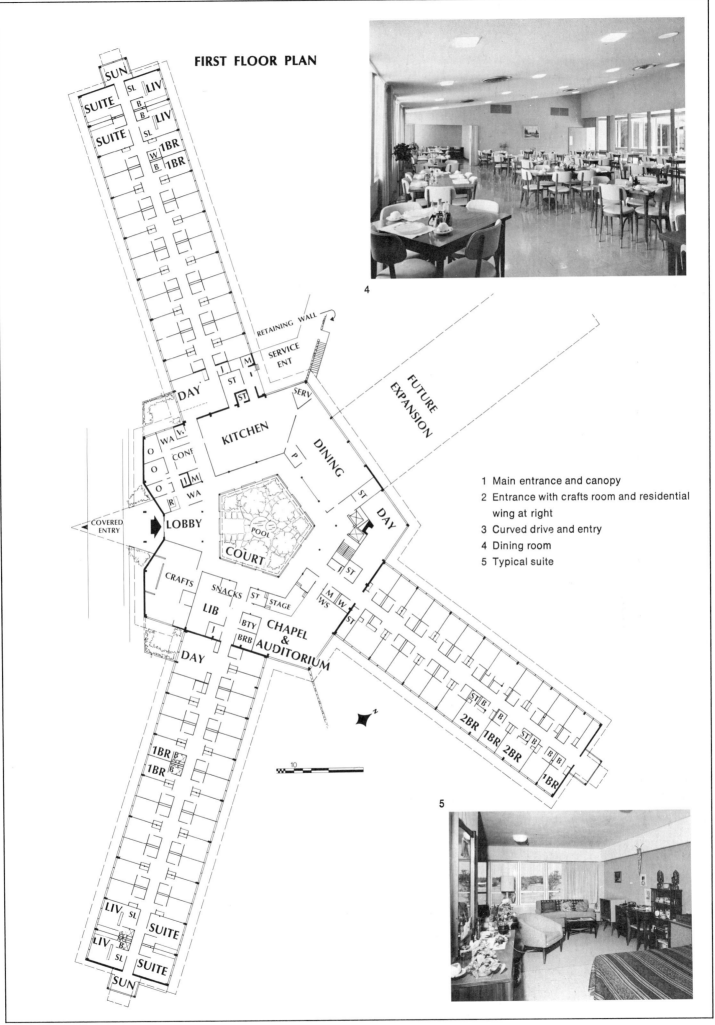

FIRST FLOOR PLAN

SUN

SUITE · SL · LIV
B
B
SUITE · SL · LIV
W · 1BR
B · 1BR

RETAINING WALL

SERVICE ENT

M
ST
ST

DAY'

SERV

KITCHEN

DINING

FUTURE EXPANSION

O · WA · W
O · CONF
O · M
R · WA

P

DAY

ST

1 Main entrance and canopy
2 Entrance with crafts room and residential wing at right
3 Curved drive and entry
4 Dining room
5 Typical suite

COVERED ENTRY

LOBBY

POOL COURT

ST

CRAFTS

SNACKS · ST · STAGE

M · W
WS · ST

LIB

BTY

J

BRB

CHAPEL & AUDITORIUM

2BR
ST · B
1BR · B
2BR
ST · B
B · B

1BR

DAY

N

1BR · B
1BR · B

10

LIV · SL
SUITE
LIV · B
SL · SUITE

SUN

4

5

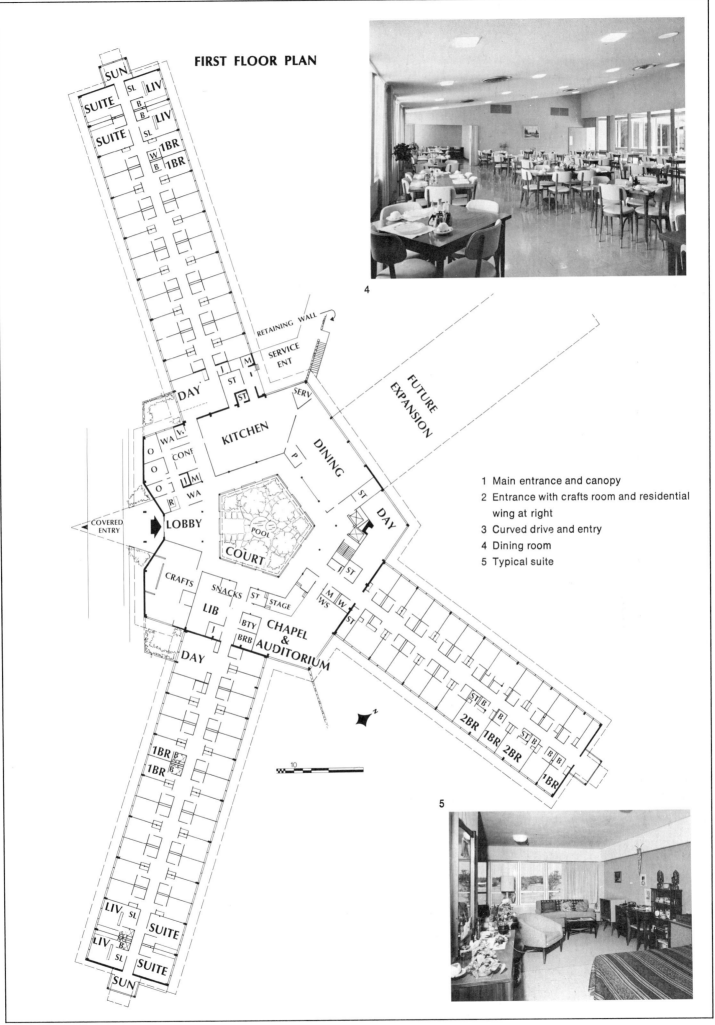

65

CRESTVIEW RETIREMENT HOME
West Des Moines, Iowa

ARCHITECT
Savage & Ver Ploeg
West Des Moines, Iowa

PURPOSE
Residential

CAPACITY
104 dwelling units

COST
$1,029,292

SPONSOR
*West Des Moines Cosmopolitan Club
(non-profit)*

The clean modern lines of this 3-story L-shaped building in West Des Moines overlie a historic past: An Indian burial ground 600 to 1000 years old was discovered on the sloping site during the excavation.

The new building, a residence for retired persons, contains a variety of room layouts. There are 26 large 1-room apartments for couples, 53 smaller 1-rooms for single occupants, and 25 1-bedroom apartments. All units have complete bathrooms but no kitchens. All three layouts are available in either wing.

The central dining room, kitchen, offices, and lounge areas are on the first floor of the larger north wing where the view, essentially into the valley area of the northwestern part of metropolitan Des Moines, is especially attractive. The first floor of the south wing contains craft rooms and apartments and also houses the boiler room, laundry, and storage areas.

The exterior walls of the building are red brick with concrete block back-up.

1

Cement plaster is used for the window spandrels.

Interiors are plastered. Steel joist framing is used for floors and roof. Floors are concrete, finished with carpeting (living areas of apartments); ceramic tile (baths); quarry tile (kitchens); and vinyl tile (corridors and general areas).

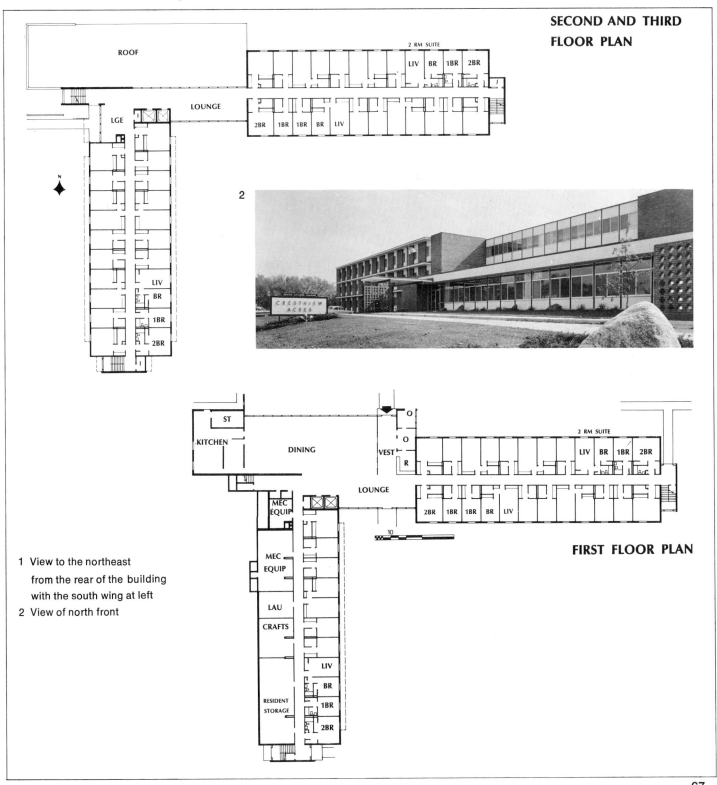

SECOND AND THIRD FLOOR PLAN

ROOF

2 RM SUITE

LIV | BR | 1BR | 2BR

LOUNGE

LGE

LOUNGE

2BR | 1BR | 1BR | BR | LIV

N

LIV

BR

1BR

2BR

2

FIRST FLOOR PLAN

ST

KITCHEN

DINING

VEST

O

O

R

2 RM SUITE

LIV | BR | 1BR | 2BR

LOUNGE

MEC EQUIP

2BR | 1BR | 1BR | BR | LIV

10

MEC EQUIP

LAU

CRAFTS

LIV

BR

1BR

RESIDENT STORAGE

2BR

1 View to the northeast
   from the rear of the building
   with the south wing at left
2 View of north front

APARTMENTS FOR SENIOR CITIZENS
Columbia, Missouri

ARCHITECT
Neville, Sharp & Simon, Inc.
Kansas City, Missouri

PURPOSE
Residential with clinic

CAPACITY
147 dwelling units

COST
$1,824,000 (excluding fees)

SPONSOR
The Public Housing Authority
Columbia, Missouri

A high-rise apartment house for the elderly has been built near the heart of a city associated with the young. Columbia is the home of the University of Missouri.

In addition to the intellectual stimulus such an environment provides, the residents of this 8-story public housing project for senior citizens are within walking distance of the downtown center, stores, transportation, and churches. Within the building itself there are facilities for demonstration cooking and housekeeping, movie

showings, television, and card games. The ground floor contains library space, party and craft rooms, and a clinic. Outdoor facilities include horseshoe and croquet courts. For the more sedentary there are patio benches and walks among flower beds.

The upper floors of the building comprise a total of 84 studio and 63 1-bedroom apartments. Each studio unit contains a kitchenette, bathroom with shower, and a large living room, part of which can be curtained off near the bath to create a small sleeping

SITE PLAN

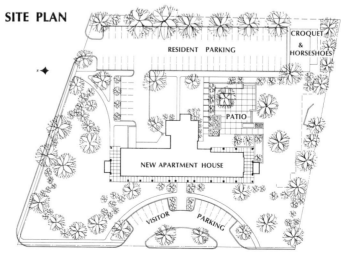

alcove. Kitchen equipment has been designed so that occupants will have little stooping to do, and bathroom showers and tubs are provided with grab bars for safety. There are television and telephone outlets in each apartment and a combined laundry and social room on each floor.

The building's main entrance is approached along a circular drive. From the front the building appears to be a simple rectangular solid. There is a short wing which extends from the center towards the rear, however. This houses the clinic and offices on the ground floor and studio apartments and laundry facilities on the upper floors.

The building is of concrete construction with monolithic poured slab floors and cavity brick and block walls. Ceilings are sprayed-on plaster. The interior of the perimeter walls is exposed painted block, and partitions are plaster over gypsum lath. The common walls between units utilize a spring clip sound control system. Floors are asphalt tile.

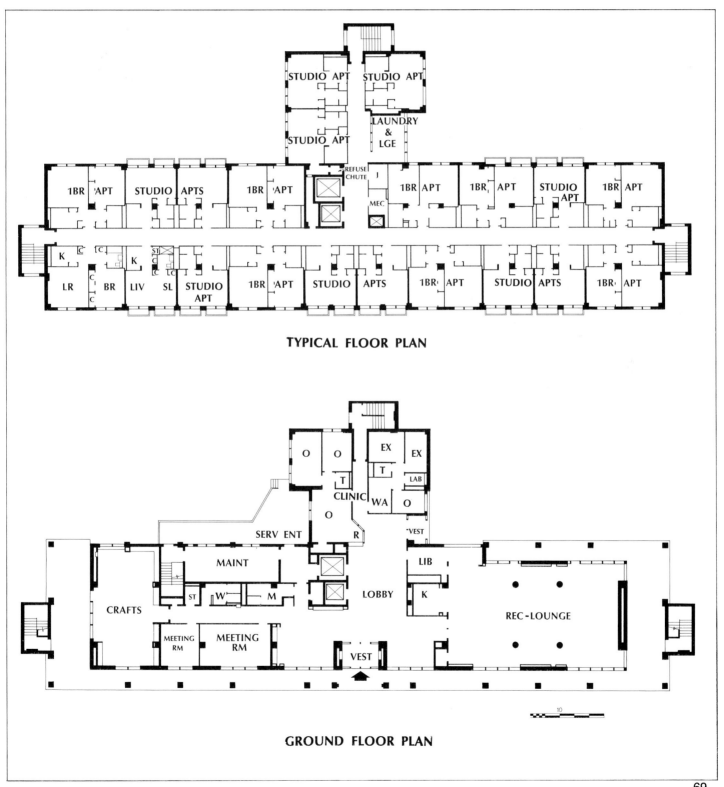

TYPICAL FLOOR PLAN

GROUND FLOOR PLAN

HOUSING FOR THE ELDERLY
Columbus, Ohio

ARCHITECT
Ireland & Associates
Columbus, Ohio
H. A. Williams & Associates,
Mechanical Engineers (Consultants)
Columbus, Ohio

PURPOSE
Residential

CAPACITY
126 dwelling units

COST
$1,600,000 (excluding fees)

SPONSOR
Columbus Metropolitan Housing Authority

Faced with the problem of creating additional housing for a municipal "Senior Village" project which already included an 11-story slab building, a 1½-story recreation building, and several older 2-story units, these Ohio architects have designed an ingenious fan-shaped 7-story residence. Not only will the building's dimensions serve to reconcile the height differences among the existing structures, but by placing the building on a continuation of the line of the diagonally sited high-rise slab, the designers can further integrate new with old. This orientation will also

permit southern exposure for the terraced apartments along the building's curved facade, which, coincidentally, parallels a bend in the river nearby.

Even without these practical virtues, the building's graceful design would still merit high praise—all the more so when it is realized that the plan had to fit the space and budgetary limitations of a public housing project. Overall costs (excluding fees) are estimated to be $18 per square foot.

All 84 efficiency units and 42 one-bedroom apartments in the building will

have terraces (or patios) and cross-ventilation. Galleried entries on the north side of the building are planned for the efficiency units, and ramps will lead down into the entryway for the 1-bedroom apartments on the lower floors. The staircase outline of the building will allow all tenants to have covered parking areas, again on the north side of the building. In addition to the individual units, each floor plan includes a lounge near the elevator. The ground floor will have a main sitting area and recreation spaces as well as the lobby and offices, a laundry, and a kitchen.

Masonry, concrete, and glass are the basic building materials to be used. Load-bearing brick masonry cavity walls will distribute all mechanical systems and provide acoustical barriers between units. Floors will be precast slabs. Insulating sliding glass units are to be used along the south facade. A penthouse will house mechanical equipment.

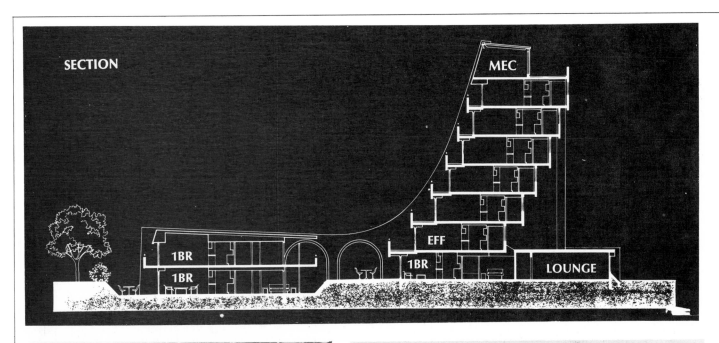

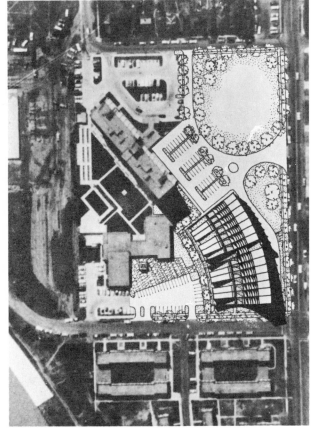

continued

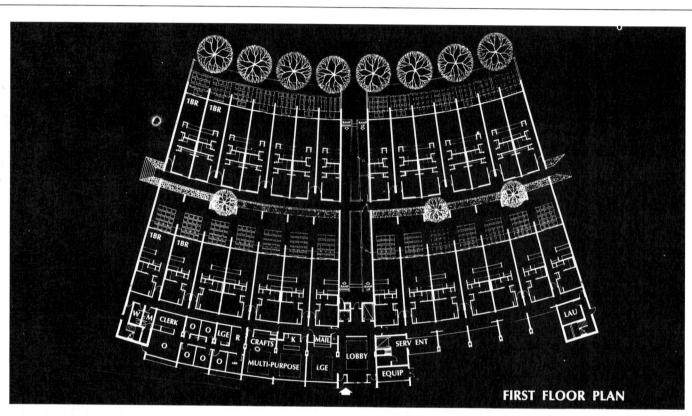

FIRST FLOOR PLAN

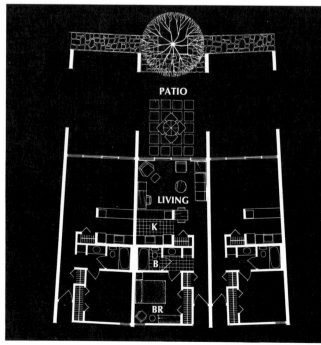

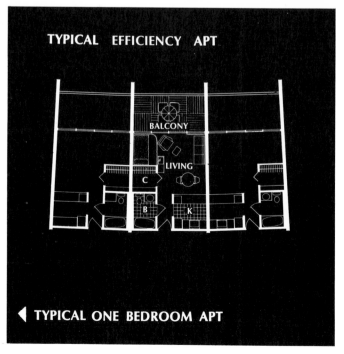

TYPICAL EFFICIENCY APT

◀ TYPICAL ONE BEDROOM APT

CANTERBURY COURT
Atlanta, Georgia

ARCHITECT
Stevens & Wilkinson and
Abreu & Robeson, Inc.
Atlanta, Georgia

PURPOSE
Residential with infirmary

CAPACITY
130 dwelling units
10-bed infirmary

COST
$2,396,980

SPONSOR
All Saints' and St. Luke's Parishes
(Episcopal Church)

A 9-story white concrete apartment house was the architects' choice for a residential building to be set in a suburban community north of Atlanta. The idea was to create a semi-urban contemporary feeling by using quiet simple lines. North and south facades are dominated by arched balconies whose filagreed railings are the major ornamentation on the building. East and west facades are pale brick rising from a precast base and topped by a cornice.

Every apartment on the eight floors above the ground level opens onto a private balcony. Half of one floor is used as an infirmary with examination and therapy rooms. All floors have lounges and utility areas.

Ground floor facilities include a walnut-paneled lounge, library, and dining room furnished in contemporary style. A chapel designed to liturgical specifications is centrally placed off the lounge.

Surrounding the ground floor is a terrace. This opens out into a garden on the south lawn with individual plots and a greenhouse for interested residents. Croquet and shuffleboard courts are also located on the south lawn. Parking has been confined to one side of the site to provide an uninterrupted green for rest or recreation.

The building is of reinforced concrete with a white precast exterior. It is centrally air-conditioned and equipped with safety devices appropriate for elderly residents.

continued

SITE PLAN

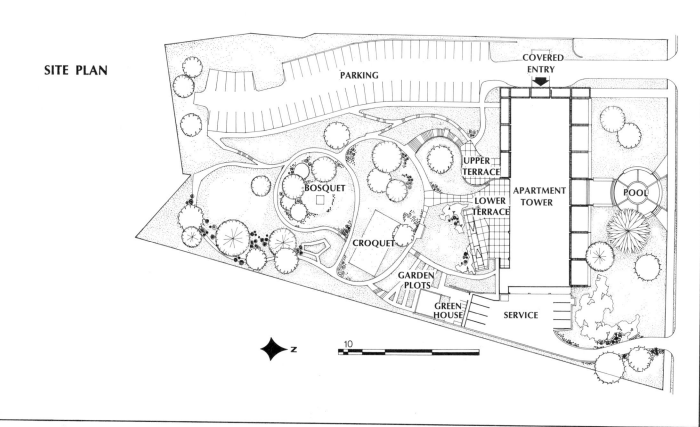

PARKING

COVERED ENTRY

UPPER TERRACE

BOSQUET

LOWER TERRACE

APARTMENT TOWER

POOL

CROQUET

GARDEN PLOTS

GREEN HOUSE

SERVICE

z

10

TYPICAL FLOOR PLAN

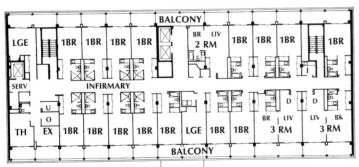

FIRST FLOOR PLAN

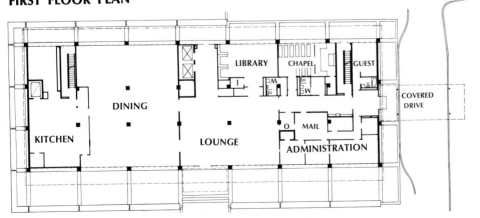

3030 PARK
Bridgeport, Connecticut

ARCHITECT
Fletcher-Thompson Inc.
Robert H. Mutrux, A.I.A.,
Associate-in-Charge
Bridgeport, Connecticut

PURPOSE
Residential with infirmary

CAPACITY
342 dwelling units
30-bed health center

COST
$6,950,000

SPONSOR
Council of Churches of Greater Bridgeport

One of the most unusual and graceful designs for an apartment house for the elderly is 3030 Park, the name (and address) of an 11-story Y-shaped building in suburban Bridgeport.

Planned to accommodate approximately 400 persons, the building is one of the largest and most modern of its kind in the country. The 98 churches in the Bridgeport area who sponsored the project sought a facility which would meet the needs of elderly persons who lead active full lives. The result is that the residence not only contains 1-, 1½-, 2-, and 3-room apartments in a

variety of layouts, but also devotes a considerable amount of space to recreational and health needs. Besides a 2-story semi-circular dining room seating 400, a 2-story lounge, a 300-seat auditorium, and the usual complement of beauty and barber shops, chapel, library, and music room, there are facilities for sewing and crafts, woodworking, painting, gardening, shuffleboard, and bowling on the green. There is a private smoking room with a billiard table for men and a separate room for ladies.

Most of these activity areas are found

1

1 Canopied main entrance of 3030 Park at left center of photo, semi-circular dining room at right

SITE PLAN

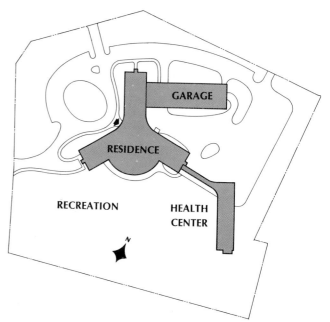

on the ground floor, the main floor, and the mezzanine. The ground floor is below the entrance level but opens onto grade at the rear of the building so that the hobby rooms are sunlit.

Adjoining the main building on the ground floor level at the east end of the east wing is a covered passageway leading to a 2-story health center. Nurses are on duty at all times in the center and residents may come for treatment for minor ailments or, in case of emergency or short-term illness, stay in the 30-bed infirmary. In addition to examination and treatment rooms,

there is a laboratory, a pharmacy, and physical therapy facilities which include whirlpool baths.

A number of apartments for semi-ambulatory patients are located in the center, along with a social area where residents may take their meals or chat in a quieter atmosphere than the main lounge.

Seven floors of the apartment building are used exclusively for apartments. All have small kitchenettes and full baths; those in central locations at the south and west elevations have bal-

conies. There is also a large lounge with a kitchenette and balcony for general use on each floor.

The corridors radiating from the central bank of elevators and the main rooms of the apartments are carpeted. Corridor ceilings are acoustical tile. Bathrooms are fully tiled and provided with handrails.

The top floor of the building houses the mechanical equipment necessary for air-conditioning and ventilating. There are also 18 two-room apartments with roof terraces and a large "family"

continued

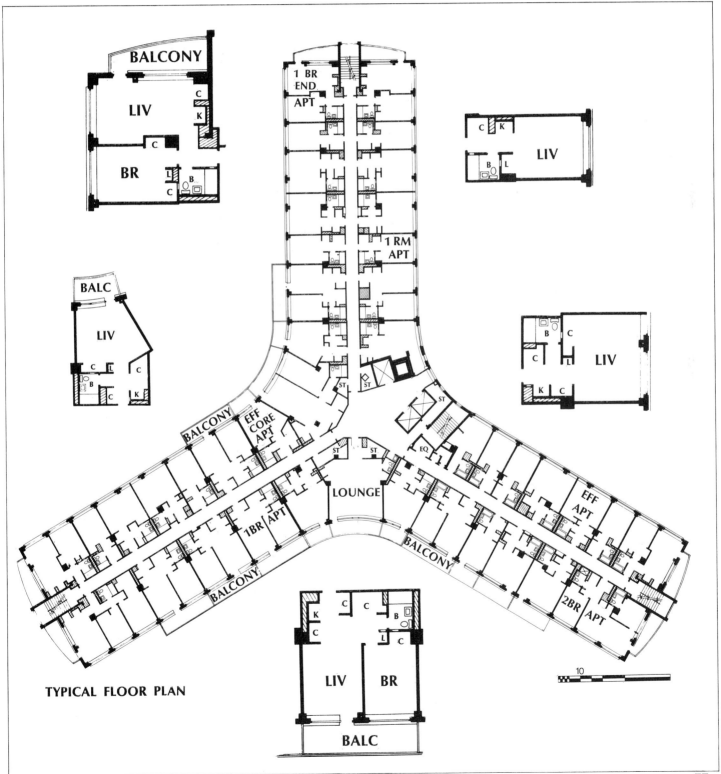

TYPICAL FLOOR PLAN

room for medium-sized gatherings. Space at the center of the floor and at the end of each wing may be used for sunbathing or star-gazing.

The building is of reinforced concrete flat slab construction. Bands of gray-buff brick set off each floor and exposed white concrete columns are used between windows. The wing of the building stemming from the dining room roughly follows a north-south orientation on a pentagonally shaped 10-acre plot. The property slopes toward the south end affording an excellent view of Long Island Sound.

1 Rear view showing 2-story dining room above ground floor and passageway leading to health center in foreground

1

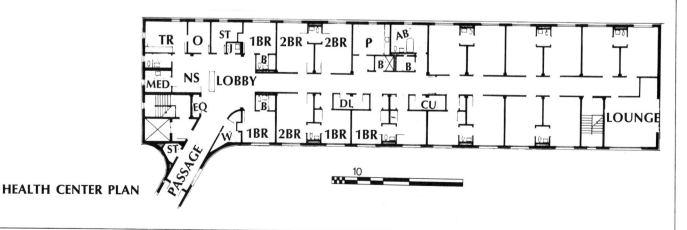

HEALTH CENTER PLAN

10

2

3

2 Typical 1½-room apartment
3 Men's club room
4 Library

4

LURIE TERRACE
Ann Arbor, Michigan

ARCHITECT
James H. Livingston Associates
Ann Arbor, Michigan
Daniel S. Ling, Structural Engineer
Benjamin Briskin, Mechanical Engineer

PURPOSE
Residential

CAPACITY
142 dwelling units

COST
$1,380,112 (excluding fees)

SPONSOR
Senior Citizens' Housing of Ann Arbor, Inc.
(non-profit)

A woman who believes that the elderly should not be led to pasture but live in the thick of things was the prime mover in the building of a high-rise apartment house in downtown Ann Arbor. After considerable research in gerontology at the University of Michigan, Mrs. Shata Ling decided it was "time . . . to stop being an expert and . . . see how a community can get what it needs."

The result is an 8-story twin pentagon apartment house for elderly persons in low-to-middle income groups which offers such amenities as:

- carpeting in apartments, corridors, dining room, and lounges
- all-electric heating and air-conditioning systems with individual room control
- electric kitchen equipment including food waste disposers
- seven apartment sizes ranging from a 311 square foot bachelor to a 2-bedroom 638 square foot size
- a top floor restaurant divided in décor into contemporary, Gay Nineties, and Early American sections
- arts and crafts room, a greenhouse, library, music room, shuffleboard courts, and flower gardening areas
- a stag club (for men only) and a luncheon room adjacent to the dining room

Mrs. Ling stressed individual touches in the finishing of the building. All seven varieties of apartments are found on each residential floor. Instead of room numbers the apartments are designated by names, and doors and corridors are painted different colors. The pentagonal shape of the building results in short branched-off corridors which "stimulate mental alertness."

Because of the all-electric design of the heating plant there is no need for a

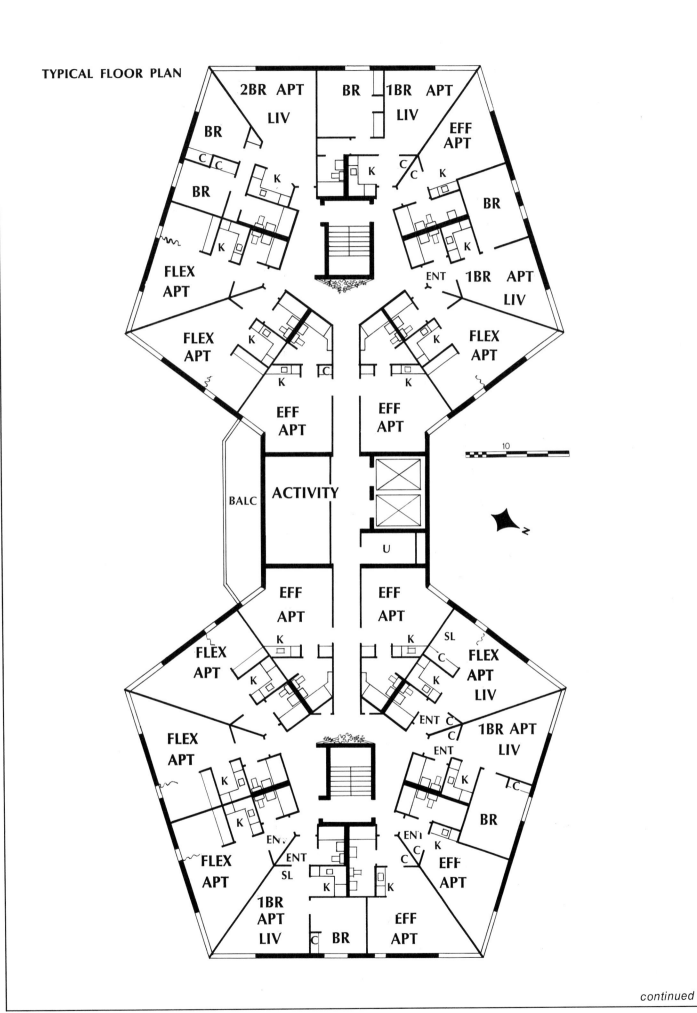

TYPICAL FLOOR PLAN

2BR APT
BR LIV
BR
C C
BR
K
FLEX APT
FLEX APT
K
K
EFF APT
BALC ACTIVITY
EFF APT
FLEX APT
K
K
FLEX APT
FLEX APT
K
K
1BR APT LIV
BR
1BR APT LIV
BR
EFF APT
ENT
EFF APT

BR 1BR APT LIV
EFF APT
C C K
BR
K
ENT 1BR APT LIV
EFF APT
EFF APT
10
U
EFF APT
SL
K K C
FLEX APT LIV
ENT C
1BR APT LIV
EFF APT
K
BR
EN ENT
SL
1BR APT LIV
C BR
EFF APT

continued

LURIE TERRACE

boiler room, chimneys, ductwork, or piping. The one basement under one of the towers is used for residents' laundry facilities.

The building is of reinforced concrete construction with exterior walls of brick on cement block, insulated with foamed plastic and finished with dry-wall. Over 25 percent of the exposed wall area is glass.

1

2

3

1 Arts and Crafts room
2 Typical apartment kitchen
3 Early American wing of dining room
4 Stag Club
5 Activity room

4

5

ARCADIA RETIREMENT HOME
Honolulu, Hawaii

ARCHITECT
John Graham and Company
Seattle, Washington

PURPOSE
Residential with infirmary

CAPACITY
287 dwelling units
27-bed nursing facility

COST
$5,600,000

SPONSOR
Central Union Church of Honolulu

Standing 13 stories high, overlooking the Waikiki area, is the broad-angled facade of an apartment house for retired persons. The 287 dwelling units, each with a balcony and individual window air conditioners, are divided almost equally into 1-room, 1½-room, and 1-bedroom apartments. Some units are situated at the angled intersections of the wings on each floor and have trapezoidally shaped floor plans. All apartments have kitchens and full bathrooms with built-in vanities. Carpeting is used in the living areas and throughout the building, in corridors and most public rooms.

General use facilities include a dining room seating 300, hobby and recréation rooms, an auditorium, main lounge, laundry, and roof solarium. A 27-bed licensed nursing facility on the second floor is available for residents who are either temporarily or chronically ill. The facilities can be expanded to a capacity of 56 beds.

Concrete is the essential structural material of the building. Pre-stressed structural members were cast at the site. Built-up asphalt roofing is used with special surfacing on walking decks. All sash is aluminum.

Interior walls are dry-wall and gypsum plaster; ceilings are dry-wall and ventilated acoustical tile.

1 Main lounge
2 Roof solarium
3 Central dining room

1

2

3

FIRST FLOOR PLAN

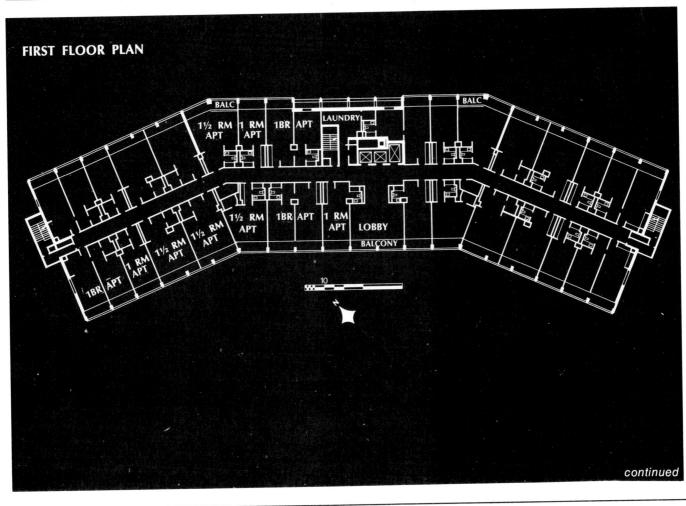

BALC

1½ RM APT   1 RM APT   1BR APT   LAUNDRY   BALC

1½ RM APT   1BR APT   1 RM APT   LOBBY

BALCONY

1BR APT   1 RM APT   1½ RM APT   1½ RM APT

10

N

continued

ONE ROOM APT

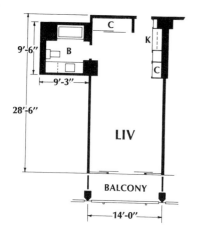

9'-6"
B
C
9'-3"
K
C
28'-6"
LIV
BALCONY
14'-0"

1

1 A one room apartment
2 A 1½ room apartment

1½ ROOM APT

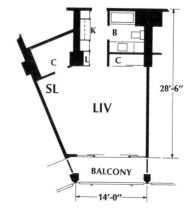

K
B
C
C
L
SL
28'-6"
LIV
BALCONY
14'-0"

2

A one bedroom apartment:
1 Balcony
2 Living room
3 Bedroom

ONE BEDROOM APT

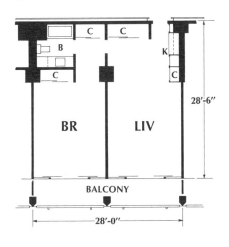

WESLEY WOODS
Atlanta, Georgia

ARCHITECT
Charles Edward Stade & Associates
Park Ridge, Illinois

PURPOSE
Residential with infirmary

CAPACITY
202 dwelling units

COST
$2,416,419 (excluding fees)

SPONSOR
Emory University, Atlanta

The formal curves of a pair of cylinders are the dominant design features of this retirement facility a mile from the campus of Emory University in Atlanta. Situated on a wooded site, flanked by a creek and a steep hill, the round white buildings seem well suited to the terrain.

More practically, the circular plan permits the placement of rooms along the perimeter. The extensive use of glass—the windows form broad horizontal bands encircling each story—assures every resident a view.

Since the 10- and 13- story buildings rise above the treetops, the view from the upper floors is extensive, and helps create a sense of spaciousness and serenity.

There are 161 single rooms, 39 1-bedroom and two 2-bedroom apartments in the buildings. A typical residential floor will include both efficiencies and 1-bedroom units surrounding a central hub area used as a lounge. A slimmer vertical unit connects the two towers, housing elevators on one side and sun rooms

on the other.

Ground floor facilities include offices and service areas as well as sewing, crafts, recreation rooms, a library, and a lounge. The storage, kitchen, and dining areas extend out from the 10-story building at the ground floor level. A large terrace runs the length of the property behind the buildings along the north side.

The residence was originally built for retired faculty of Emory University. The reinforced concrete and glass complex now includes a small nursing home at the east end of the property, screened by trees.

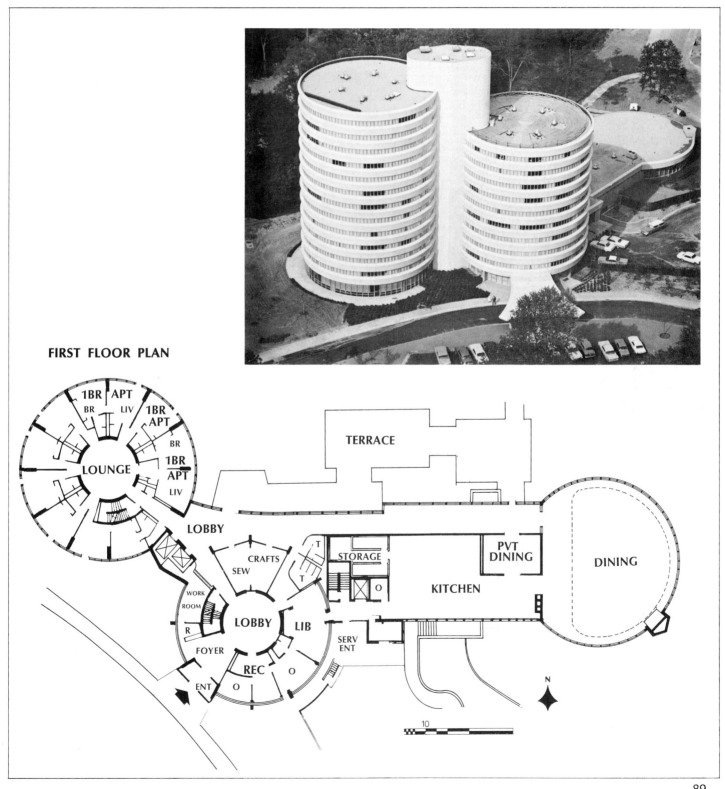

FIRST FLOOR PLAN

THE ADMIRAL—ADDITION
Chicago, Illinois

ARCHITECT
Mittelbusher & Tourtelot
Chicago, Illinois

PURPOSE
Residential with infirmary

CAPACITY
25 residents

COST
$775,000 (excluding fees)

SPONSOR
The Trustees of The Old Peoples Home of the City of Chicago

The recent history of the Admiral, a residence for retired persons which overlooks Lake Michigan and Lincoln Park in Chicago, began in 1960. At that time an 11-story hotel at the site was converted to a residence for the aged with a capacity of 110. A small infirmary was included in the plan, and two 1-story-plus-basement additions provided space for a dining room and a solarium. In 1966 a 3-story and basement extension was completed, bringing the residential and infirmary capacity up to 135.

The new wing is set at right angles to the older tower building, and a new canopied main entrance placed on a diagonal where the buildings meet, links the two. The entrance leads up to the first floor containing a large meeting room overlooking a garden, and managers' apartments. The basement is used for recreational facilities, (shuffleboard and game tables), as well as for the heating plant, laundry, and storage.

Above the first floor is the infirmary level connected to the existing facility

1

2

1 The main entrance to the Admiral is a part of the new wing and is approached along a circular drive   2 The side of the tower building opposite the new wing contains the 1-story glassed-in dining room (left), and solarium (right). These additions were made earlier

SITE PLAN

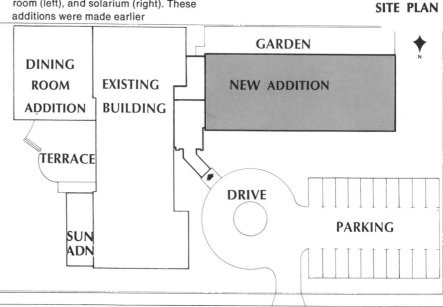

in the tower. The original nursing station has been replaced by a waiting room outside doctors' offices, and a new station has been placed at the intersection of the old and new wings to allow supervision of both areas.

Unlike infirmaries which house patients on a temporary or emergency basis, the new facilities are primarily for long-term patients who may not be seriously ill, but who require attention. For this reason care has been exercised to give these areas as well as the rest of the addition a home-like atmosphere. Rooms and corridors are fully carpeted, windows are equipped with double draperies, and colonial-style furniture is used.

The infirmary rooms are all private and include toilets which are fitted with emergency door stops. This enables an attendant to open the door in case a patient loses consciousness or otherwise finds himself locked in. Central bathing facilities consist of tubs which are equipped with electrically or manually operated chair lifts. A day room is also provided on the infirmary floor.

The third floor consists of eight apartments, each double the size of the infirmary rooms. Again colonial décor is followed, but the extra space permits residents to add furniture or things of their own. The corridor walls are used for bathrooms, dressing spaces, closets, and wardrobes.

In order to harmonize with the tower building, the reinforced concrete

continued

1

1 Dining room interior. A yellow and green color scheme was selected to emphasize an out-of-doors feeling

FIRST FLOOR PLAN

extension is finished in buff brick. Like the earlier solarium and dining room additions, the new building also makes extensive use of glass. To underscore the horizontal lines of the building, ebony granite has been used along the base course and fascia.

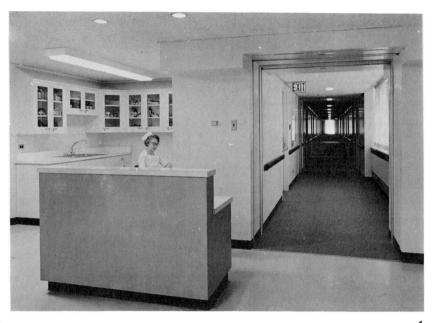

1

1 The view of the nurses' station looking into the new wing. A mirror on a column directly ahead of the corridor enables nurses to observe activity. Handrails and cushion-backed carpeting are safety features   2 Typical residential room on the third floor of the Admiral addition. Door opens into an area containing a dressing room with walk-in closet and the bathroom

SECOND FLOOR PLAN

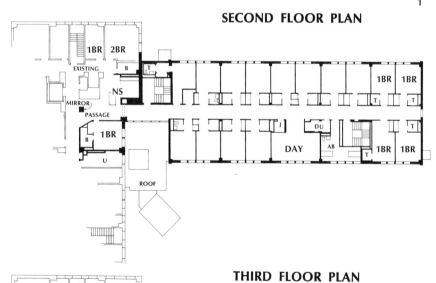

THIRD FLOOR PLAN

2

Combined Residential and Nursing Care Facilities

The facilities in this category are generally larger than independent residences or nursing homes for the aged and more space has been devoted to each of them. Usually the infirm residents are housed in separate buildings or on separate floors of a building along with clinical and therapeutic facilities. "Well" residents may be offered a choice of housing from independent living to more sheltered care. Adaptability is an important concept in the design of these facilities. In some cases the architect has provided for the easy conversion of some residential units to full nursing care facilities. Sometimes the heating plant or other central services have been specified with a clear view toward expansion or extension of present services. The examples presented here are arranged from low to high-rise buildings.

FOUR SEASONS HOME
Columbus, Indiana

ARCHITECT
The Architects Collaborative Inc.
Norman C. Fletcher, F.A.I.A.,
principal in charge
Cambridge, Massachusetts

PURPOSE
Residential and nursing

CAPACITY
160 residents
100-bed health center

COST
$1,500,000

SPONSOR
Baptist Homes and Hospitals, Inc.

A random pattern of pitched roofs and courtyards, games and gardening areas, a bird sanctuary and an arboretum, putting greens and a man-made pond...these are a few of the elements in a total plan the architects conceived to create interest and a suburban residential feeling on a long, flat, 44-acre site.

The result is a pleasing complex of land and interconnected 1-story buildings that is appropriate for a well population whose average age is 80 years. Each residential building contains about a dozen 1- or 2-room apartments for single or married persons.

At the heart of the complex is a chapel whose sharply peaked roof towers above the other buildings on the site. Nearby is the central core facility which houses the kitchen and a series of small dining rooms surrounding a landscaped interior court. In addition, the core contains administrative offices, a lounge with a library and music room, a center for arts and crafts, and barber and beauty shops. A gift shop and soda fountain to be managed by the residents is also included.

At the north end of the site is a health center with separate dining and kitchen facilities. The 16 double rooms for patients needing intensive care and the 68 single rooms for the chronically ill are arranged around a pair of interior courts to be used for relaxation or exercise. There is a municipal hospital a mile away in case of emergency.

Wood, glass, and brick are used for the exterior of the buildings, which are light steel frame with bar joist roofs. Interior partitions are dry-wall and flooring is vinyl asbestos tile. There is carpeting in the central core areas and circulation corridors. Special hardware for the convenience or safety of the residents is employed throughout. All buildings are air-conditioned.

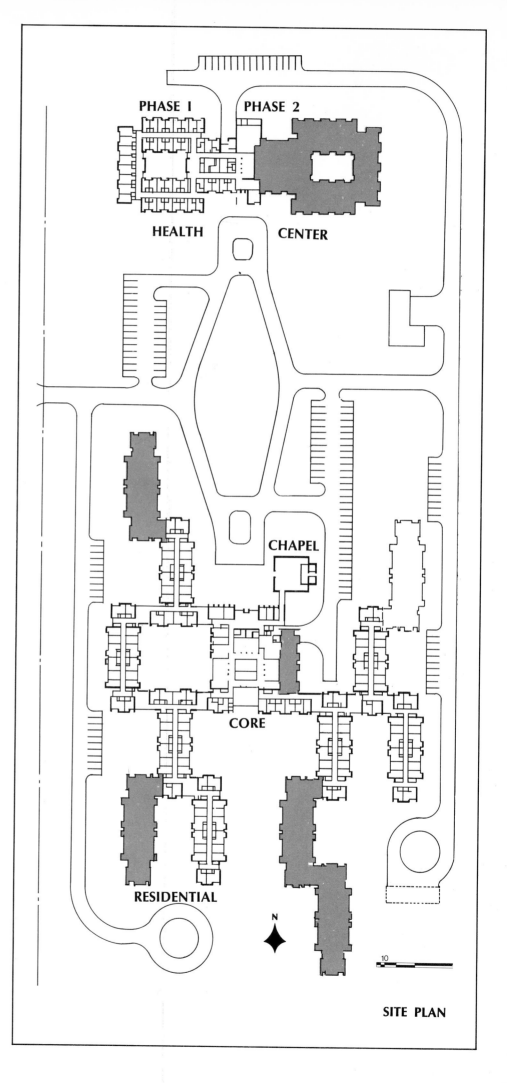

PHASE I   PHASE 2

HEALTH   CENTER

CHAPEL

CORE

RESIDENTIAL

N

SITE PLAN

continued

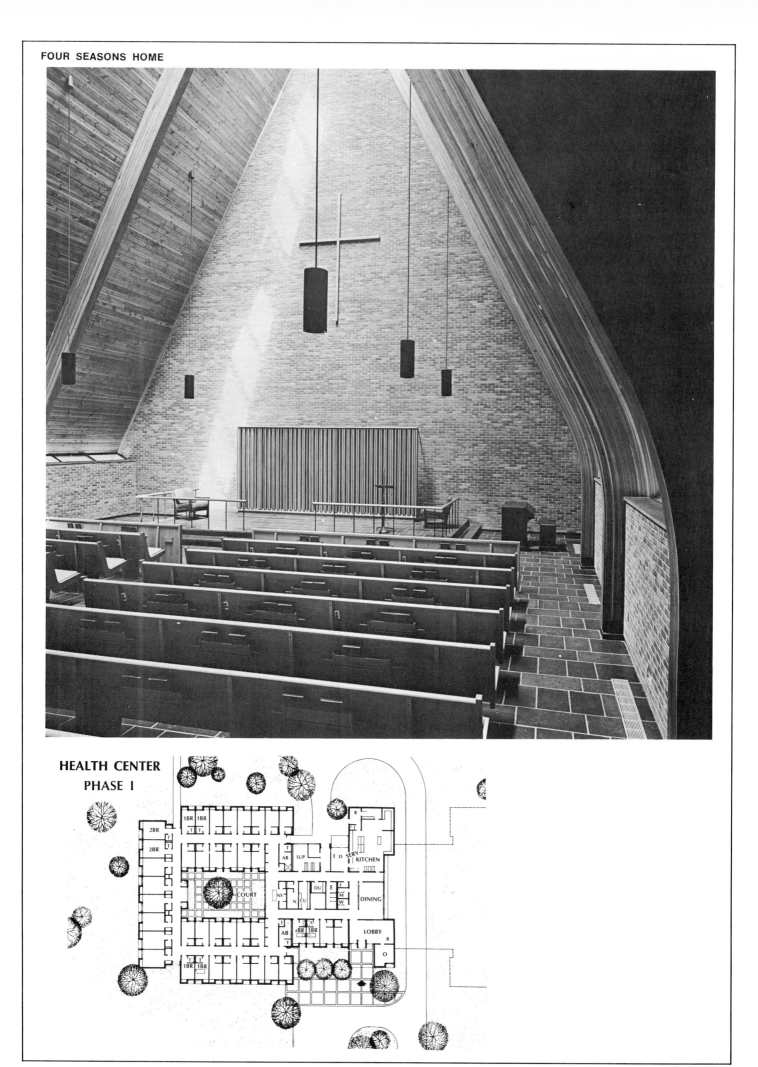

HEALTH CENTER
PHASE I

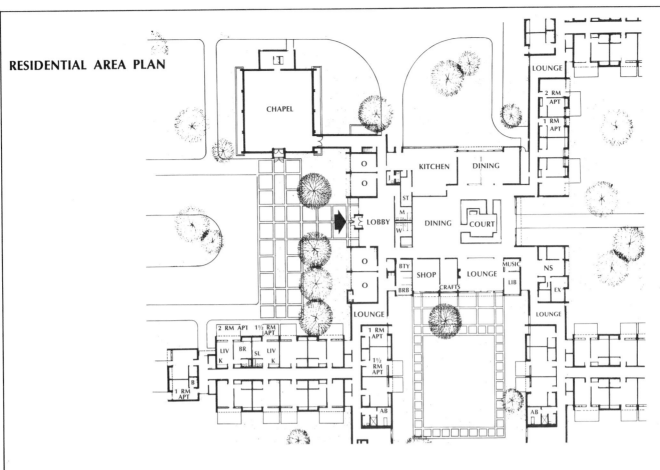

RESIDENTIAL AREA PLAN

EAST RIDGE RETIREMENT VILLAGE
Dade County, Florida

ARCHITECT
Steward-Skinner Associates
Miami, Florida

PURPOSE
Retirement village

CAPACITY
396 residents
40-bed health center

COST
$3,460,000

SPONSOR
Federation of Lutheran congregations
of the Florida-Georgia District of the
Lutheran Church-Missouri Synod

One of the first retirement villages to be built in the U.S. was East Ridge, completed in 1963. Located in an area much favored by the elderly, southeastern Florida, the village gets its name from a 70-acre tract of land on a natural coral rock ridge. The generally flat terrain lies off U.S. Highway 1 about 20 miles south of Miami. Bus service from the village extends to all parts of Dade County, and shuttle service exists for transportation on the site. Upper income residential areas border two sides of the village; undeveloped

pineland the two other sides.

The project was financed through a Federal Housing Administration insurance program, and won an award from that agency in 1964 for excellence in residential design. Not only is a variety of housing arrangements for the elderly offered, but also enough nursing, recreational, religious, and shopping facilities for the village to be self-sufficient.

A key to understanding the layout is the Founders Square and Fountain near the center of the site. The

1

1 Aerial view of the village

2 Type I residential building at right contains six efficiency apartments

cross-shaped fountain is oriented according to the compass points and serves as a convenient reference marker. Due north of it lies the main recreation area, including putting and bowling greens, and a recreation and industrial activities building. This houses a large auditorium as well as a workshop where residents may be gainfully employed. Beyond this is an outdoor swimming pool and sunbathing area.

Due south of the fountain is a "Hospitality Center," a general store for residents who may not want or be able to take a specially provided bus to nearby shopping areas.

Three buildings at the southwest end of the site house administrative offices and a post office, a dining hall and chapel, and a 40-bed health center. The remaining areas of the site are residential. The buildings are arranged in clusters, each cluster containing its own parking area, lawns and gardens, and frequently a laundry building and shuffleboard facilities. All buildings in the village are 1-story and there are no steps anywhere on the site.

Seven of the 12 residential clusters consist of garden apartment buildings with from four to six units each. These may be efficiencies or 1- or 2-bedroom apartments. Two clusters are composed of detached houses; two others of 2-unit buildings connected in pairs. The twelfth residential cluster, just west of the Founders Fountain, is made up of five "Residence Clubs." These were designed for single

continued

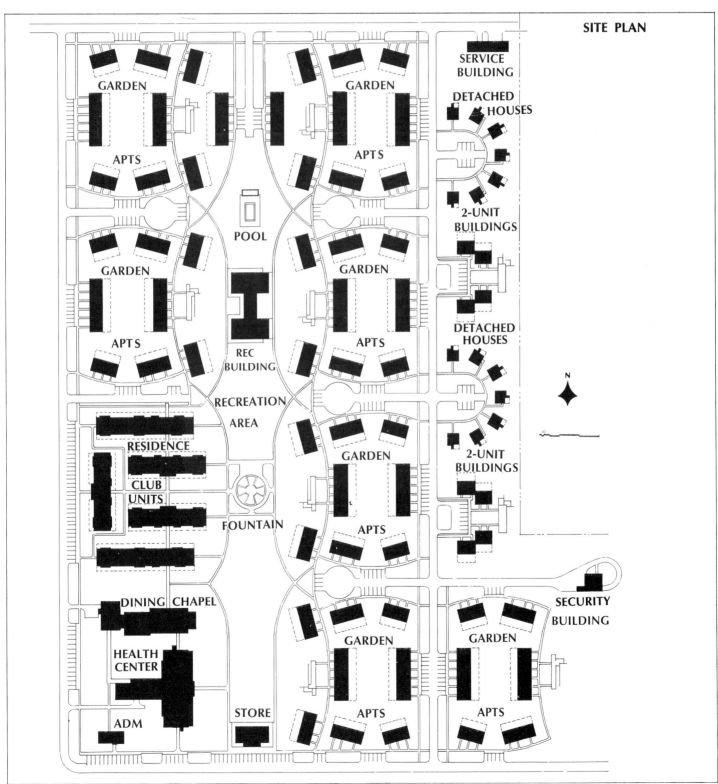

EAST RIDGE RETIREMENT VILLAGE

persons or couples who want privacy and independence but only limited housekeeping chores. A small kitchenette is included in these units which are typically efficiency or 1-bedroom size, but it is presumed that these residents are more likely to take their meals in the dining hall. The club units open onto private terraces. Other units in the village typically open onto screened porches and private gardens.

If a resident becomes ill he may avail himself of the health center facilities. In addition to the 40-bed infirmary, there is a diagnostic and treatment clinic, and visiting service for individuals in their homes.

The residents of East Ridge are 62 years or over. Applicants for admission pay a founder's fee, (in a lump sum or by installments), which entitles them to lifetime occupancy in the type of accommodation chosen. There is also a monthly maintenance fee. An endowment fund is available to assist individuals who would otherwise be unable to apply.

All buildings at East Ridge have reinforced concrete foundations. Floors are concrete slab on grade; tie beams and columns are concrete, designed to meet hurricane specifications. Other construction elements include wood truss rafters, built-up gravel roofs and concrete block interior partitions. Exteriors are finished in brick or stucco in pastel shades. Interior walls are plastered; floors are covered with non-slip materials (including carpeting).

1

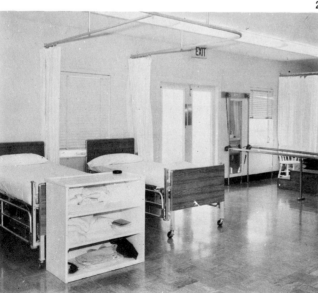

2

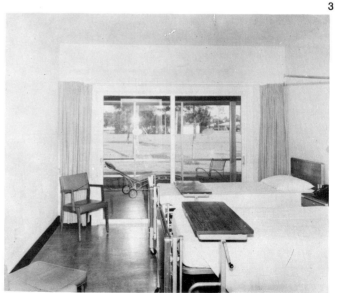

3

Doors are wood in integral metal
frames and trim. Aluminum awning
windows and glass jalousies are also
used.

Health Center:
1 Exterior
2 Therapy Room
3 A double room
4 Reception and nursing station

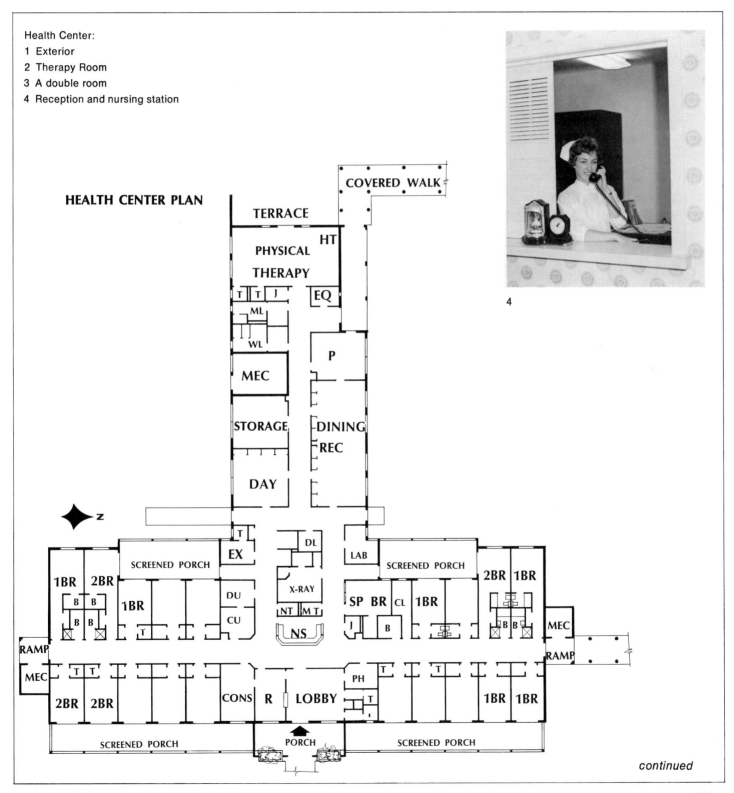

HEALTH CENTER PLAN

4

continued

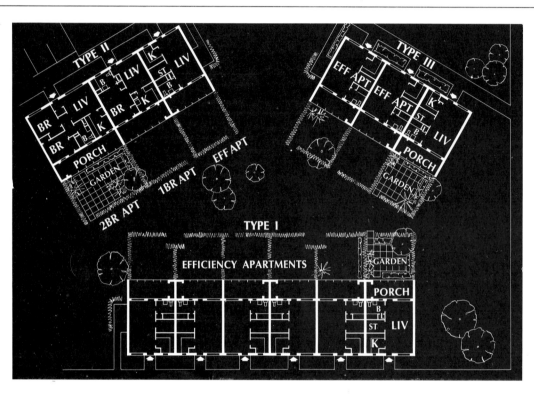

2

1 Type II residential building with three efficiency apartments

2 Detached houses. Note electric cart at right

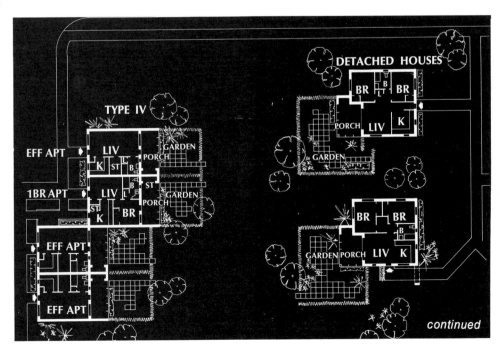

continued

EAST RIDGE RETIREMENT VILLAGE

1

2

3

104

5

4

1 The village swimming pool

Dining and chapel building:
2 Library
3 Dining room
4 Kitchen

5 Founders Fountain

**JEWISH ORTHODOX HOME
FOR THE AGED**
Beechwood, Ohio

ARCHITECT
*Gruzen & Partners
New York, New York*

PURPOSE
Residential, nursing, and day care facilities

CAPACITY
281 beds

COST
$5,670,000

With the aim of establishing a sense of privacy and a residential rather than an institutional feeling, the architects of this multi-purpose nursing home designed a series of 1-story pavilions surrounding a main activities building. The individual units, each with a nursing staff to serve 25 to 35 residents, offer a range from minimal to maximal medical and intensive psychiatric care.

The buildings are grouped around landscaped courtyards and linked by covered walkways. They occupy the highest point on the site. Retaining walls made of railroad ties and filled

with plantings lie at the west end of the property. Next to the main parking lot an artificial lake has been created for esthetic reasons but also to collect rain water.

The central building serves day care patients as well as permanent residents. This extends the function of the home to that of a community geriatric center. Among the facilities available are a sheltered workshop, occupational and physical therapy departments, an X-ray unit and laboratory, and a variety of special medical clinics including dental and

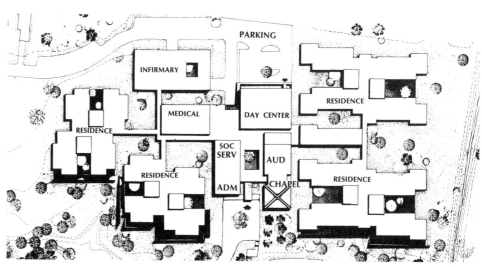

SITE PLAN

podiatry services. There is also a chapel and an auditorium, a snack bar and gift shop, a religious library, and suites for administrative and volunteer personnel.

All the buildings are of precast concrete construction with folded plate and double T members at the roof. The voids left between the structural columns are filled with brick and glass to complete the enclosure. Interiors are generally of metal stud construction with plaster on rock lath. A vinyl covering is added in bedrooms and in some other areas.

Care has been taken in the choice of color and furnishings for the home. Instead of the metallic dressers, beds, and desks that are the hallmark of many institutions, warm wooden wall units were chosen for the bedrooms. The activity rooms, which face the courtyards, were kept light and airy with furnishings that would be appropriate in or out of doors. With due consideration for the failing eyesight of the aged, wall colors are generally light to increase reflectivity and to contrast with darker floors. All colors are more vivid than normal.

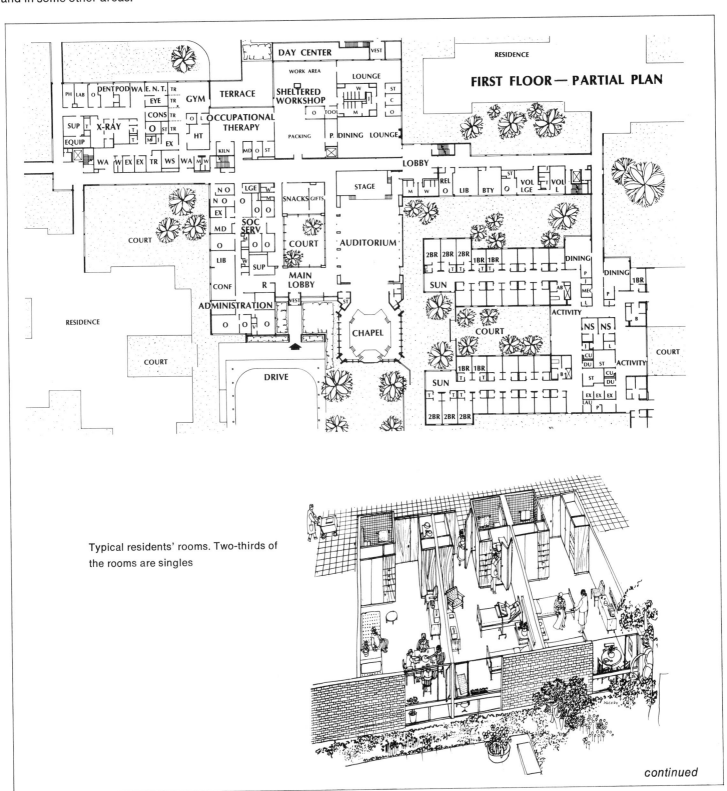

Typical residents' rooms. Two-thirds of the rooms are singles

continued

1

2

1 View towards the main entrance and
  chapel from landscaped courtyard
2 The folded plate roofs were chosen to
  convey a residential feeling
3 Sunny activities room flanks courtyard

3

1

1 Looking from the nurses' station toward
  a lounge in one of the maximum care
  pavilions
2 View across the central court from the
  main lobby

2

HOME FOR RETIRED PRESBYTERIANS
Washington, D.C.

ARCHITECT
Mills, Petticord & Mills
Washington, D.C.

PURPOSE
Residential and nursing

CAPACITY
80 residents
60-bed nursing facility

COST
$2,000,000

SPONSOR
Presbyterian Church

A 3-story brick residence adjoining a 2-story nursing facility comprises the Home for Retired Presbyterians in Washington, D.C. The 12½-acre site, with variations in elevation of as much as 60 feet, overlooks the capital's lovely Rock Creek Park. The residence, completed in 1960, has the distinction of having been dedicated by then President Eisenhower.

The steel frame buildings follow traditional lines in design and construction materials. Cast stone trim, Georgetown Colonial brick, and cement tile shingles were the materials selected for the exteriors of the buildings. Walnut paneling and plaster walls were used inside, which, along with furnishings, lighting, and rugs in soft pastel colors help to create a warm home-like atmosphere.

The residence is cross-shaped in layout with a pitched-roof central section nestled between wings which project out at 45-degree angles to it. The southwest wing at the ground floor level houses a chapel; the southeast wing contains a medical suite

Main entrance of the residence

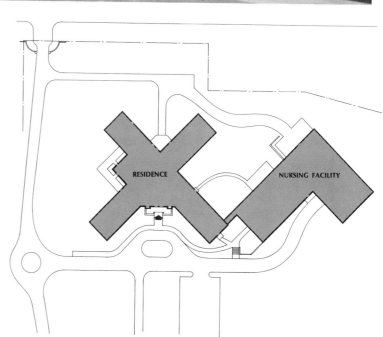

SITE PLAN

RESIDENCE

NURSING FACILITY

and infirmary wards and bedrooms. The other end of this wing houses storage and mechanical equipment and several staff bedrooms. The fourth wing on the ground floor and all but one of the wings on the upper two floors are reserved for residents' bedrooms. These are supervised from nurses' stations placed just to the right of the central core of the building. One wing on the second floor is used for resident and staff dining and kitchen facilities.

The L-shaped nursing addition is connected to the residence at the southeast wing (which contains the medical suite). Additional medical offices and examining rooms and the patients' dining rooms are placed at the first floor level in the nursing facility, with occupational therapy facilities and the superintendent's apartment in the basement. The remaining sections on the first and second floors of the addition are given over to patients' bedrooms on either side of a central space. In the short leg of the L this central space contains an island of work, storage, and utility areas ending at the intersection in a nursing station and staff area.

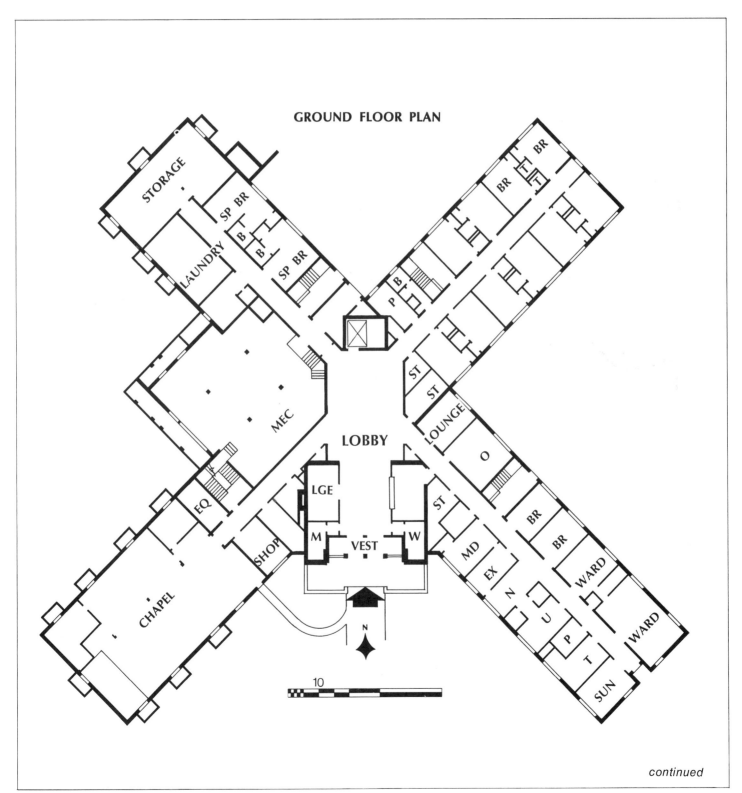

GROUND FLOOR PLAN

continued

1

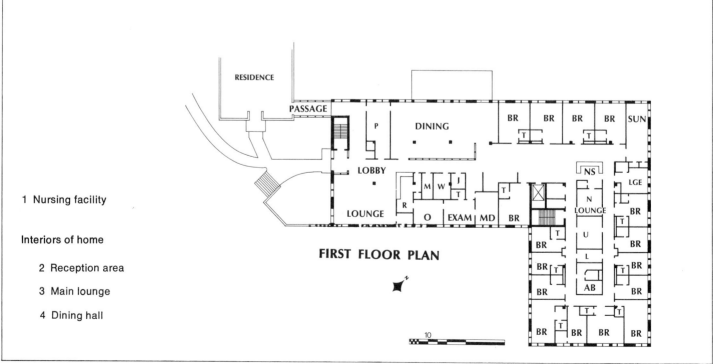

1 Nursing facility

Interiors of home

   2 Reception area

   3 Main lounge

   4 Dining hall

FIRST FLOOR PLAN

2

3

4

GOOD SAMARITAN HOME
FOR THE AGED—Building I
St. Louis, Missouri

ARCHITECT
Manske and Dieckmann
St. Louis, Missouri, and
Hellmuth, Obata & Kassabaum, Inc.
St. Louis, Missouri

PURPOSE
Residential and nursing

CAPACITY
130 beds

COST
$1,045,598

SPONSOR
Good Samaritan Hospital, Inc.
(affiliated with the United Church of Christ)

The design of the Good Samaritan Home was strongly influenced by the site: a wooded slope overlooking the Mississippi River in southern St. Louis. The entrance, public rooms, lounges, and dining area have been placed on the second floor on a line with the street height of the slope. Bedrooms for ambulatory residents are on the first and third floors, while the fourth (top) floor has been reserved for bed patients, medical suites, and a clinic.

The bedrooms are disposed along the long facades of the rectangular-shaped reinforced concrete building, parallel to the river. The glass and brick curtain walls at these levels are broken up into a series of broad V's, creating architectural interest and at the same time slightly increasing the floor area of the single or double rooms. A horizontally folded entrance canopy reflects the V motif at the second floor level. Here the exterior walls are largely flat expanses of glass. A series of balconies punctuate the river side of the facade.

The reinforced concrete frame building uses brick and glass curtain walls with ceramic tile accents. Masonry block walls are finished with acoustical plaster in public areas.

1

SITE PLAN

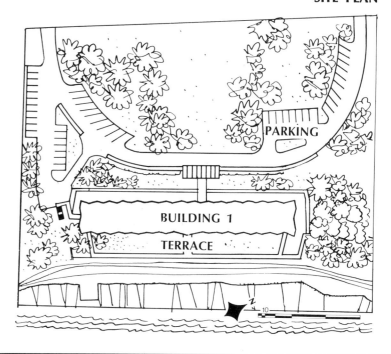

PARKING

BUILDING 1

TERRACE

2

3

1 The building profile on the river side.
View is at the second floor level

2 Street side of home with entrance at
second floor level

3 Dining room on second floor overlooking
river

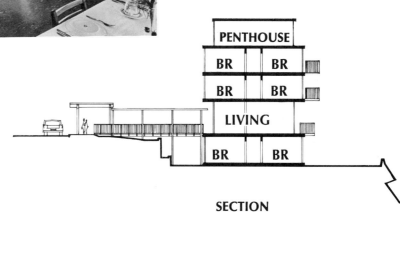

SECTION

TYPICAL FLOOR PLAN

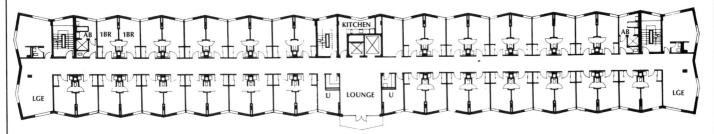

continued

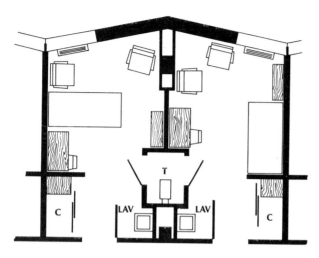

TYPICAL SINGLE ROOM PLANS

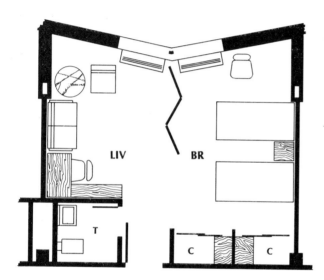

TYPICAL DOUBLE ROOM PLAN

1

1 Typical single residential room. Note variations possible in furniture placement (see plan). Double occupancy room for ambulatory residents uses folded partition to separate living from bed areas

2 Four-bed infirmary room

2

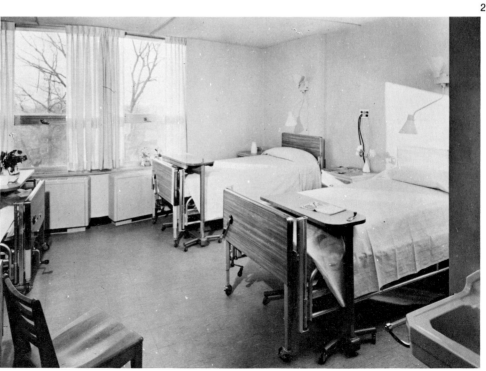

**GOOD SAMARITAN HOME
FOR THE AGED—Building II**
St. Louis, Missouri

ARCHITECT
Manske and Dieckmann
St. Louis, Missouri

PURPOSE
Residential

CAPACITY
78 beds

COST
$1,034,500

SPONSOR
Good Samaritan Hospital, Inc.
(affiliated with the United Church of Christ)

This 3-story addition to the Good Samaritan Home for the Aged can offer guests rooms which either overlook the river or face a landscaped park.

The single or double rooms are placed along the broad cross-bar of the T-shaped building. Each room is furnished with chairs, a reading desk, closet, wardrobe, and lavatory. Controls for the individual regulation of heating and air-conditioning are also provided. A number of snack kitchens, lounges, and utility rooms are included in this part of the building, which is topped by a penthouse containing mechanical equipment.

The stem of the T houses the common rooms, primarily an auditorium.

The reinforced concrete building has brick exterior walls and aluminum windows. A steep slope at the edge of the bluff made a long retaining wall necessary, and poured-in-place concrete piers were keyed into bedrock to keep the building from "slipping" off the bluff.

Interior finishing includes plaster walls, rubber tile floors, and acoustical tile ceilings. The addition is connected to the older building through a glassed-in walkway.

1 New residential building (center) extends Good Samaritan facilities along Mississippi River bluff

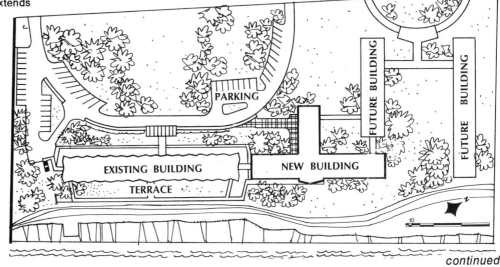

SITE PLAN

continued

1

1 Second floor lounge overlooks river.
  In foreground is a portion of the lobby
  separating the lounge from the chapel
2 Chapel interior. The large auditorium and
  stage on the first floor occupies the
  same area as the lobby and chapel above
3 View from street with chapel at left.
  Entrance to auditorium, (below chapel
  doors), is through an open passageway
  under the patio

2

TYPICAL SINGLE ROOM PLANS

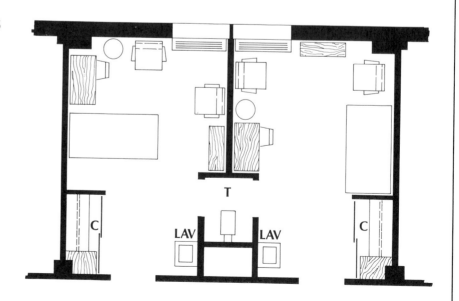

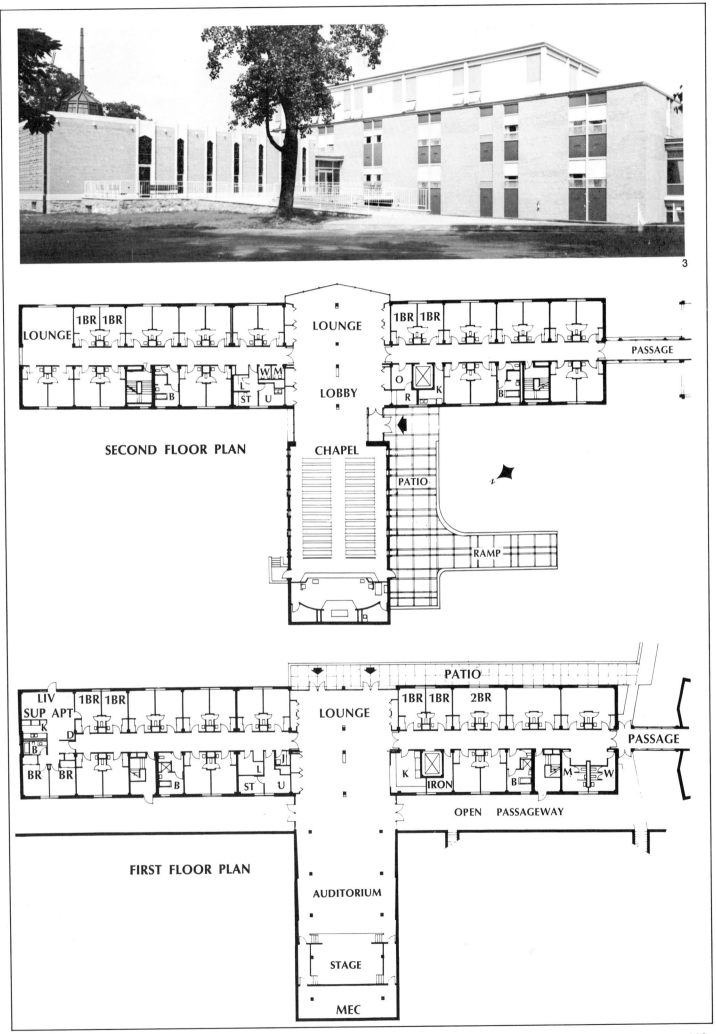

3

SECOND FLOOR PLAN

LOUNGE 1BR 1BR

WM
B
L
ST U

LOUNGE

LOBBY

1BR 1BR

O
R
K
B

PASSAGE

CHAPEL

PATIO

RAMP

FIRST FLOOR PLAN

LIV
SUP APT
K
D
B
BR BR

1BR 1BR

B
ST U
L

PATIO

LOUNGE

1BR 1BR 2BR

K
IRON
B
M W

PASSAGE

OPEN PASSAGEWAY

AUDITORIUM

STAGE

MEC

ISABELLA HOUSE
New York, New York

ARCHITECT
Joseph Douglas Weiss and Associates
New York, New York

PURPOSE
Residential and nursing

CAPACITY
233 dwelling units
114-bed infirmary

COST
$5,716,000 (including site development; excluding fees)

SPONSOR
Isabella Geriatric Center (non-profit)

Isabella House is a 17-story reinforced concrete building in upper Manhattan, adjacent to Isabella Home, a domiciliary facility which is traditional in design. The new building, completed in 1965, was designed to serve independent elderly residents who live in efficiency or 1-bedroom apartments, and nursing patients who live on three infirmary floors. Separate entrances and elevators are used for the two categories of residents.

The building was planned so that floors 6 through 10, currently used for efficiency apartments, can be readily converted to nursing units. All wiring and plumbing have been built in for immediate future use, and only minor alterations and the addition of a day-dining room are needed for full conversion.

Residents lease their apartments by the year and pay a monthly fee to cover electricity, cleaning service, and linen. All apartments have small kitchenettes for preparing breakfast or snacks. Residents take their main meals in the central dining room,

1 North facade.

2 South facade with existing Isabella Home in the foreground

3 Detail of south facade showing entrance to Isabella Nursing Home

4 North facade. Bay-windowed stories are residential floors which can be converted to nursing floors with only minor alterations

1

making selections from menus at each meal.

The residential hotel atmosphere continues with a reception desk in the lobby, a tea shop, beauty and barber shops, a bar, and a large auditorium with stage and movie equipment.

If a resident becomes ill he may call a doctor whose offices are located in a physician's suite in the lobby, or he may call his own doctor. Nurses are on call at all times in case of emergency.

On all floors where elderly persons are likely to be living alone in efficiency apartments there is a communal living room with a kitchen attached to promote socializing, and also a community automatic laundry room with lounging space and fine views.

The clinical facilities for the nursing patients are on the second floor and are available to any resident on doctor's orders. In addition to examination and treatment rooms, there are X-ray facilities, medical, dental, podiatry, and ophthalmology offices, a social service department, rehabilitation medicine and occupational therapy facilities. If long-term care is recommended a resident may apply for admission to the Isabella Nursing Home or any other nursing facility.

Floors 3 through 5 house the nursing patients in single and double rooms. All rooms have toilet facilities which in the singles also includes tubs. Furnishings were chosen to emphasize a home-like atmosphere.

2

3

SITE PLAN

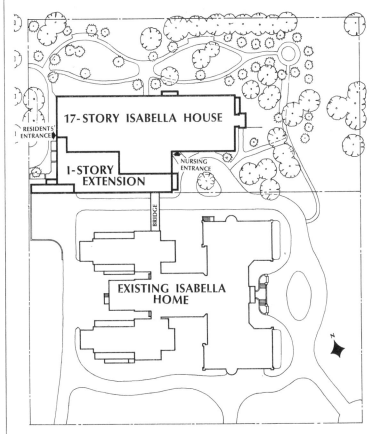

RESIDENTS' ENTRANCE

17-STORY ISABELLA HOUSE

1-STORY EXTENSION

NURSING ENTRANCE

BRIDGE

EXISTING ISABELLA HOME

N

4

continued

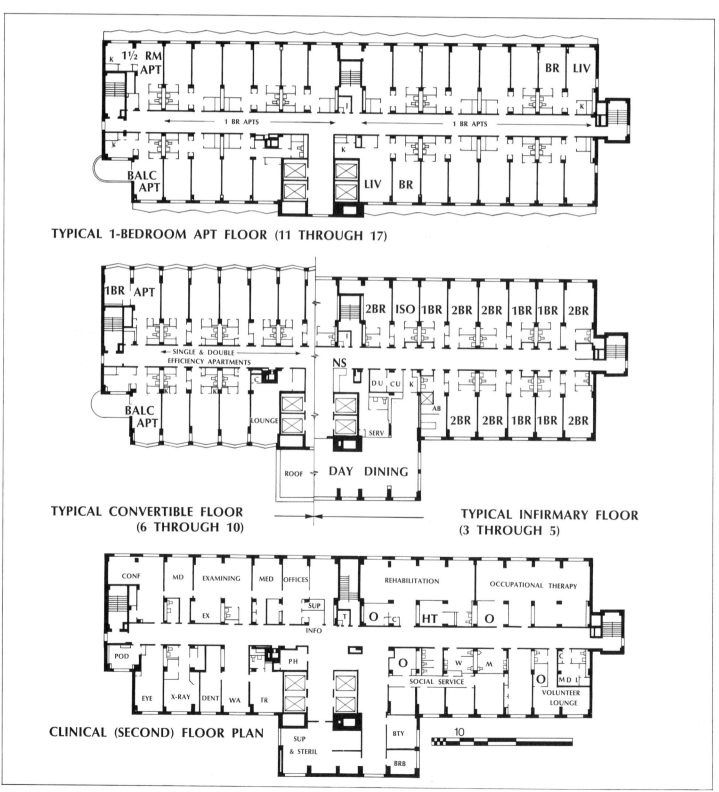

TYPICAL 1-BEDROOM APT FLOOR (11 THROUGH 17)

TYPICAL CONVERTIBLE FLOOR (6 THROUGH 10)

TYPICAL INFIRMARY FLOOR (3 THROUGH 5)

CLINICAL (SECOND) FLOOR PLAN

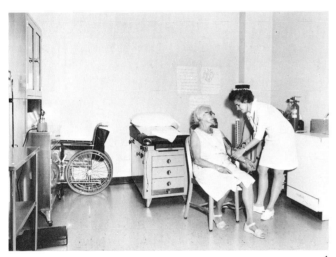

1

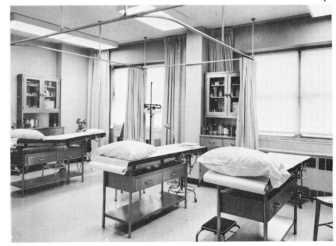

4

3

5

6

1 Examining room in the clinic, emergency section

2 Medical desk in the clinical area

3 Bay window area in an efficiency apartment

4 Examining room in the clinic

5 Kitchenette in an efficiency apartment

6 Single room in the infirmary

ST. ANTHONY CENTER
Houston, Texas

ARCHITECT
Goleman & Rolfe
Ernest L. Youens, A.I.A., Partner
Houston, Texas

PURPOSE
Residential and nursing

CAPACITY
137 dwelling units
192-bed nursing facility

COST
$7,500,000

SPONSOR
The Sisters of Charity of the
Incarnate Word

"A conservative estimate has it that by 1970, Harris County alone will contain over 100,000 people over 65," states a brochure of the St. Anthony Center in Houston. With such a forecast in mind, the Sisters of Charity of the Incarnate Word, owners of St. Anthony as well as some 20 other homes and hospitals in the southwest, have drawn up long-range plans for their 40-acre Houston property. In addition to the newly completed Center, (which replaces a smaller home on the grounds), the Sisters' building program calls for a day care center, a 150-bed

geriatric hospital, and a psychiatric unit. These facilities will encourage the expansion of already existing teaching and research affiliations between St. Anthony's and nearby Texas Medical Center.

The immediate need to be filled, however, was for a large multi-purpose facility, one that would provide apartments for elderly well persons and also nursing facilities for the chronically or acutely ill. The 10 stories and basement of the T-shaped St. Anthony Center are designed to do

1

just that. The basement is the clinical floor, fully equipped with a pharmacy, laboratory, classrooms, X-ray facilities, and a dental suite as well as the usual offices and treatment rooms. This level also contains a laundry and a workshop for residents, a snack bar, and beauty and barber shops.

The ground floor houses the major communal facilities of the Center: a 500-seat auditorium, the main dining hall, music and club rooms, physical and occupational therapy facilities, parlors, a guest suite, and a library.

A short foyer leading off the main corridor at one end of the building connects the Center to a modern 2-story circular chapel seating 250. The circular design with a centrally placed altar was planned to aid the hard-of-hearing. The balcony will accommodate wheelchair patients.

The second through the fifth floors are used to house chronically ill patients in single or double rooms. The nurses' station is at the center of the cross-bar of the T. A feature of St. Anthony's nursing care is a 6-bed intensive care

unit placed immediately behind the nurses' station on each nursing floor.

The four floors above the nursing units are residential, with room layouts generally following the plan of the nursing floors. The rooms are furnished in keeping with a high-rise modern apartment. Each residential floor includes a lounge and TV area and pantry and dining facilities. There are 29 single and 9 double rooms on floors six, seven, and eight. The ninth floor is

continued

1 The front of the building showing the porch. At the left is the circular chapel
2 Exterior with St. Anthony statue in the foreground

2

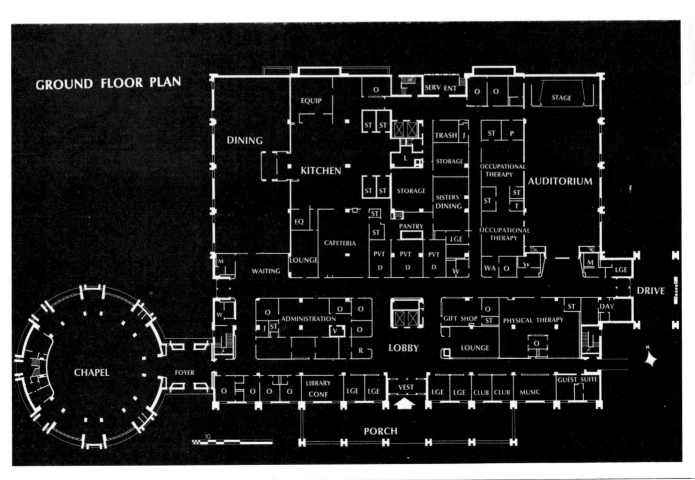

GROUND FLOOR PLAN

divided into 23 suites, each the size of a double room and consisting of a living room, bedroom, bath, and storage areas. The tenth floor serves as the Sisters' convent but may be converted to provide additional residential capacity.

The reinforced concrete building uses conventional pan and joist floor slabs. The exterior is brick and Indiana limestone. Windows are bronze colored anodized aluminum, recessed for sun control.

Interior partitions are plaster with heavy-duty vinyl covering in the corridors and bedrooms. Floors are terrazzo in the public areas, ceramic tile in bath areas, and vinyl in bedrooms. Acoustical ceiling tile has been used where sound control was a factor.

A "happy feature of the building," according to the architect, was the addition of a wide covered porch that runs along the front of the building. "On a day when the weather is even halfway good, there is almost an exodus from the breakfast table to the porch, where residents may spend most of the day."

1

2

TYPICAL FLOOR PLAN

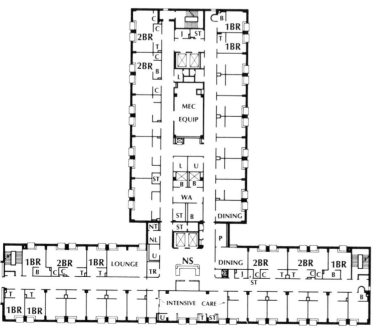

3

1 Lounge with game room beyond folding partition
2 Wooded grounds provide pleasant walks for residents
3 TV and game room

1 A corner of the front porch looking
   toward the chapel
2 An antique fountain in the lobby

continued

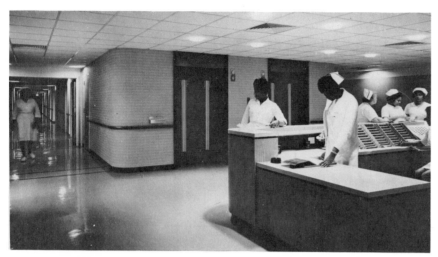

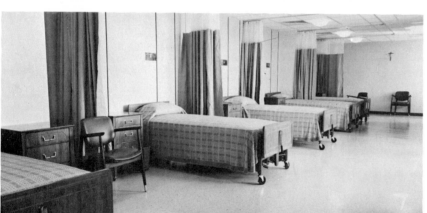

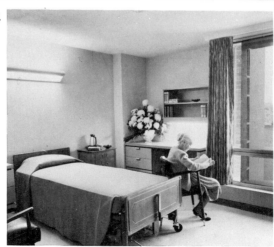

1 Typical nurses' station
2 A 6-bed intensive care unit
3 The 2-story circular chapel
4 Typical single room

Residential and Nursing Care Facilities in Other Countries

The structures described in this section represent major residential and health care facilities in Canada and Europe. In the English example the elderly are treated as a special sub-group of a community planned for all ages. The Italian example focuses on complete medical and surgical care for the elderly. It is a modern geriatric hospital, a type of institution more common abroad than in the United States. The other projects depicted fall between the classifications of residential and hospital orientation, and were selected for their variety of settings, architectural styles, costs, and services provided.

RESIDENCE FOR THE AGED
Blackeberg, Sweden

ARCHITECT
Carl Nyrén, S.A.R.
Stockholm, Sweden

PURPOSE
Residential

CAPACITY
130 dwelling units

COST
1,800,000 kronor

SPONSOR
The City of Stockholm

Blackeberg is a suburb of Stockholm on the west branch of the subway about six miles from the downtown center. The site for the *pensionarshem* (home for pensioned or retired) is small, so the architect designed an 11-story apartment house to provide sufficient dwelling units. The high-rise solution is still unusual in Sweden where the trend in housing for the elderly has been toward low-rise no-elevator buildings.

The site does adjoin a public park and recreation area, however, so that pleasant views and leisure time facilities are readily available.

The typical residential floor of the reinforced concrete building has 11 1-room efficiency apartments and one 2-room apartment. The rooms flank a central hallway with closets and bathrooms nearest the hall, and small kitchens and alcoves near the windows. At one end of the hall is a large circular staircase and two elevators; at the other, the fire stairs.

There is a small meeting room, laundry, and two clubrooms in the basement, and on the 12th, or roof floor, two rooms for weaving or other crafts, and storage space for every apartment.

1

TYPICAL FLOOR PLAN

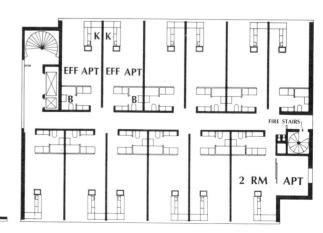

On the ground floor near the entrance is a clinical area. At fixed hours residents may come for examinations or treatment by visiting health workers provided by the government. Hot and cold meals for residents who may not want or be able to cook are also available as part of the centrally organized care for the aged. These are delivered daily and kept in hot or cold storage units.

The building's frame is poured-in-place concrete on which light-weight concrete facade elements were hung.

2

1 Exterior
2 North facade with door to basement level

SECTION

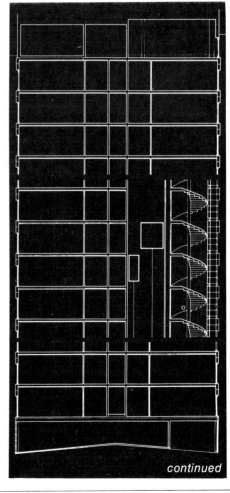

continued

1 Site adjoins a public park (foreground)
2 Typical single room with kitchen at left
  and alcove at right
3 Club room opens onto grounds at grade

HOME FOR THE AGED AT KRESSBRONN
Ottenberg, Germany

ARCHITECT
Wilfried Beck-Erlang, B.D.A.
Stuttgart, W. Germany

PURPOSE
Residential

CAPACITY
120 beds

SPONSOR
A Roman Catholic Mutual Aid Organization

One of the prime considerations in the design of this 5-story home for the aged was that the rooms face Lake Constance. The site lies along one of the southern slopes leading down to the lake east of the village of Kressbronn at Ottenberg. The resulting plan, which called for a broad Y-shaped structure with projecting chapel and dining room extensions at lower levels, not only succeeds in this aim, but scores esthetically as well. The finished reinforced concrete building is handsome and dramatic. The architect has made the most of the

clean lines and texture of concrete. The use of louvered sun-screens, wind-protected inner courts, modern sculpture, gardens, and pools has further enhanced the design, and helped create an altogether successful and livable building.

The position of the building on a slope made it possible to place the basement and sub-basement below ground. Here are the garages, storerooms, main laundry, sewing, and other maintenance or utility areas. The sub-basement houses the heating plant

continued

The residential wings; at right, the projection of the dining room

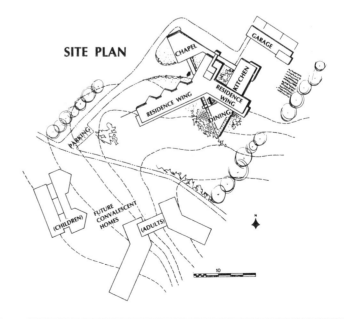

ORIENTATION DIAGRAM

VIEW OF LAKE

MAIN WIND DIRECTION

LAKE VIEW TOWARDS SWITZERLAND

LAKE VIEW TOWARDS BREGENZ

SITE PLAN

CHAPEL
GARAGE
KITCHEN
RESIDENCE WING
RESIDENCE WING
DINING
PARKING

(CHILDREN)
FUTURE CONVALESCENT HOMES
(ADULTS)

HOME FOR THE AGED AT KRESSBRONN

and auxiliary facilities.

The entrance floor above these is also partially below ground, and, one might say, partially incorporates the grounds. For in addition to the lobby and concierge's office, three guest rooms, ample storage space for residents, and other auxiliary facilities, there are several inner garden courts, one with a sheltered seating space and an upper gallery, and several smaller

wind-protected areas with sculpture and pools. A passageway at this level leads to the 150-seat chapel at the northwestern side of the building. A separate outside entrance makes it possible for townspeople to attend services without having to pass through the home.

Stairs, a ramp, and an elevator all lead from the 2-story lobby at the entrance level to the terrace floor. The main dining room forms a glassed-in triangular projection at this level, again providing residents with clear views

of the lake and landscape. A smaller dining room extends beyond it. In addition to kitchens and pantries, this floor also contains three double rooms for residents, four large social rooms, and the apartments of the managers and superintendent of the home.

Above the terrace floor are three residential floors the uppermost of which is an attic floor, set slightly back from those underneath. Each of these floors contains single and double rooms, day rooms, a living room,

1

2

3

4

tea kitchens, staff quarters, and appropriate service or utility facilities. The lowest residential floor has a large 1,100-foot terrace over the larger dining room. All single rooms and most of the doubles have balconies with sun-screens. Opaque glass partitions are used to separate the balconies for each room. Light-colored plaster and pebble surfaces contrast with the concrete finish to create color and textural interest on the facades of the building not dominated by the balconies and sun-screens. The flat roof is gravelled roofing board over an insulating cork layer.

Care has been taken to sound-proof interiors. Floors of rooms and passageways are linoleum over a floating-floor system. Hung ceilings use sound-absorbing insulating panels. Double-wall partitions are used between rooms.

The halls of the longest corridors are illuminated in part by natural light from false balconies on one side. These have been placed between the three triangularly projecting double rooms.

Natural wood has been used in window frames, in some interiors, and for much of the furniture, in order to create a warm residential feeling. The entrance floor is tiled.

Convalescent homes for young people and adults are also planned for this site, but they will be placed so that they will not interfere with the views or traffic to and from the home for the aged.

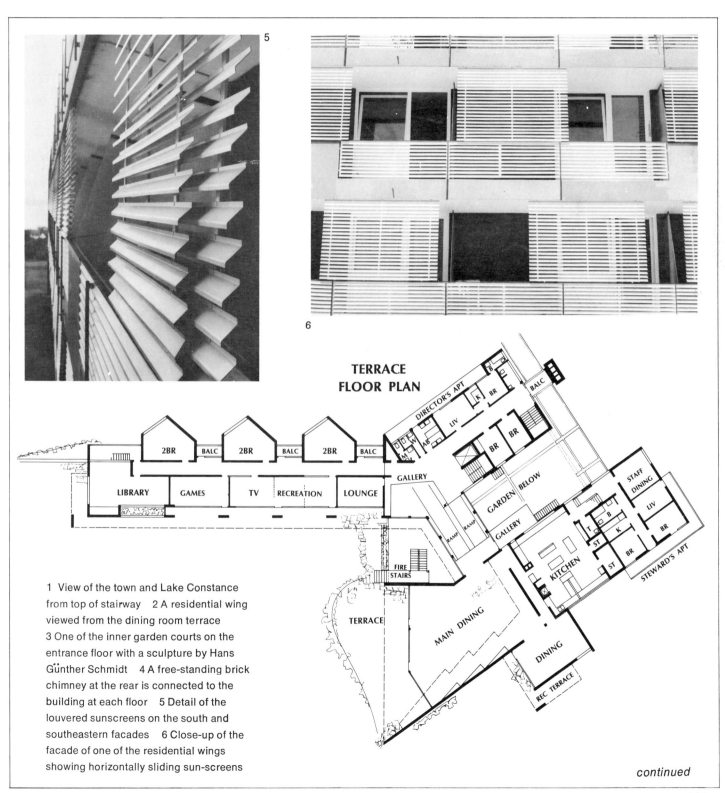

TERRACE FLOOR PLAN

1 View of the town and Lake Constance from top of stairway 2 A residential wing viewed from the dining room terrace 3 One of the inner garden courts on the entrance floor with a sculpture by Hans Günther Schmidt 4 A free-standing brick chimney at the rear is connected to the building at each floor 5 Detail of the louvered sunscreens on the south and southeastern facades 6 Close-up of the facade of one of the residential wings showing horizontally sliding sun-screens

continued

1 Corner of a typical day room

2 Section of the larger dining room

3 The interior of the chapel with abstract stained glass window designed by the painter Fritz Ruoff

4 Steel sculpture by Kurt Frank in the pool next to the covered passageway leading from the main entrance to the chapel

1

TYPICAL TWO BED ROOM

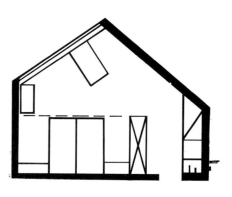

2

4

3

5

5 Chimney and covered passageway
leading to sloping-roof chapel

6 Non-skid rubber-surfaced ramp leads
from the entrance level to the dining
rooms

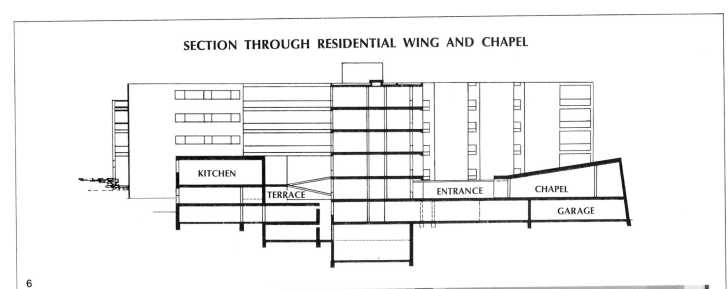

SECTION THROUGH RESIDENTIAL WING AND CHAPEL

KITCHEN

TERRACE

ENTRANCE

CHAPEL

GARAGE

6

SELVALE ESTATE
Felixstowe, England

ARCHITECT
Peter Barefoot and Associates
London, England

PURPOSE
Residential

CAPACITY
126 dwelling units

COST
£344,589

SPONSOR
Felixstowe Urban District Council

The 1-, 2-, and 3-story dwellings of Selvale Estate were designed with a mixed-aged community in mind. About half the units will accommodate old people, the other half, younger families needing up to three bedrooms. The estate, owned by the Felixstowe Urban District Council, will provide housing for about 350 persons in 1-bedroom apartments, 2-story houses or "maisonettes" over apartments, and 1-story row houses exclusively for the elderly. Some of the 3-story units were intended to house three generations, with young children and grandparents under the same roof.

No automotive traffic will be allowed within the site. The existing roads surrounding the property can be used for access, services, deliveries, and parking, (one car per two dwellings was stipulated in the program).

As a focus of social activity the architect proposed a central path leading to a court about 75 feet square. Near the square is a clubhouse for the elderly with a kitchen attached. This is used for the preparation of welfare meals which are delivered to infirm persons living alone in the area.

The accommodations for older persons

1

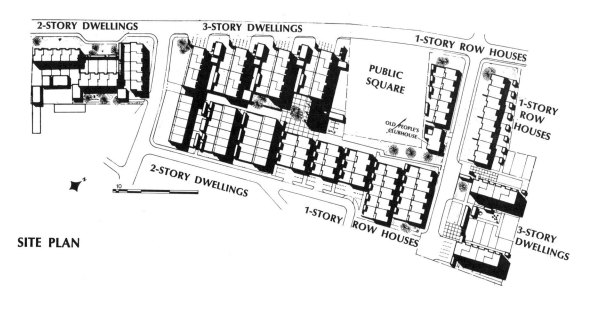

SITE PLAN

incorporated convenience and safety features. The 1-story houses can be used by persons in wheelchairs. Storage space, equipment, and fittings are within easy reach, and safety handrails are provided in bathrooms.

The prohibition of vehicular traffic permitted considerable space to be devoted to landscaping and play areas. There are sand-pits, climbing poles, and equipment for very small children near each block of maisonettes, and a larger playground with swings, parallel bars, and tunnels near the central square. Most of the dwellings have private gardens and outside storage space for tools and bicycles. The private gardens in the backs of houses are screened, and grass lawns in front have been planted and maintained by the local authority. Trees and shrubs have also been planted, and an official lime tree-planting ceremony for the central square was arranged to encourage tenants to take an interest in the landscaping plans.

Traditional construction and materials were used throughout in keeping with the surrounding countryside. Gray brick load-bearing walls with white mortar, concrete floors, and gray tile roofs were selected.

A variety of heating systems are being tried for comparative cost purposes. These include solid fuel; under-floor electric heating (in old persons' accommodations); and warm air convection, both by gas and electric power.

2

1 View of a 3-story and part of a 2-story unit at the west end of the site
2 The old people's clubhouse with kitchen beyond (under construction)
3 Open log-burning fireplace in old people's common room.

3

L-SHAPED FLATS FOR OLD PEOPLE

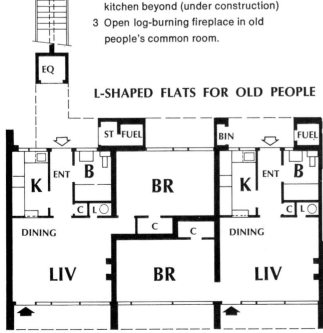

continued

Entry hall of a 2-story 3-bedroom dwelling.
The houses and the maisonettes over old
people's flats follow similar layouts

TWO-PERSON DWELLING

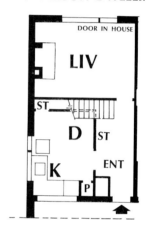

LOWER FLOOR

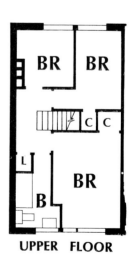

UPPER FLOOR

SECTION THROUGH 3-STORY DWELLING

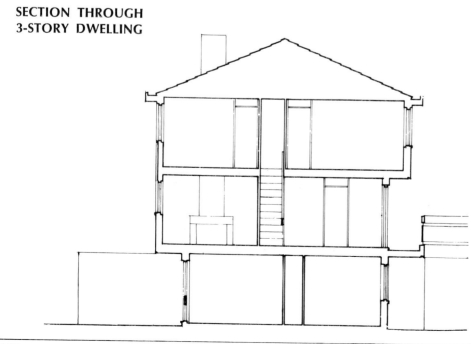

140

TYPICAL FLOOR PLAN FOR ROW HOUSES

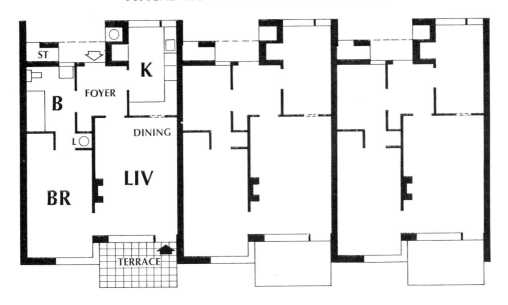

1 Front of a row house for elderly persons,
  bedroom on left; living room, right
2 Garden at the rear of a row house

JEWISH HOME FOR THE AGED & BAYCREST DAY CARE CENTRE
Toronto, Canada

ARCHITECT
Marani, Rounthwaite & Dick
Toronto, Canada

PURPOSE
Nursing and residential
with day care facilities

CAPACITY
425 beds
350 day care patients

COST
$7,250,000

SPONSOR
Baycrest Centre for Geriatric Care
(non-profit)

The aim of the four phase building program of the Baycrest Centre for Geriatric Care is to keep "the individual as independent as possible and functioning to the best of his ability alone, but with the knowledge that, when and if the time comes that he requires a more protective environment, it is available to him." The two facilities planned for the first stage, the Jewish Home for the Aged and the Baycrest Day Care Centre have now been completed.

The new home is a 10-story reinforced concrete building which can accommodate over 400 residents on the upper eight floors, with activity areas and offices on the first two. The day care unit forms part of a lower level extension of the rectangular-shaped high-rise building linking it to the existing home and hospital. About 350 patients a week can make use of the day care facilities.

The two types of services represent some but not all the aspects of care the Baycrest Centre ultimately hopes to provide. The second phase of building calls for a new 200-bed rehabilitation and chronic illness

1

1 View of the home from the southwest, showing roof gardens and main dining room

2 Outdoor courtyard adjacent to the main dining room with stairs leading to roof terrace

3 Typical bays on the south side with precast sunshade device

hospital to be built on the site to replace the older home and hospital, which in Phase III will be converted to a 160-bed nursing home. Phase IV will consist of a 400-suite apartment house for the elderly. This is scheduled for completion in 1974 at which time the Centre will be able to offer almost any kind of living arrangement for the elderly, from very independent to completely sheltered care.

The first facilities to be completed fall between these two extremes. The Day Care Centre is planned for individuals who live in the community but who can benefit from the combination of therapy and social and recreational activities the Centre provides. Persons of any faith can come from one to four or five times a week and participate in arts and crafts, outings, or other group activities. The Centre has its own large meeting room (divisible into four smaller rooms), lounge, lobby, and entrance connected to the main entrance of the home by a covered walkway. Day Care participants also may share in major programs of the home, and take two meals a day in the central dining room. This arrangement works to the advantage of the day care participant as well as staff, for if the full facilities of the home are ever needed, the individual is already familiar with the physical arrangement and knows and is known by the staff.

The floor above the day care facilities houses a large 500-capacity auditorium with a spacious foyer and an adjacent servery. Other facilities at the lower levels of the new building include the kitchen, dining room, staff cafeteria, snack bar, sundries shop (staffed by volunteers), gift shop, arts and crafts

continued

2

3

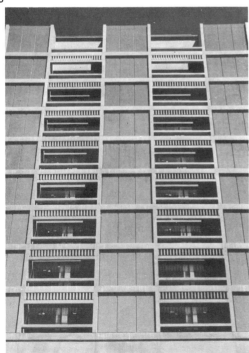

SITE PLAN

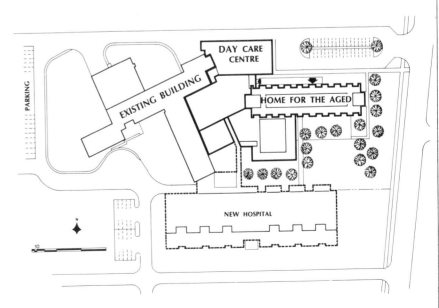

JEWISH HOME FOR THE AGED

facilities, various lounges, a board room, and a library. A basement houses a sheltered workshop in addition to the boiler room, mechanical equipment, and storage areas.

The dining room is a largely glassed-in rectangular-shaped extension of the first floor of the home with views of a garden or terraces along two sides and a busy thoroughfare on the third. The roof garden over it along with adjacent areas are accessible directly from the outside by stairs.

The residential floors of the home have been organized according to the degree of nursing care needed. "Special Care" patients— either mentally or physically deteriorated— are placed on floors 3 and 4; "Nursing Care" patients—mentally alert but needing occasional nursing or aid in dressing or bathing are on the top two floors. These floors have their own dining rooms, lounges, and solariums. The "Standard Care" patients on the floors in between take their meals in the main dining room but also have lounges and solariums on their floors.

About 70 per cent of the rooms are doubles, the rest singles. All rooms have toilet and lavatory facilities which have been placed at the exterior walls and form bays along the facade. The windowed areas between have special concrete sunshades.

One of the reasons for the exterior placement of washrooms was to avoid a narrow corridor upon entering a room. The architects also wished to avoid narrow hall corridors so they

1 Main dining room with view towards street

2 Typical corridor with built-in lighting in handrails

3 Day Care Centre lobby

4 Mezzanine lounge area

5 Main entrance lobby and lounge area (adjacent to dining room at right)

(Note these pictures were taken prior to completion of the building)

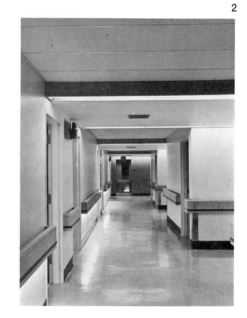

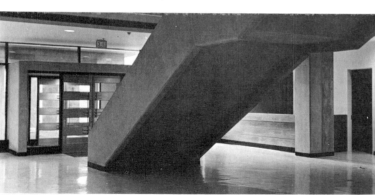

have arranged the nurses' station, central bathing and other supportive services along one side of the hall in a series of projections. The doors to the patients' rooms have been placed in the niches in between. The rooms themselves have been designed to emphasize a feeling of domesticity with built-in cabinet work and soft but adequate lighting. Music and synagogue services can be piped in.

Doors will accommodate wheelchairs and in central activity areas open automatically. Lighted handrails are used in corridors.

Among the facilities available in the older building are physical and occupational therapy, a dental clinic, laboratory, pharmacy, and synagogue.

It is interesting to note that admission to the home or day care facilities is not restricted according to faith or finances. Approximately 30 percent of the residents pay the full cost of care. Another 33 percent pay their old age pension only, and the remaining 37 percent pay only what they and their families can afford. The deficit is made

up through government grants, through the United Community Fund, and by funds raised by the Woman's Auxiliary and the Men's Service Group.

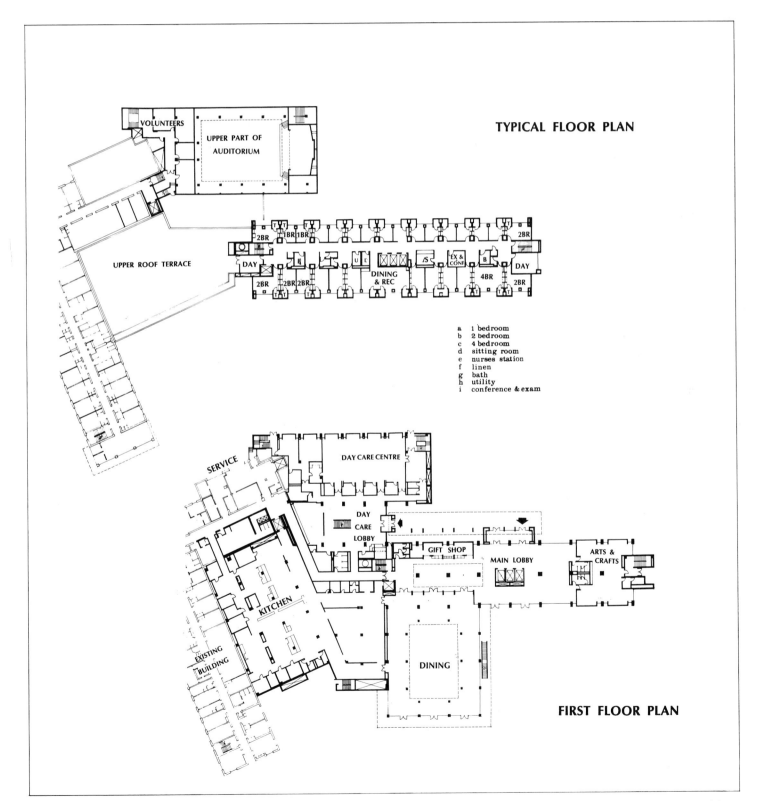

TYPICAL FLOOR PLAN

a   1 bedroom
b   2 bedroom
c   4 bedroom
d   sitting room
e   nurses station
f   linen
g   bath
h   utility
i   conference & exam

FIRST FLOOR PLAN

GAMMELBYN'S HOME FOR THE AGED— NEW BUILDINGS
Stureby, Sweden

ARCHITECT
Anders Tengbom, S.A.R.
Stockholm, Sweden

PURPOSE
Residential and nursing

CAPACITY
52 residents
270-bed nursing facility

COST
8,000,000 kronor

In a country celebrated for its advances in social legislation it is not surprising that old people are referred to as "pensioners," for old age in Sweden does not evoke the economic fears it does elsewhere in the world. Retirement means leisure with a comfortable pension and services provided by the government.

At Stureby, the architect Anders Tengbom has designed four new buildings for a home for the aged. Two smaller connected 2-story buildings are residences with single rooms for 52 pensioners and central dining and commons rooms.

The two other buildings are virtually identical lozenge-shape 3-story nursing homes. Each nursing floor accommodates 45 patients—21 in single rooms, and 24 in six 4-bed wards for the chronically bedridden. It was felt that this arrangement would make for maximum efficiency in caring for the large number of patients the home maintains. The lozenge shape was chosen to break up the corridor lengths and create a more home-like atmosphere.

Running the length of the floors and following the building's outline is a central core "island." In addition to a nursing station, treatment room, storage areas, and bathing facilities, the core unit contains a coffee kitchen and a room for cleaning utensils and arranging flowers.

Balconies for airing clothes have been placed at either end of the building. Adjacent to these is a row of bays and balconies which extend from the 4-bed rooms and a lounge on either side of the building.

A laundry building, kitchen, chapel, and two residential buildings were part of the existing structures.

1

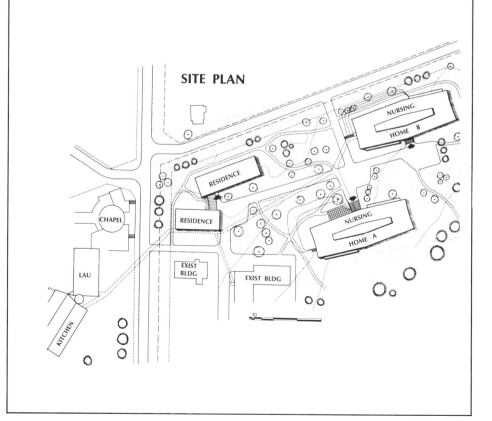

SITE PLAN

2

1 Nursing home entrance

2 Balconies for airing clothes have been
placed at the ends of each floor of the
home

NURSING HOME — TYPICAL FLOOR PLAN

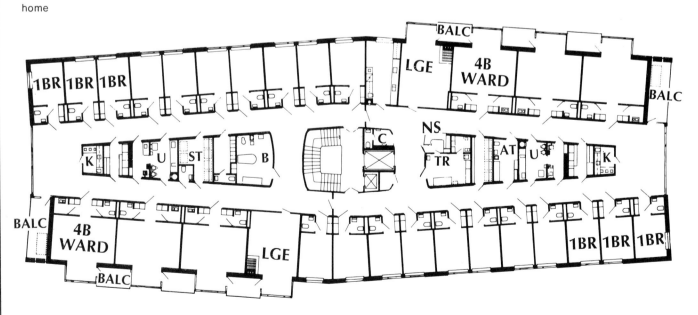

continued

GAMMELBYN'S HOME FOR THE AGED— NEW BUILDINGS

1

1 View into a projecting bay from a balcony of the nursing home

2 Central bathing facilities in core area

NURSING HOME — 4-BED WARD PLAN

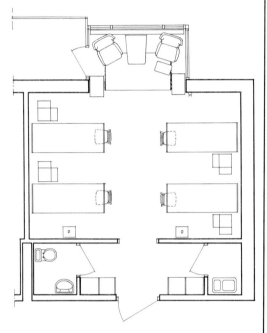

RESIDENTIAL BUILDING —
TYPICAL FLOOR PLAN

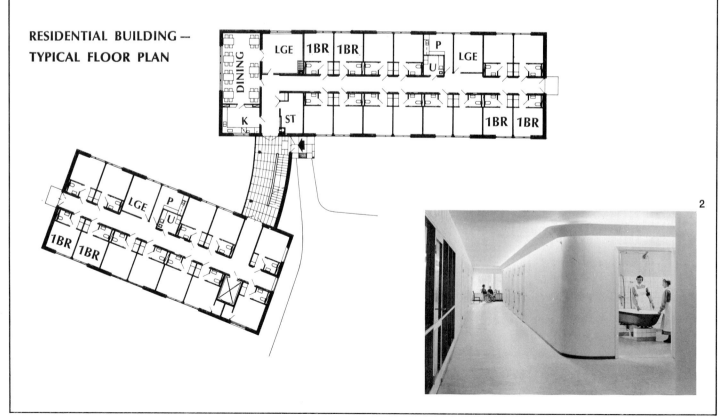

2

LA COURNEUVE CENTER FOR THE AGED
Paris, France

ARCHITECT
*Paul Chemetov, D.P.L.G. and
Jean Deroche, D.P.L.G.
Paris, France*

PURPOSE
Residential with infirmary

CAPACITY
30 dwelling units and infirmary

A limited budget, a small site, a poor suburb of Paris—these were the unpromising beginnings of a building program of apartments for the elderly. The end product, a central building connected by ramps to a pair of residences, is a handsome solution to the problems. The architects chose economical building materials and let their choices work esthetically for them. They exposed the concrete structural elements and used unglazed brick as facing material along with large areas of wood and glass. The combination of these textures echoed in the design of interior and exterior gardens have a charm and simplicity which blends well with the old stone houses of the neighborhood.

The central building has been designed around a circular patio open to the sky. Dining and meeting rooms, offices, lounges, and a library radiate from this hub which acts as a focus for the complex. The building's position on the site is close to the street in order to invite use of the facilities by non-residents.

Ramps at the side and rear of the building lead to the 2-story residential wings with a total of 30 living units plus a small infirmary and staff quarters. The majority of rooms are singles with toilets and lavatories. The rooms have been arranged in step fashion, each set a certain distance back from its neighbor. The effect is one of privacy and intimacy which is enhanced by the mode of entry. Glass-louvered passageways run the length of the wings so a resident may have the feeling that he is strolling on a quiet (covered) street and turning into his own private doorway. Once inside, he can view the garden or other parts of the complex from the window areas on the opposite wall. The position of one of the horizontal glass sections allows residents to see outside while seated.

A concrete cupola caps the central building. It has been sound-treated with an asbestos spray which will also insure heat insulation.

Wooden benches and brick paving were used in the exterior garden open to the public

View of the glass-louvered wall of the passageway of the longer residential building

continued

1

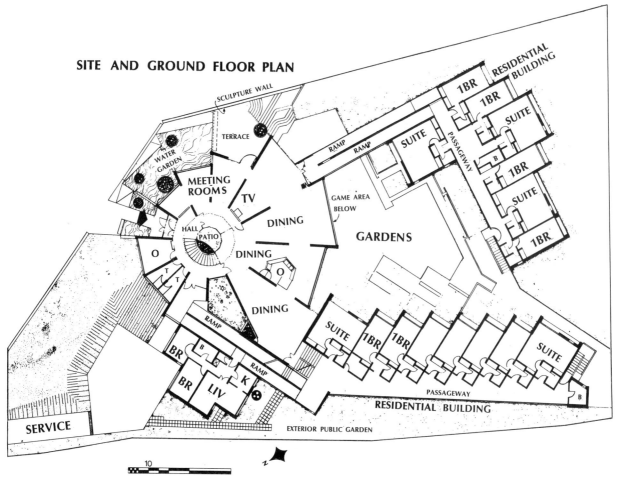

SITE AND GROUND FLOOR PLAN

2

3

4

1 The south facade of the longer residence faces the interior garden

2 The dining room (above, right) in the central building overlooks the interior garden. Covered area below may be used for ball games

3 View of the complex from above. The two residential wings are in the foreground

4 View of the ramp leading to the shorter residence as seen from the television room. In the background are typical neighborhood houses

continued

LA COURNEUVE CENTER FOR THE AGED

SECTION

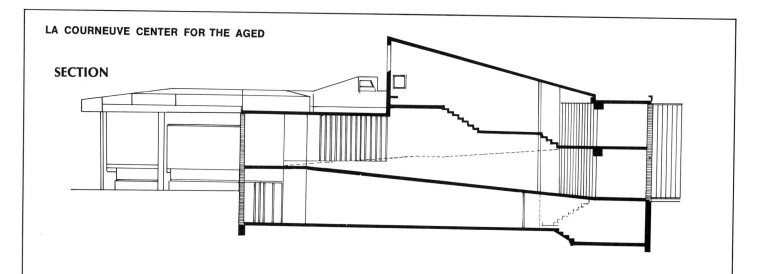

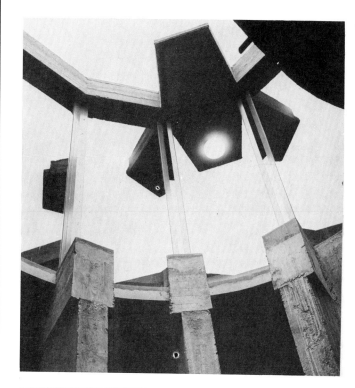

1

1 Roof gutter, reflected in glass panels, projects rainwater into the patio below. The effect is like a fountain

2 Glassed-in semi-circular passage overlooks patio. Dining and other group activity rooms radiate from this area

3 Dining room ceilings have been sound-proofed with an asbestos spray

2

3

1 Dining room with serving pantry. The small tables can be used individually or grouped for banquets

2 Mosaic designs set in a concrete wall can be seen from meeting rooms in the central building

3 View from the dining area across the glassed-in well towards the lobby

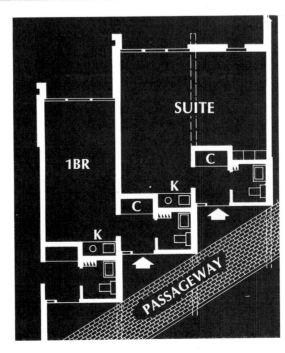

TYPICAL ROOM PLANS

MAIMONIDES HOSPITAL AND HOME FOR THE AGED
Montreal, Canada

ARCHITECT
Greenspoon Freedlander Plachta & Kryton Montreal, Canada

PURPOSE
Complete geriatric care

CAPACITY
247 beds

COST
$4,000,000 (excluding fees)

SPONSOR
Federation of Jewish Community Services

This modern 5-story hospital dedicated to the care and rehabilitation of elderly indigent patients is a model of careful planning for the patient's comfort and for ease of operation. Even future needs were thought of, for the building's mechanical and service equipment will serve three additional floors (200 more beds) some day, so that the transition may take place with a minimum of disturbance to patients and staff.

Privacy was a prime factor in the building layout. The "lazy H" pattern

makes it possible to divide each floor into five short-length sections so that patients may be grouped according to sex or type of illness. A majority of rooms—147—are singles. These and the 42 double rooms all have their own toilet facilities. Strong primary colors contrasting with a basic off-white color scheme were chosen for the interior. The colors vary from wing to wing and floor to floor. Such features, along with separate dining rooms and pantries, lounges, group activity rooms, balconies and solariums on every patient floor combine to create a

1

2

3

4

residential rather than an institutional flavor, a difficult assignment in a building this large.

A considerable amount of space has been assigned to physiotherapy and occupational therapy facilities. There is a large gymnasium, a hydrotherapy unit, a speech therapy clinic, and a sewing room, for example. Other ancillary facilities such as the small chapel, large auditorium, beauty and barber shops, snack bar, library, and "quiet" and "noisy" rooms make the building one of the most complete of nursing homes. In addition, of course, full hospital facilities are provided. There are departments of medicine, urology, gynecology, laryngology, and dermatology. There is an operating room and a fracture room, a dental clinic, a pharmacy, an X-ray department, and so on.

So that patients may feel secure and free to move about on their own, a number of safety features have been incorporated in the design. Solid grab bars have been placed on both sides of corridors. Special consideration has been given to wheelchair patients. Toilet rooms allow maneuvering on wheelchairs, and the toilets themselves have been raised on 4-inch bases and provided with heavy-duty grab bars. There are no steps anywhere in the building except at the fire stair towers which were required by the city code.

The building is of reinforced concrete construction. White Bentonite was used as a finish for the structural beams. Exterior walls were precast

continued

1, 2 Views of main entrance seen from one wing and in detail   3 End wall of a typical wing   4 Side view of main entrance
5 Wall detail showing multi-colored rock surfaces, white structural members, and aggregate panels

GROUND FLOOR PLAN

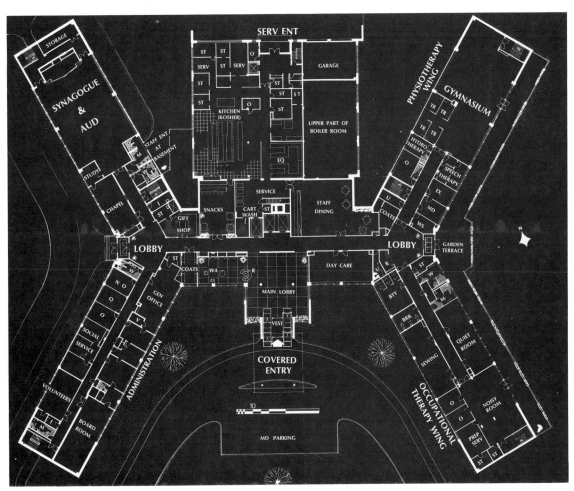

MAIMONIDES HOSPITAL AND HOME FOR THE AGED

granite chip aggregate panels
alternating with floor-to-ceiling
glazed units.

Black Bentonite was used at the base
and head of windows on the ground
floor. Broad areas of multi-colored
rock at the lower level provide
additional color and textural variety.

1

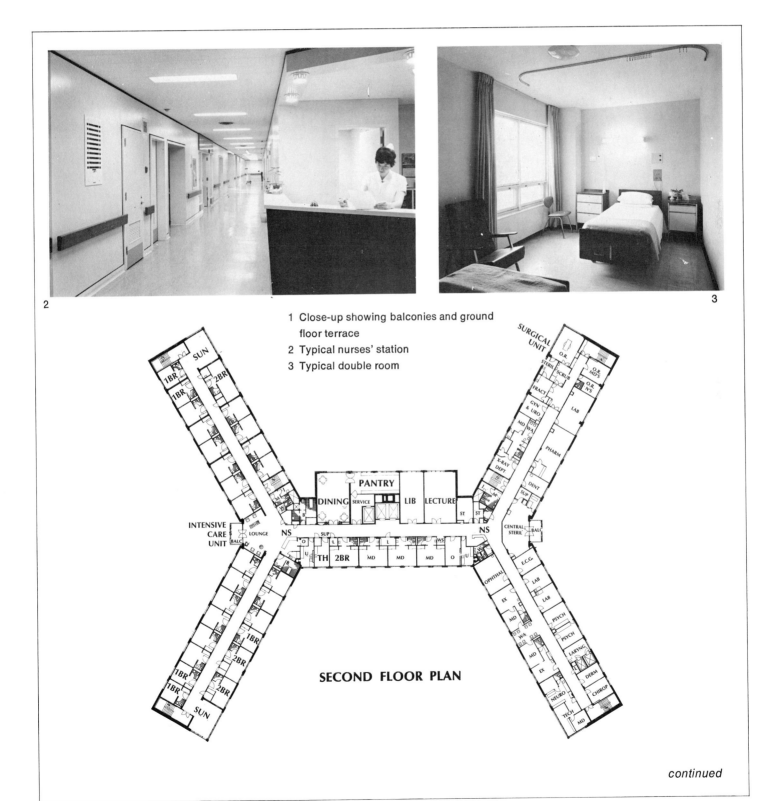

1 Close-up showing balconies and ground floor terrace
2 Typical nurses' station
3 Typical double room

SECOND FLOOR PLAN

continued

Waiting room in main lobby

Board room

Kitchen

Auditorium

LA MARTINIÈRE HOME FOR THE AGED
Sablé-sur-Sarthe

ARCHITECT
Guy Bisson, D.P.L.G.
Paris, France

PURPOSE
Residential and nursing

CAPACITY
80 residents
99-bed nursing facility

The romantic site for this large combination residence and nursing home is a vast woods which was once a castle park. The modern "castle" consists of a 2-story residence for 80 persons, a 3-story nursing home divided into three 33-bed units, a general services building which connects to both, and a separate chapel. All buildings are reinforced concrete with glass curtain walls in the patient wings.

Each residential or patient floor has two dining rooms and a pantry, a day room, and a television room. All floors

end in sun decks along the south facade. Several day rooms are two stories high in part, the remaining volume being occupied by the day room of the floor above, which, in effect, becomes a mezzanine overlooking the lounge below.

The nursing wing includes a library on the roof which opens onto a grass-covered terrace. Other facilities in this building are a medical treatment area including an X-ray department, the main kitchen, storage areas, the

continued

1

2

1 A view of La Martinière and its wooded site

2 The general services building is at the center connecting the 3-story nursing wing with the 2-story residence. In the right foreground is the chapel. Beyond the sheep meadow is the town of Sablé

LA MARTINIERE HOME FOR THE AGED

boiler room, electric generating equipment, and staff lockers and dining room.

The basic floor plan for both residential and nursing units consists of single rooms along the west side and doubles on the east. Some single rooms are arranged with a sliding partition which may be opened to permit occupancy by couples.

Tile floors and pine-laminated ceilings —often sloping and curved as in the library or main activities room—are a feature of the interior finishing. The contemporary furniture was designed specifically for the home and includes, in each patient room, a bed with a height-adjustable frame, an easy chair, a movable wall table which also serves as a night table, and a movable cupboard-closet. A wash basin and bidet have been placed in the dressing corner of each room and there is storage space for luggage in a compartment located above the

corridor outside.

A variety of measures were undertaken to minimize sound transmission. Bathing and toilet facilities have been centrally placed; plumbing from patients' rooms is routed through corridor ducts (accessible for easy maintenance); and all heating and electrical ducts have been embedded in concrete, either underground or in heavy partitions. The sliding partitions between individual rooms are thick and curtained on one side. Sound-absorbent materials have been used

1

2

for the walls in the day rooms.

A multi-color décor throughout the home makes use of natural materials and restful colors. It was based on recent research by Swiss and German psychologists.

1 West end of the complex. At the left is a bicycle shed; in the center, the chapel. Part of the residential wing shows in the right background, and the general services building is in the right foreground

2 View of the residence at the east end of the site. In the background is the nursing wing with the roof library and chimneys showing

3 A detail of the facade of the residential wing and the connecting passage. Room windows are wood sash set in aluminum sections. Shutters in the horizontal wood wooden strip separating upper and lower glassed areas provide ventilation

4 Curved and sloping library ceiling is pine-laminated. The room opens onto a grassed roof terrace

3

4

GROUND FLOOR PLAN

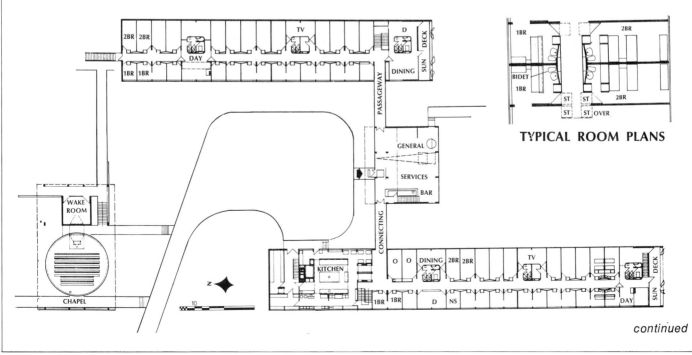

TYPICAL ROOM PLANS

continued

1 Several day rooms are 2-stories over part of their extent

2, 3, 4 The main living room in the general services building was designed to be a multi-purpose area. Facilities include a billiard room, beauty salon, dental suite, bar (lower center of 2 and continued in 3), and equipment and space for staging plays or projecting films

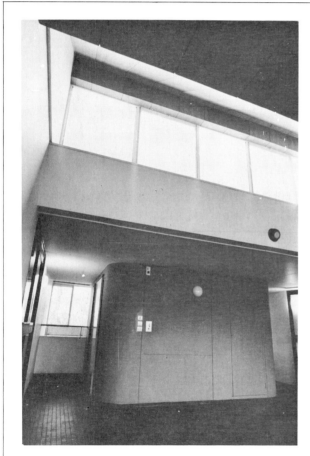

1

2

SECTION

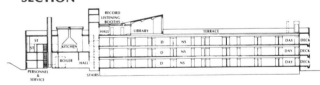

4

3

1 A dining room and sun deck. A sunken tub for flowers has been placed at the edge of the deck just beyond the railing

2 The chapel includes the altar room, a mortuary, and a room for holding wakes

3 Metal and glass ventilating hood above the central oven in the kitchen. The low gutter houses lighting fixtures and acts as a drain for condensation

4 Chapel interior

CHAPEL SECTIONS

LONGITUDINAL

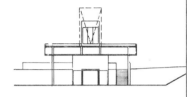

TRANSVERSE

1

2

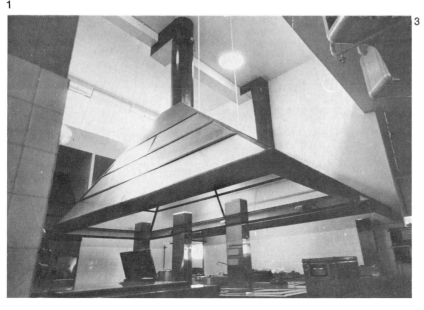

3

4

OSPEDALE GIUSTINIAN DI VENEZIA
Venice, Italy

ARCHITECT
Giorgio Zennaro
Venice, Italy

PURPOSE
Medical and surgical geriatric care

CAPACITY
400 beds

SPONSOR
Fondazione Opera Pia
G. B. Giustinian

Behind the walls of this classic Renaissance *palazzo* in Venice lies a completely modern geriatric hospital. Built as a monastery in 1472, the complex of buildings hemmed by canals on three sides retains only its exterior walls. The interiors were gutted and converted to an up-to-date facility catering to the special needs of the elderly. A staff of 23 full-time physicians renders medical service, augmented by outside consultants for such specialties as dermatology, gynecology, neurology, psychiatry and dentistry.

On the first floor there is an out-patient clinic with diagnostic and X-ray facilities, and a large department of cardiology. The upper two floors house the department of medicine, primarily treating gastro-intestinal and chest disorders), and the department of surgery.

There are two fully equipped general operating suites in the surgery department; a third, currently being built, will be used for ear, nose, and throat surgery. A pathology laboratory and

164

autopsy facilities are also available.

As in any hospital, patients are admitted for treatment and discharged when they are able to leave. The chronically ill or infirm are moved to other institutions. (An exception is made for 100 patients who, if they have no other resources, may reside in a special wing.)

In converting the buildings all wood construction was replaced by reinforced concrete and masonry. Elevators were installed, along with completely modern electrical, plumbing, air-conditioning, and mechanical systems. All patient rooms are equipped with oxygen piping.

The hospital is supported by the *Fondazione G. B. Giustinian.* While the institution is non-denominational, nursing services are furnished by a Roman Catholic nursing order.

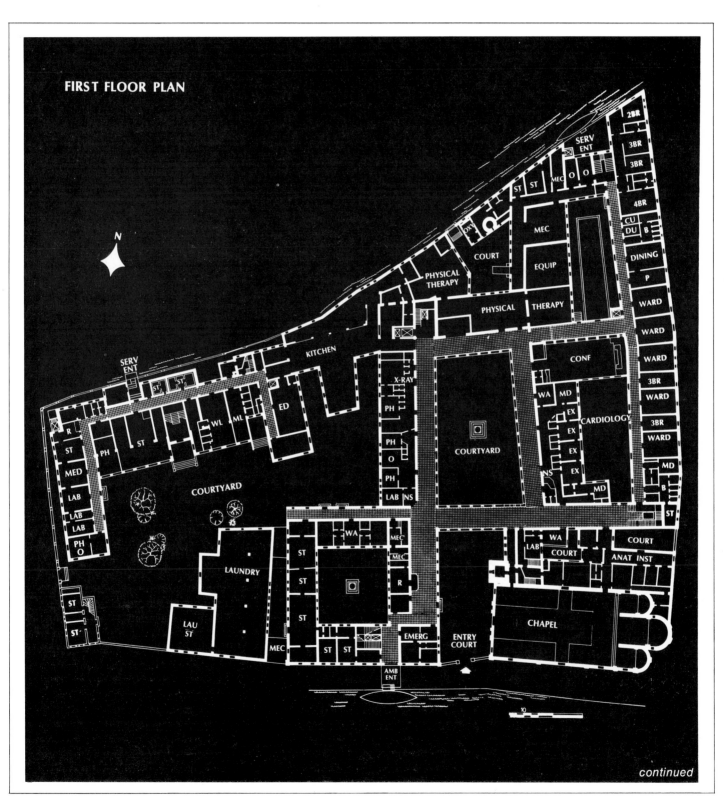

FIRST FLOOR PLAN

continued

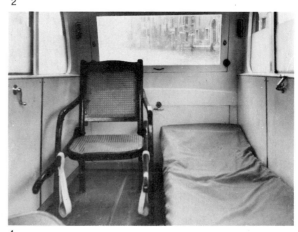

1, 2 Main entrance and detail
3 Floating ambulance
4 Interior of ambulance

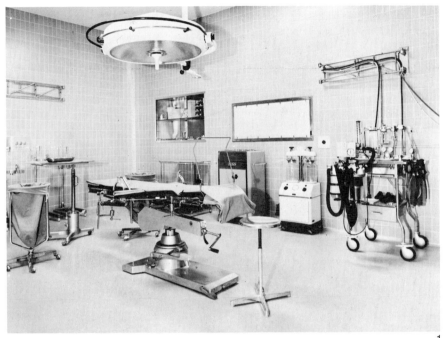

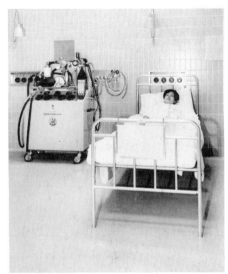

1   2

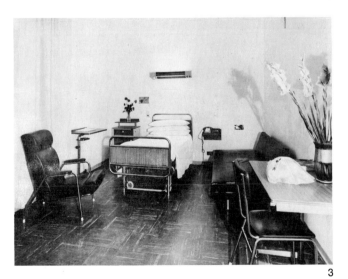

3   4

1 Operating room
2 Recovery room
3 Single room
4 Medical lecture room

AN EXPLANATION OF ABBREVIATIONS APPEARING IN THE FOLLOWING SECTION

AB	assisted bath		LGE	lounge
ACT	activity room		LIB	library
AD	admission		LIV	living room or area
ADM	administration		M	men's
APT	apartment		MAINT	maintenance
AT	assisted toilets		MD	doctor
AUD	auditorium		MEC	mechanical
B	bath		MED	medicine preparation
BALC	balcony		ML	men's lockers
BLDG	building		N	nurse
BP	bedpans		NEURO	neurology
BR	bedroom		NL	nurses' lockers
1 BR	one bed room		NS	nurses' station
2 BR	two bed room		NT	nurses' toilet
3 B Ward	three bed room		O	office
BRB	barber shop		OBS	observation
BTY	beauty shop		OPHTHAL	ophthalmology
C	closet		OR	operating room
CENT	central		OT	occupational therapy
CHIROP	chiropodist		P	pantry (serving)
CL	clean linen		PH	pharmacy
CONF	conference		PSYCH	psychiatry
CONS	consultation		PT	physical therapy
CU	clean utility		R	receptionist
D	dining		RAD	radiology
DAY	day room		REC	recreation
DENT	dental		RM	room
DERM	dermatology		S	staff
DL	dirty linen		SD	staff dining
DU	dirty utility		SERV	service area
E	employee's		SERV ENT	service entrance
E.C.G.	electrocardiology		SEW	sewing
ED	employee's dining		SL	sleeping area
EFF	efficiency apartment		SOC SERV	social service
ENT	entrance		SP BR	special bedroom
EQ,EQUIP	equipment		STERIL	sterilizer
EX	examination		SUN	sun room or solarium
FLEX	flexible		SUP	supply
FRACT	fracture		ST	storage
GCW	garbage can wash		T	toilet
GEN	general		TECH	technician
GYN	gynecology		TH	therapy
HT	hydrotherapy		TR	treatment
INCIN	incinerator		TV	television
INFO	information		U	utility
ISO	isolation		URO	urology
J	janitor		V	vault
K	kitchen		VEST	vestibule
L	linen		VOL	volunteer
LAB	laboratory		W	women's
LARYNG	laryngology		WA	waiting
LAU	laundry		WL	women's lockers
LAV	lavatory		WS	wheelchair storage

Nursing
Homes

Structures in this category are divided into two main
groups. The first group consists of independent nursing
facilities. Buildings in the second group are additions
either annexed or adjacent to an existing residence
facility or hospital. Generally, all the facilities described
in this section have sufficient staff and services to qualify
as skilled nursing homes. Individual differences are
detailed in the accompanying text.

THE MARIN CONVALESCENT AND REHABILITATION HOSPITAL
Tiburon, California

ARCHITECT
Duncombe, Roland, Miller
Santa Rosa, California

PURPOSE
Nursing

CAPACITY
56 beds

COST
$130,000

SPONSOR
(proprietary)

Perched on a rugged promontory seven miles north of San Francisco, the Marin Hospital is visible evidence that a nursing home needn't look like one. The sharp peaks of the triangular-shaped redwood and concrete building frame broad expanses of glass overlooking dramatic views of San Francisco and Sausalito, Mt. Tamalpias, and San Francisco and San Pablo Bays.

The floor plan of the 1-story building can be thought of as a trio of rectangles positioned along the sides of an equilateral triangle. Patients' rooms in 2-, 3- and 4-bed units, nursing stations, offices, and sitting rooms fill the rectangles. The corner sections left at the vertices house the dining room and kitchen; a solarium with an adjacent library and a television room, and a gymnasium next to X-ray and treatment rooms. The center of the building is dominated by a large open court cut off near the gymnasium corner by a swimming pool used for physical therapy.

The unusual design of the building was

not an extravagance. The triangular shape enabled the architects to position the building optimally on the bare and windy site, and at the same time provide patient rooms with exposures that would avoid the hot afternoon sun. The use of native materials which would weather well—redwood, and brown-colored concrete block masonry from Napa, California—helped reduce costs. Clear water-proof coating was the only protection required.

The block sizes vary from 8″ by 8″ by

16″ in the patient wings to 12″ by 12″ by 16″ in areas where heavier walls are needed. The blocks run up to window level where a continuous sill encircles the building. The wall above is redwood and glass.

Interior walls are either plastered or exposed concrete. Ceilings are acoustical plaster for sound control. Floors are integrally colored concrete scored in 4-foot squares. The slab is radiantly heated with a closed hot water system.

continued

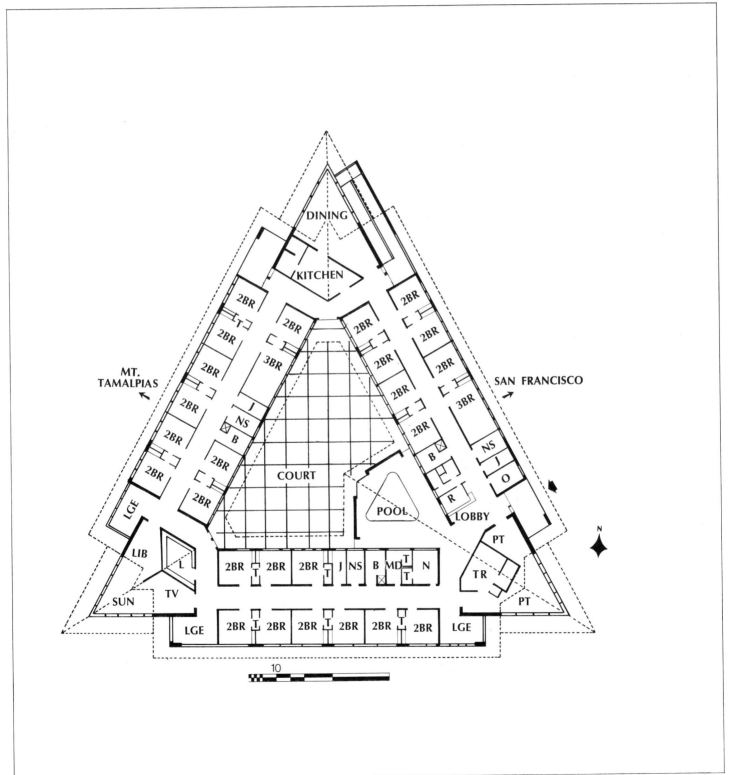

SITE PLAN

MENARD COUNTY NURSING HOME
Petersburg, Illinois

ARCHITECT
Pearce and Pearce, Inc.
St. Louis, Missouri

PURPOSE
Nursing

CAPACITY
41 beds

COST
$473,622 (excluding fees)

SPONSOR
Menard County

At first glance this 1-story nursing home appears to follow the popular cruciform pattern in layout, with patients' rooms in wings that are set at right angles to a central nursing station. Closer inspection shows a far more unconventional plan. The Menard home incorporates three nursing "pods." The semi-private rooms in each pod are formed by splitting a square along the diagonal and placing pairs of beds in each of the resulting triangles. The far corner of each triangle has been cut off to make room for a garden area outside; the near corner provides the entryway. Toilet and lavatory facilities are disposed along the diagonal, to be shared by the occupants of adjoining rooms. The nursing station is centered at the intersection of the three pods.

The fourth wing leads to the main entrance on the north side. This wing also houses offices, a conference room, and the recreation-dining room which opens onto a porch on one side and into a central court on another. In addition this area of the building houses the heating plant and other service facilities.

Each pod is a self-contained unit with its own ventilating and cooling system. A builder may add one or more when and where he will. From the patient's and administrator's point of view, the pods provide a means of grouping people according to interests or states of health. Nursing care and supervision are also simplified since a greater number of rooms are controlled from the station and corridor lengths are reduced.

An unusual feature of the masonry and steel frame building is the use of mansard roofs, sheathed in plywood and finished with asphalt shingles. The exterior is brick with light-weight block back-up exposed on the interior.

Interior walls are painted or vinyl fabric. Floors are carpeted in the public areas, sheet vinyl in corridors, and elsewhere asphalt or ceramic tile. Ceilings are dry-wall and acoustical tile.

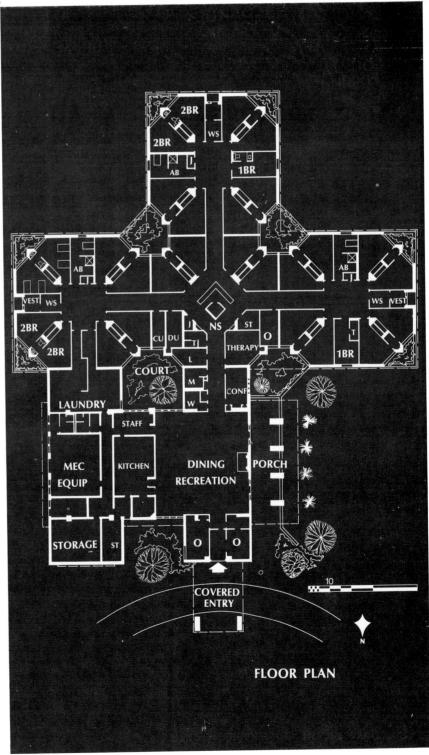

FLOOR PLAN

STEUBEN COUNTY INFIRMARY
Bath, New York

ARCHITECT
Sargent—Webster—Crenshaw & Folley
Syracuse, New York

PURPOSE
Nursing

CAPACITY
105 beds

COST
$2,481,579

SPONSOR
Steuben County Board of Supervisors

The crisp lines of pitched- and flat-roofed buildings, courts, and L-shaped wings will create an interesting architectural contrast to the gently rolling farmland area of upstate New York. This site for a nursing home is part of county property which also includes a jail. Architects solved the unhappy contiguity problem by placing the service drive, facilities, and administrative offices of the home on the west side of the site with sufficient landscaping to screen the buildings from each other. This portion of the

site is on a slope so that all offices and service areas of the home are at a lower level. The upper floor Is exclusively reserved for nursing units and related activities.

Each of the two L-shaped patient wings consists of 18 double rooms and four singles supervised by nursing stations at the corners of the L's. There is a solarium at the end of each corridor and a TV room opposite each nursing station. A third and fourth nursing unit at the opposite sides of the building are planned for

Model viewed from main entrance showing all planned facilities

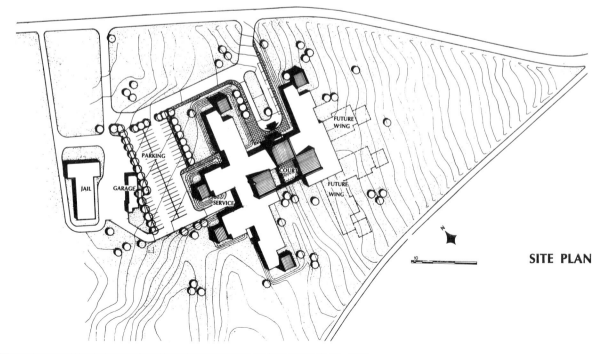

SITE PLAN

the future, and a leg of one of these L's, a 25-bed unit, will be included in the first stage of construction.

Poured-in-place concrete was used for the frame of the buildings with precast concrete planks for decking. The exterior walls are finished in brick and asphalt shingles are used on the pitched roofs.

Interior finishes include plaster walls and radiant ceilings in patient rooms, brick and plastic wall coatings in corridors, dining room, and solariums. Acoustical tile ceilings and vinyl

asbestos tile and carpeted floors are used in corridors. Ceilings in dining rooms and solariums are acoustical plaster.

An interesting feature of the design is that all the pitched-roofed buildings are used for communal activities—chapel, meeting room, physical and occupational therapy rooms—in contrast to the flat roofs which mark the nursing units. Thus the shape of the roof not only keys the function but also provides extra light and air in the areas where they are most needed.

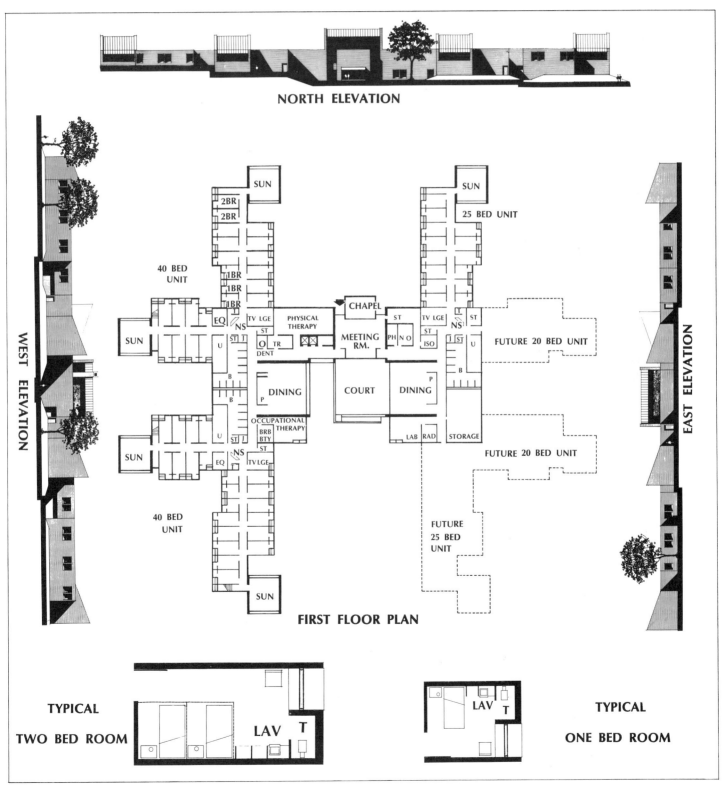

NORTH ELEVATION

WEST ELEVATION

EAST ELEVATION

FIRST FLOOR PLAN

TYPICAL TWO BED ROOM

TYPICAL ONE BED ROOM

THE IOWA COUNTY HOME FOR THE AGED
Dodgeville, Wisconsin

ARCHITECT
Ames-Torkelson and Associates
Madison, Wisconsin

PURPOSE
Nursing

CAPACITY
86 beds

COST
$592,000

SPONSOR
Iowa County

An extensive survey of conditions in Iowa County in 1957 pointed to the need for a home for the aged. Five years later, following recommendations from the State Department of Public Welfare and the architects' own research in the field, a home for bedfast, chairfast, and ambulatory patients was built. It is located on the grounds of the Iowa County Hospital and Home, five miles west of the town of Dodgeville.

A sloping site made it possible to arrange the 2-story and basement building so that the kitchen, dining room, therapy, and utility services are placed at the basement level. The upper two floors are reserved for patients' rooms, all with outside windows. Each patient floor also contains a serving pantry, three day rooms, a nurses' station, and supervised bath and shower facilities. There is a medical examining room and a public lounge opening into a chapel on the main floor, and an apartment for the administrator on the second floor.

The T-shaped building is of concrete and steel frame construction with

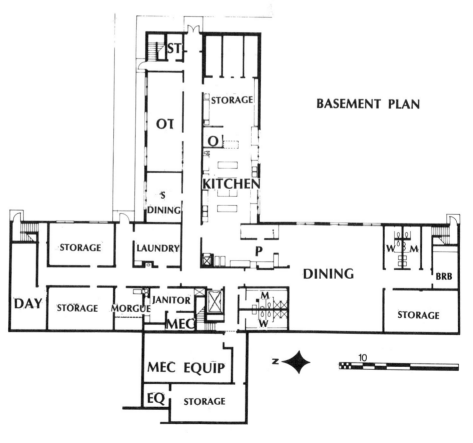

BASEMENT PLAN

precast floors and roof decks. Exterior walls are brick veneer with fiber glass blanket insulation. They are finished with lath and plaster inside.

Budgetary considerations dictated the choice of durable materials for interior finishes. Floors of corridors, nursing stations, and some bed areas are terrazzo. Quarry tile is used in the kitchen and ceramic tile in bath areas. A vinyl fabric is used as a wall covering, eliminating the need to paint. Expansion strips and picture molds are used liberally to control cracking of plaster.

A radiant heating system is integrated into the metal acoustical tile ceiling of all rooms on the patient floors.

Safety features include corridor handrails and grab bars in toilet and bath areas. The door knobs are square-shaped for easy gripping and all door widths will accommodate wheelchairs, beds, or cots. Stairways are wide and a large hospital-type hydraulic elevator and a dumbwaiter serve all floors.

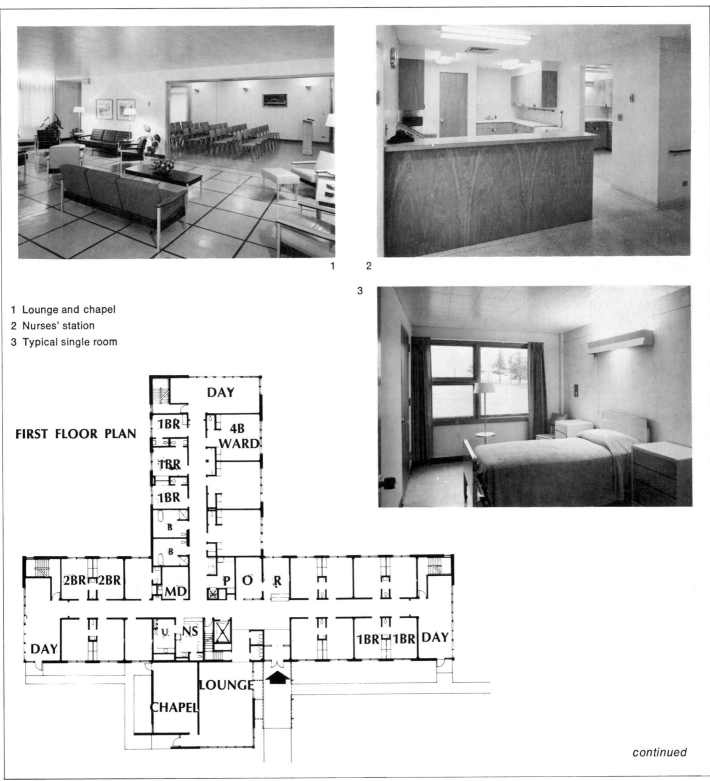

1 Lounge and chapel
2 Nurses' station
3 Typical single room

FIRST FLOOR PLAN

continued

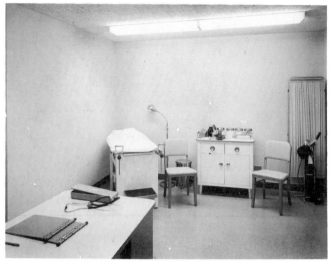

1   2

3

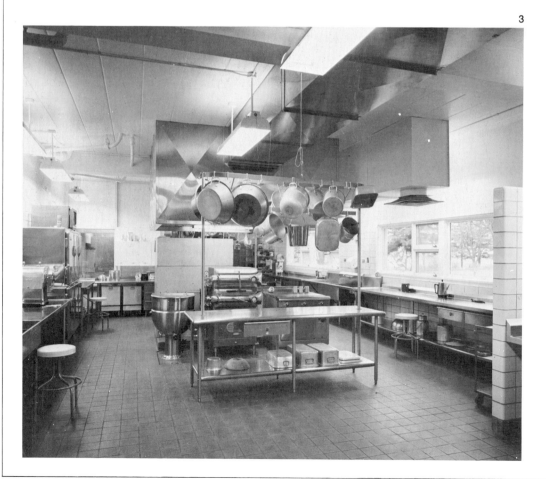

1 Four-bed ward
2 Examining room
3 Kitchen

OAK MEADOW NURSING HOME
Alexandria, Virginia

ARCHITECT
Cross and Adreon
Washington, D.C.

PURPOSE
Nursing

CAPACITY
62 beds

COST
$434,000

SPONSOR
Oak Meadow, Inc. (proprietary)

"Oak Meadow," named for a stand of mature willow oaks on the grounds, is a modern 1-story facility composed of twin circular wings connected by a curve-shaped administration building. The site, an abandoned farm in the Mount Vernon country of Virginia, is on a plateau overlooking a community recreation club and swimming pool. It is screened by woods and a stream on one side, and bordered by main roads along the other two. The combination of activity, accessibility, and natural beauty is considered especially felicitous from a therapeutic point of view. The architects report that patient morale is excellent and there is a high rate of rehabilitation and discharge.

The nursing wings are mirror images in layout. Each has a nurses' station at the hub within a few steps of the wedge-shaped patient rooms. These rooms, the majority doubles, have sliding doors at the perimeter, inviting attention out-of-doors and providing fast exits if necessary.

The central building serves both wings

continued

1

OAK MEADOW NURSING HOME

with dining room-auditorium, rehabilitation, and service facilities. There is also a beauty parlor, a lounge, recreational facilities, and, connected to the building near the side of the entrance a conically shaped orangery. Here patients may garden or retire for solitude or meditation.

The architects state that a number of devices or design features of value to geriatric patients were invented for,

or installed quite early at Oak Meadow. Among them: "wicket" wheelchair stops; pivoted bathroom doors with hardware on both sides; safe control systems for toilet and room privacy; sitting, standing, or wheelchair showers, lavatories and wardrobes; and controls usable by arthritic patients. "Disappearing" (no ceiling track) room dividers and baffled light valences are other features incorporated in the finishing details.

The outer rings of the nursing buildings are steel-framed; the nursing core

is reinforced concrete. Exteriors are brick and plywood. Roofing is poured gypsum and walls are multi-layered gypsum over steel studs. Penthouses for mechanical equipment are clad in porcelain enamel on aluminum. The center wing uses exposed double bulb angle beams to support acoustical panel roof deck. The exterior is brick and porcelain enamel. The orangery is framed in aluminum sections. Radiant heating in slabs and heat pumps in walls permit close control of heating.

2

1 The orangery

2 The front of one nursing wing and the orangery

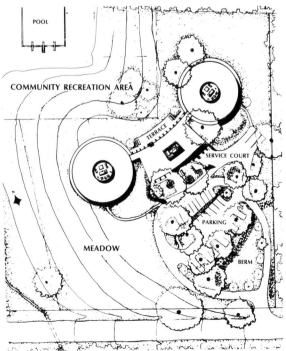

SITE PLAN

View from the lounge toward the
dining room

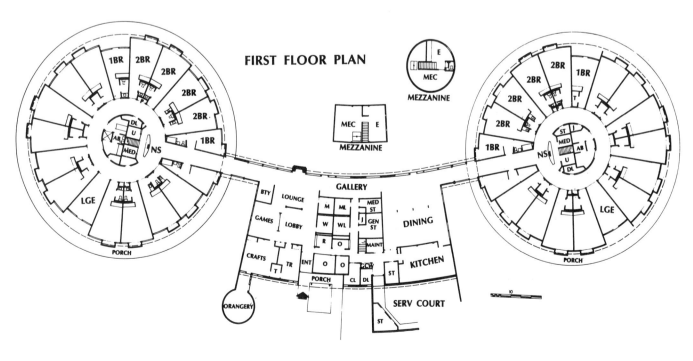

FIRST FLOOR PLAN

MEZZANINE

MEZZANINE

1BR 2BR 2BR 2BR 2BR 1BR

DL U AR MED NS

LGE

PORCH

BTY LOUNGE GALLERY MED ST

GAMES LOBBY M ML J GEN ST DINING

W WL

CRAFTS ENT R O O MAINT

TR T O O G CW KITCHEN

PORCH CL DL ST SERV COURT

ORANGERY ST

2BR 1BR 2BR 2BR 2BR 1BR

ST MED AB NS U DL

LGE

PORCH

NEWAYGO COUNTY MEDICAL CARE FACILITY
Newaygo, Michigan

ARCHITECT
Daverman Associates, Inc.
Grand Rapids, Michigan

PURPOSE
Nursing

CAPACITY
110 beds

COST
$913,290

SPONSOR
Newaygo County

One of the signs of changing attitudes towards the elderly can be seen in the replacement of the dismal county farms and poorhouses of a generation ago by modern buildings and facilities which put the emphasis on the comfort and well-being of the aged.

The Newaygo County Medical Care Facility, which received a First Honor Award in the 1966 A.I.A. Grand Valley Chapter Honor Awards Program, occupies part of the original county farm site a short distance east of the city of Fremont, Michigan. It was

designed to meet the County Welfare Department's aims of modern rehabilitation and re-motivation. The 1-story winged building has substantial physical and occupational therapy facilities and a number of social and recreational rooms in addition to the centrally located dining and day rooms.

The structure of the building—a series of L-wings grouped around inner courts—makes expansion comparatively easy and a 35-bed addition is currently planned. No patient wing is

longer than 100 feet. This, combined with the central arrangement of nursing stations and supply rooms, results in maximum efficiency.

Individual rooms are large enough to permit access to each bed from both sides. Door widths, toilet facilities, corridor handrails, and furniture arrangement throughout the building are suited to the wheelchair patient.

Exterior materials for the steel and concrete frame building were selected for beauty as well as durability.

A dark bronze finish aluminum was chosen for the roof fascia to complement the buff brick, while blue-green ceramic tile was the choice for the window spandrels.

Most interior walls are plaster, ceilings are acoustical tile, and flooring is vinyl asbestos. Generous contributions from local citizens made it possible to furnish the building completely and to landscape the grounds.

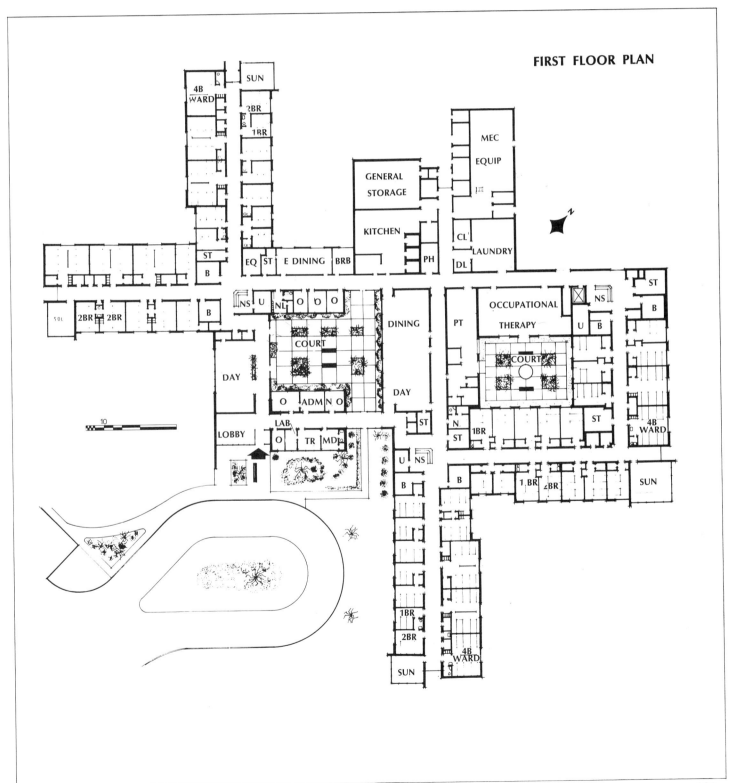

FIRST FLOOR PLAN

SIMPSON HOUSE LTD.
Elgin, Illinois

ARCHITECT
Kaltenbach and Rennie
Elgin, Illinois

PURPOSE
Nursing

CAPACITY
68 beds

COST
$704,000

SPONSOR
(proprietary)

Space and comfort are featured in the design of Simpson House, a 2-story convalescent and intensive care facility in Elgin, Illinois. The plan of the building is a broad U-shape. The majority of patients' rooms are placed along the base; the main entrance and some of the ancillary facilities in the shorter arms. The latter areas are topped by pitched roofs in contrast to the flat roof over the patient wing. The building, which encloses a large landscaped court, is situated on a bluff overlooking the Fox River. A director's residence on the north side may eventually be removed to allow for the building of a duplicate facility to meet future needs. The property is in an older suburb of Elgin which has many large Victorian estates.

Each of the 34 patient rooms is 16 feet square, a space and shape which allows flexibility in layout. About half the rooms are used as singles, but their size permits them to be converted to doubles if necessary. The nurse station on each floor is at the intersection of the base and side wing.

1

2

3

A generous amount of space has been allotted to ancillary facilities. In addition to the dining and service areas on the first floor, there is a library, several sitting areas, and a therapy and crafts room. On the second floor there is a large lounge with a screened porch, a small infirmary, and a treatment room. The full basement houses a chapel, beauty and barber shops, games areas, and a laundry and storage area for the residents.

In contrast to the Victorian neighborhood, the lines of the reinforced concrete building are simple and uncluttered. SCR brick is used as infill allowing complete expression of structural elements.

Interior finishes are plaster on steel studs and concrete block. Wood and exposed brick add textural accents. Ceilings are acoustical tile. Floors are carpeted throughout. Simpson House has the distinction of being the first fully carpeted nursing home in Illinois. Prior to this, carpeting was prohibited by law. After extensive tests with the newer synthetic fibers, the state permitted the installation.

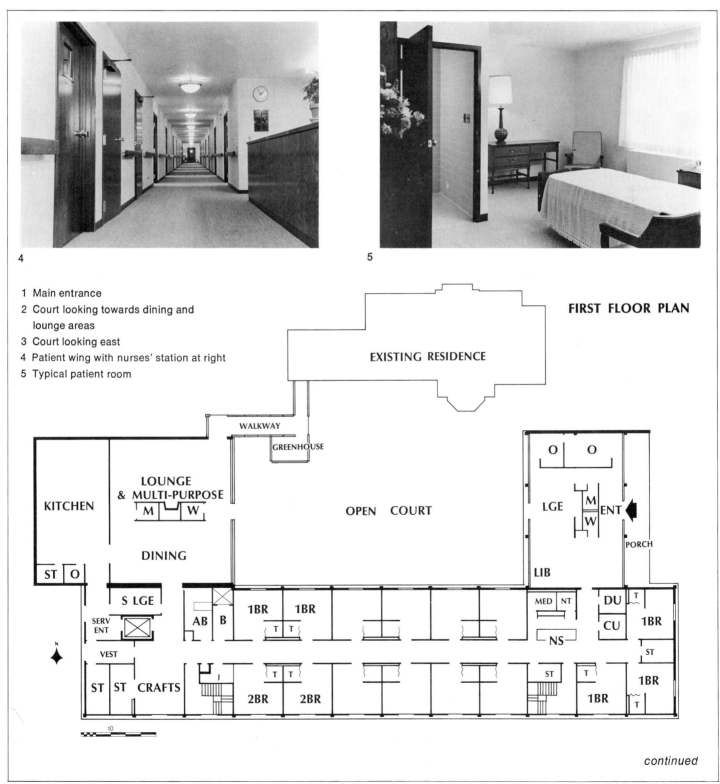

4

5

1 Main entrance
2 Court looking towards dining and lounge areas
3 Court looking east
4 Patient wing with nurses' station at right
5 Typical patient room

FIRST FLOOR PLAN

EXISTING RESIDENCE

WALKWAY

GREENHOUSE

KITCHEN

LOUNGE & MULTI-PURPOSE

M   W

DINING

OPEN   COURT

LGE

ENT

M
W

PORCH

LIB

ST O

S LGE

AB B

1BR 1BR

T T

MED NT

NS

DU T

CU

1BR

SERV ENT

VEST

ST

N

ST ST CRAFTS

J

2BR 2BR

T T

ST T

ST

1BR

1BR

1BR

T

O O

10

continued

1

2

3

4

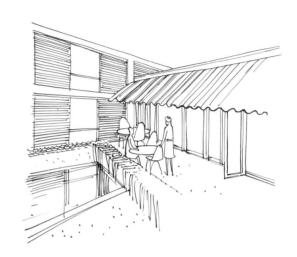

5

1 Lounge and multi-purpose room
2 Barber shop
3 Library and lounge
4 Dining area
5 Chapel

MISSOURI SLOPE LUTHERAN NURSING HOME
Bismarck, North Dakota

ARCHITECT
Leonhard and Askew
Bismarck, North Dakota

PURPOSE
Nursing

CAPACITY
80 beds

COST
$1,316,949

SPONSOR
Missouri Slope Lutheran Homes, Inc.

In their desire to create a nursing home with the accent on home, the architects of the Missouri Slope project designed a series of 1-story hip-roofed buildings which give the overall impression of a group of garden apartments. The residential feeling is enhanced by the site location: The buildings lie on a promontory overlooking the Missouri River valley on the north edge of the city of Bismarck. The chapel, lounge, dining room, and other gathering places for residents were specifically oriented to take advantage of the view along the

western rim. Considerable grading and contouring was necessary to modify the site to suit the design, but it was agreed that the advantages of a 1-story structure for the elderly outweighed the site modification difficulties.

The buildings are interconnected and grouped in right angles around a rectangular court used for recreation or strolling. The court's enclosure on all four sides provides protection against the strong prairie winds.

The patient wings and treatment areas

in the eastern half of the complex are arranged so that nursing stations can be strategically placed at the intersections. In addition to a large main lounge, day rooms have been placed where two or three wings come together. A large centrally located combination physical therapy and crafts room flanks the east side of the inner court. Mechanical facilities including the boiler room and an emergency generator, the laundry, and storage areas are in a basement beneath the intersection of the south and southeast wings.

The buildings' exteriors are finished in two kinds of brick with precast concrete projections at periodic intervals. These accents are actually boxes which form the clothes closets in the patients' rooms.

The flat roofs are standard built-up gravel and pitch. The slopes of the hipped roofs are covered with plastic material, while the sides of the flat center sections are shingled in natural red cedar.

In keeping with the home-like intent of the basic design, most interior walls

are plaster and ceilings are of acoustical plaster. Vinyl flooring is used in major utility areas and in one patient wing designated for intensive care. Otherwise all floors are to be carpeted with wool carpet according to U.S. Public Health Service specifications.

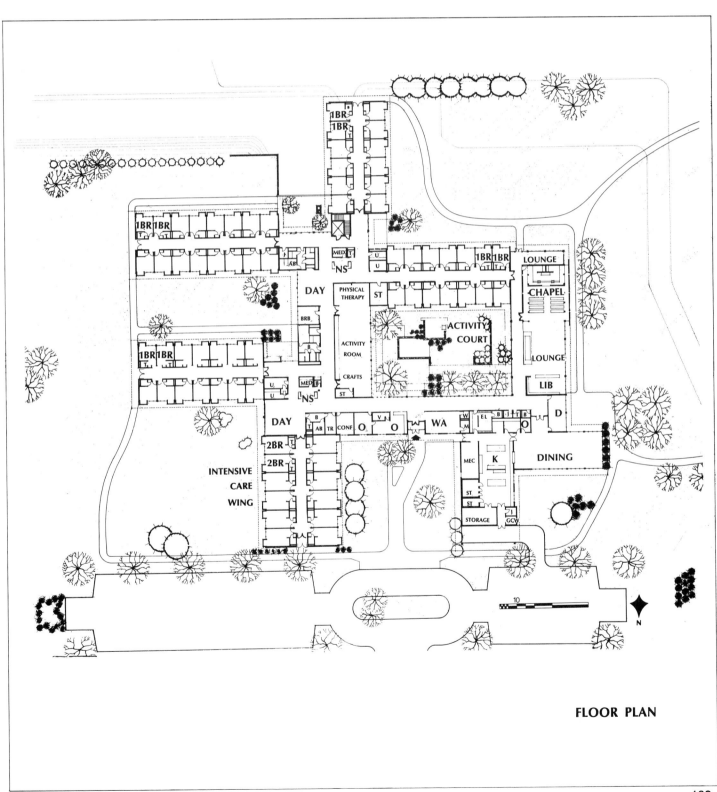

FLOOR PLAN

NEWPORT NURSING HOME
Newport News, Virginia

ARCHITECT
Forrest Coile and Associates
L. Duane DeBlasio, A.I.A.,Project Architect
Newport News, Virginia

PURPOSE
Nursing

CAPACITY
50 beds

COST
$280,000 (excluding fees)

SPONSOR
Newport Nursing Home, Inc. (proprietary)

The use of natural stone, brick, and colored cement asbestos panels adds variety and textural interest to the facade of this nursing home in Virginia, complementing a basically simple design. The floor plan of the 1-story building consists of three rectangles arranged parallel to each other along their lengths. The smallest rectangle in the middle houses the main entrance and common rooms. It connects to a long patient wing on one side and a shorter maintenance and utility wing on the other. A landscaped court lies at the center of the mid-rectangle, flanked by a reception area and the dining-recreation room.

Outdoor activities for patients have been oriented toward the rear of the building, away from a busy thorough-fare paralleling the main entrance. The rear site adjoins a wooded area which is part of the property of a city museum. An outdoor terraced space placed off the dining room takes advantage of this view. To augment the feeling of openness and the outdoors, as well as to add importance to this part of the building, the architects have added

clerestory windows on three sides. The interior court itself is open to the sky.

The building is of steel frame construction with masonry bearing walls and concrete slab floors. Interiors include painted masonry walls and terrazzo, vinyl asbestos, or ceramic tile floors. Acoustical tile ceilings are used in the nursing unit. Patients' rooms, the majority semi-private, have built-in closets, dressers, desks, and bookcases. In most cases toilet and lavatory facilities are shared between rooms.

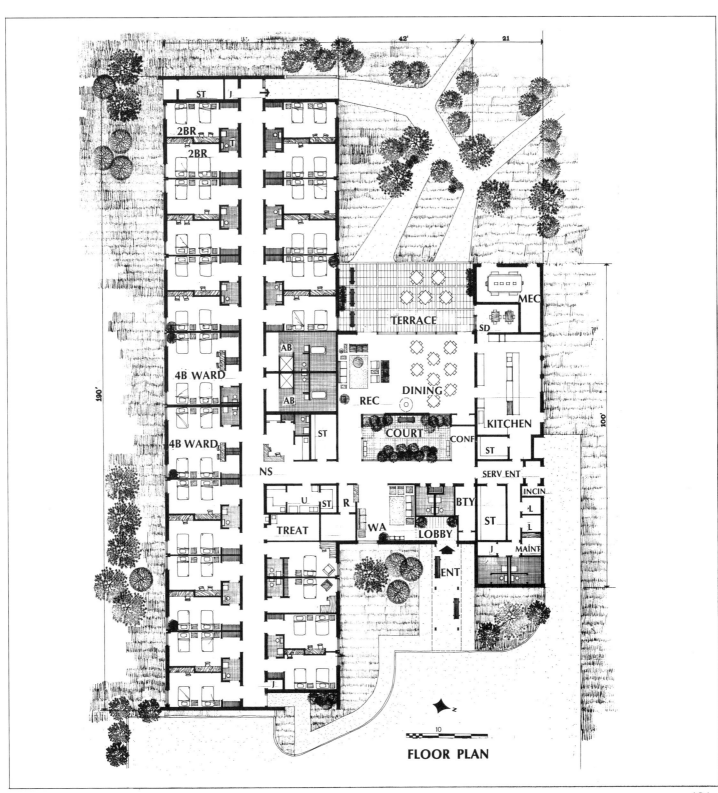

FLOOR PLAN

EARTHA M. M. WHITE NURSING HOME
Jacksonville, Florida

ARCHITECT
Freedman and Clements
Jacksonville, Florida

PURPOSE
Nursing

CAPACITY
122 beds

COST
$687,000

SPONSOR
Eartha M. M. White Nursing Home, Inc.
(non-profit)

A creek cutting across a wedge-shaped site imposed a major design problem for architects planning a maximum service facility for a low to middle income clientele. Their solution was a 3-story brick building whose length parallels the creek. Patients' rooms in single, double, and 3-bed units extend along the building lengths on the upper two floors. A dual nursing station in the center of each patient floor allows a nurse-to-patient ratio of approximately 1 to 30.

To provide more interior space and at the same time enliven the long facades, designers placed the toilet facilities for the patients' rooms in bays which project at the second and third story levels. The central bay on each floor, across from the nurses' station, houses a large day room. The first floor has been left free for administrative offices, a dining room and a lounge, occupational and physical therapy rooms, recreational facilities, and a chapel.

The concrete building uses exposed soffit slab construction with brick and block exterior cavity walls and block interior partitions.

FIRST FLOOR PLAN

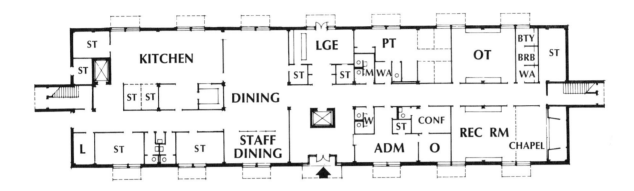

ST
ST

KITCHEN

LGE   PT   OT   BTY
                   BRB
                   WA   ST

ST   ST   **DINING**   ST   ST   M WA   W

L   ST   ST   ST   **STAFF DINING**   W   ST   CONF   **REC RM**   **ADM**   **O**   CHAPEL

SECOND AND THIRD FLOOR PLAN

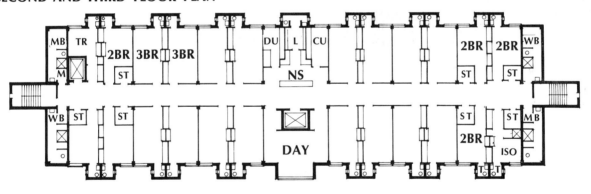

MB   TR   2BR   3BR   3BR   DU   L   CU   2BR   2BR   WB
M   ST   ST
                           NS
WB   ST   ST   ST   ST   ST   MB
                           DAY   2BR   ISO
                                        T T

10

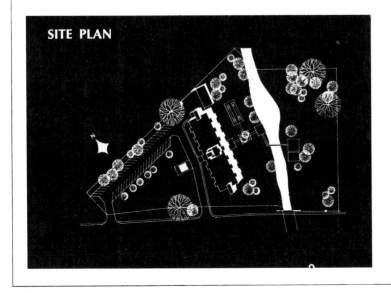

SITE PLAN

N

FOLEY NURSING HOME
Foley, Alabama

ARCHITECT
Dietz, Prince & Fischrupp
Mobile, Alabama

PURPOSE
Nursing

CAPACITY
83 beds

COST
$426,120

SPONSOR
(proprietary)

Proximity to a hospital or major medical facility is an asset for a nursing home. The Foley home is within the town's medical center, occupying a little over half a square block between the hospital and a doctors' clinic. The remainder of the block will eventually be used for a 1-story residential apartment building to be integrated with the nursing facility.

The patients' rooms are disposed along two L-shaped wings, a popular design which allows a single nursing station at the intersection of the L to control rooms along both segments. Most of the rooms are semi-private, but there are several 4-bed rooms and a few special care singles. All rooms are equipped with individual fan coil units for heating and cooling, and each bed is supplied with a pillow television speaker and control system.

Centered between the patient wings are the home's administrative offices, dining and recreation area, the chapel, reception area, and beauty shop. There are a number of land-

scaped interior courts, with portions of some earmarked for future additions of crafts or physical therapy facilities.

The building is of concrete construction with a prestressed concrete roof, load-bearing block exterior walls, and slab on grade floors. Exterior surfacing is 4-inch brick veneer. Interior surfacing is gypsum wallboard, on metal studs for partitioning. Suspended ceilings are fiber glass and floors are covered with vinyl tile, carpeting, or ceramic tile.

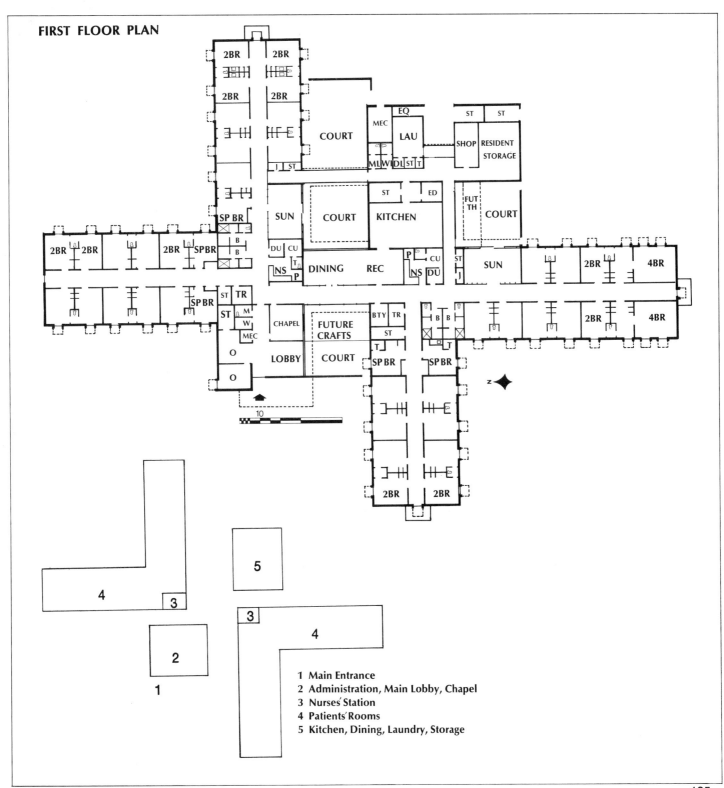

FIRST FLOOR PLAN

1 Main Entrance
2 Administration, Main Lobby, Chapel
3 Nurses' Station
4 Patients' Rooms
5 Kitchen, Dining, Laundry, Storage

HAROLD & GRACE UPJOHN COMMUNITY NURSING HOME

Kalamazoo, Michigan

ARCHITECT
G. E. Diekema & Associates
Kalamazoo, Michigan
Edward Coe Embury, A.I.A.,(Consultant)
New York, New York

PURPOSE
Nursing

CAPACITY
60 beds

COST
$504,067 (Phase I building)

SPONSOR
(non-profit)

When architects examined the 5-acre site for the Upjohn Home in residential Kalamazoo, they noted that a portion of the land bordered a major artery leading into town. Residents would probably enjoy watching the traffic and activity, the designers felt, but would not appreciate the noise or fumes. For this reason, they set the 1-story building 100 feet back from the street and added landscaping to act as further insulation against noise. In order that the main entrance would be parallel to the street, however, the axis of this part of the building was placed at an angle. The result is a slight skewing of one wing of an essentially cruciform floor plan.

This skewing had the effect of reducing the apparent length of the corridor. It also provides clear visibility into all four wings from the centrally placed nursing station. The lounges, a meditation room, a beauty and barber shop, and physical and occupational therapy facilities are also clustered in this central area.

The building is the first of a 2-part project planned to house 120 patients in all. The second phase building will be almost a mirror image of the first, joining it at the kitchen-dining room extremity. The utility and maintenance facilities and the kitchen and boiler rooms of the Phase I building will accommodate the needs of the completed project.

The building is constructed with masonry walls and has a steel frame roof with a poured-in-place gypsum deck covered with shingles. The exterior brick face alternates with cut stone panels at the window spandrels. Interior walls and ceilings are plaster, with acoustical ceilings in heavy traffic areas.

Patient rooms—singles, semi-privates, and 4-bed wards—are equipped with call systems and individual controls for heating and air-conditioning.

FLOOR PLAN

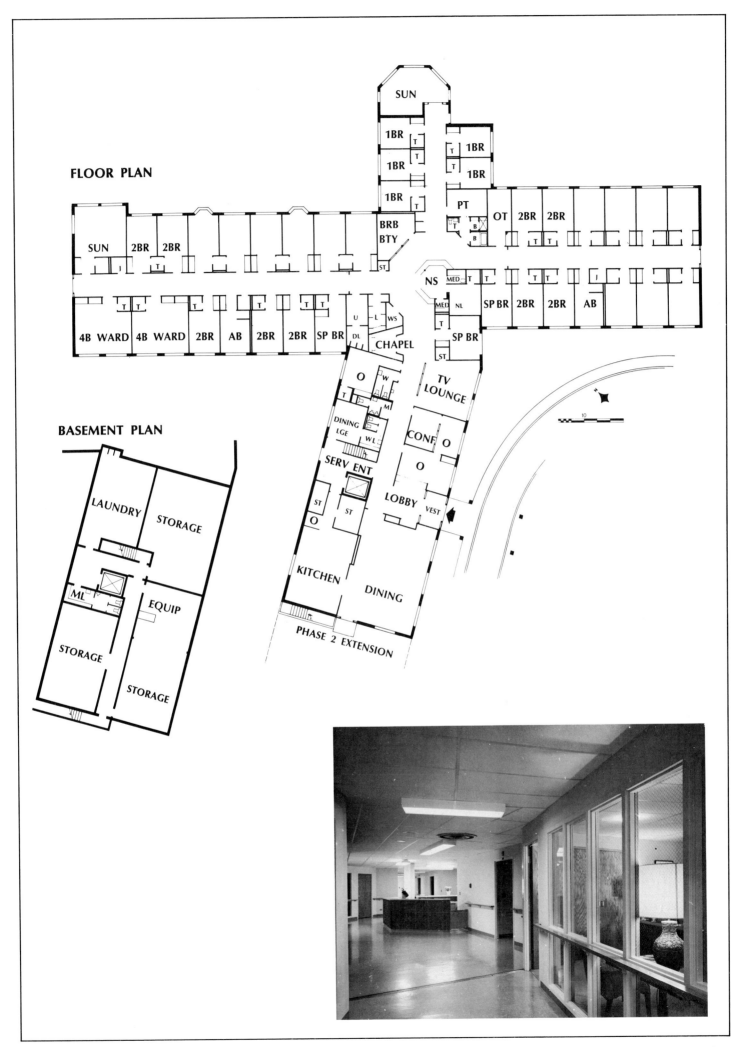

SUN

1BR
1BR

T
T

1BR

T
T

1BR
1BR

PT

OT 2BR 2BR

BRB
BTY

ST

NS
MED T T

T T

J

SP BR 2BR 2BR AB

MED
T

NL

SP BR

ST

SUN 2BR 2BR

J

T

4B WARD 4B WARD 2BR AB 2BR 2BR SP BR

T T

T

T

T T

U L WS

DL

CHAPEL

O W

T M

DINING LGE WL

SERV ENT

ST

ST O

O

KITCHEN

TV LOUNGE

CONF O

O

LOBBY VEST

DINING

BASEMENT PLAN

LAUNDRY STORAGE

ML

EQUIP

STORAGE

STORAGE

PHASE 2 EXTENSION

197

FAIRFAX NURSING HOME
Fairfax, Minnesota

ARCHITECT
Kenneth H. Walijarvi, A.I.A.
St. Paul, Minnesota

PURPOSE
Nursing

CAPACITY
64 beds

COST
$316,347 (excluding fees)

SPONSOR
Fairfax Nursing Home, Inc. (proprietary)

The problem of this prairie site is typical. It's flat. There are no woods, valleys, hills, or brooks to complement a building or hide its faults. Faced with designing a nursing home in such a terrain, this Minnesota architect decided to concentrate interest on the building's interior. He designed a Y-shaped 1-story structure in which three equal-length wings meet in a central triangularly shaped area containing the day room, dining room, chapel, and nursing station. The architect writes that the area has no particular orientation: "It's comparable to being in a Cinerama movie house or out-of-doors, in a park. The walls do not seem to enclose, and one can see out the windows, down the halls, or look up at the ceiling which seems to undulate." Residents find the area attractive, and use it as a meeting ground, market place, atrium—a pleasant place to gather.

The wings house patients' rooms, mostly doubles, and such ancillary facilities as a beauty and barber shop, doctor's examining room, and offices. Each wing ends in a pentagonally

shaped sun or activities room, which in the west wing is shortened at one side to accommodate the sitting room of a deluxe suite for a couple.

The building's exterior is brick with concrete block back-up. Roof construction is bar joist and metal deck. Built-up roofing is topped with white marble chips to reflect the hot summer sun.

Colored glass has been used extensively in the building; blue-green for the hot western walls of the dining room, warmer colors in the day room.

The combinations cast variegated shadows on the walls over the course of the day, thus serving esthetic as well as practical ends.

All windows are double glazed and screened. Patients' windows are designed so that they may be opened without creating a draft. The patient's comfort has also been a consideration in installing heating pipes. They have been placed in a tunnel under the floor, thus maintaining a constant warm temperature underfoot even at the exterior walls.

continued

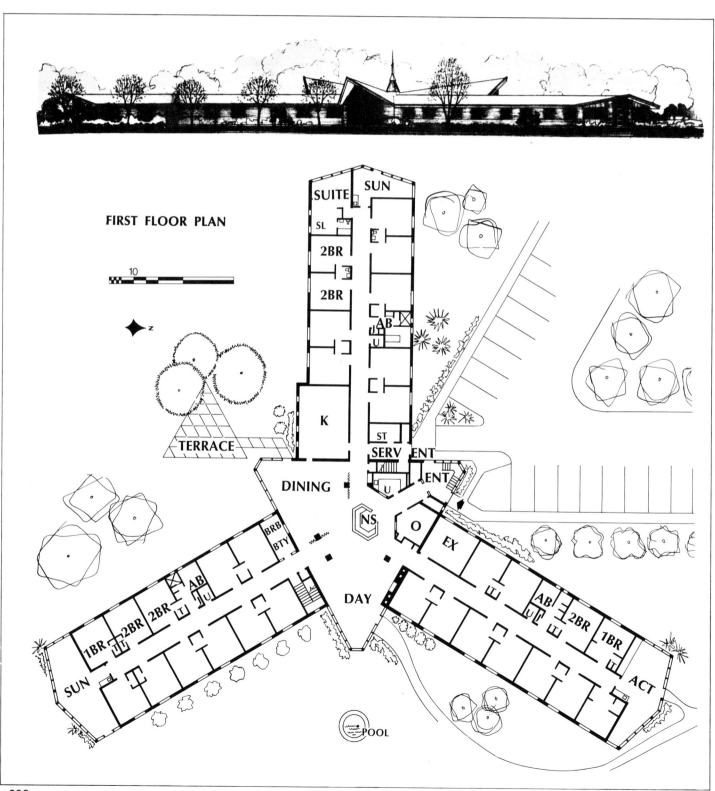

FIRST FLOOR PLAN

10

z

SUITE   SUN

SL

2BR

2BR

AB
U

K

ST

TERRACE

SERV   ENT

DINING   ENT

NS

O

EX

BRB
BTY

AB
U

DAY

AB
U   2BR   1BR

1BR   2BR   2BR

ACT

SUN

POOL

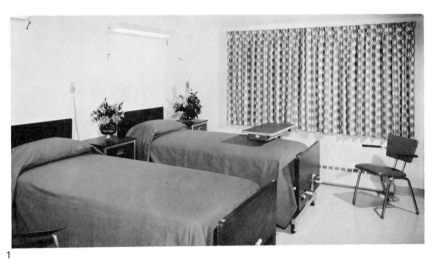

1 Typical double room

2 Nurses' station

3 West elevation

4 South sun room—east end

5 Day room windows

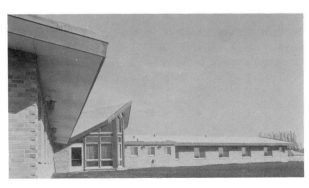

POWHATAN NURSING HOME
Arlington, Virginia

ARCHITECT
Mayne, Oseroff, Van Besien & Associates
Arlington, Virginia

PURPOSE
Nursing

CAPACITY
167 beds

COST
$2,000,000

SPONSOR
Powhatan Associates (proprietary)

Symmetrical cross-shaped patient pavilions flank the administration and general use building of this 2-story nursing home in Virginia. The canopied main entrance, approached via a horseshoe drive, is placed at the side of a dramatic window wall which fronts the building. The center section of the main building is accented by a folded plate roof, a motif which is repeated on the connecting wings of the patient pavilions.

The main building is used for most ancillary facilities of the home—offices, staff and resident dining, chapel, lounges, and the like. Short passageways lead from the main building into the patient pavilions on either side. The shorter wings of these pavilions, nearest the main building, contain solariums which open onto balconies or terraces. The remaining wings house patients' rooms, mostly doubles, flanking a central corridor. There is a separate door for each bed in a double room, and a centrally placed shared toilet and lavatory. The nurses' station is at the intersection of the wings, along with examination rooms, bathing, and service facilities.

The exterior of the reinforced concrete building is brick veneer. Floors are concrete slab. Interior walls are plaster over masonry or dry-wall on steel studs. Corridor walls are equipped with wooden handrails for safety.

SECOND FLOOR PLAN

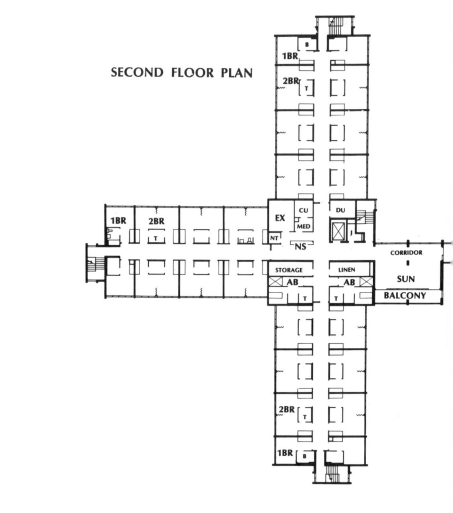

FIRST FLOOR PLAN

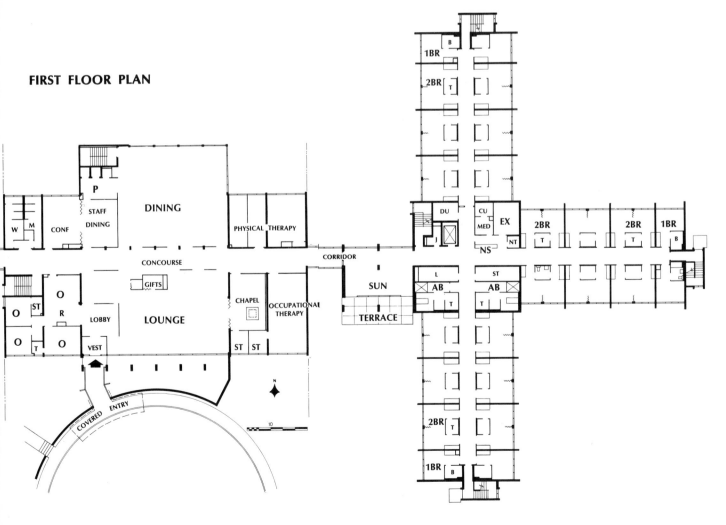

GREENBOUGH CONVALESCENT CENTER
Clarksdale, Mississippi

ARCHITECT
Brewer, Skewes & Godbold
Clarksdale, Mississippi

PURPOSE
Nursing

CAPACITY
32-64 beds

COST
$211,619

SPONSOR
Greenbough Nursing Center (proprietary)

The use of a pitched roof on this 1-story nursing facility gives a traditional residential feeling to the building at the same time that it adds a comfortable spatial quality. The entry, dining hall, and lounge have high ceilings; patients' rooms have sloping ceilings. All rooms are large enough to permit double occupancy.

The building plan follows the popular cruciform pattern, with a large central nurses' station supplemented in this case by a smaller station at the end of the longest wing.

Construction is reinforced concrete slab with integral footings on compacted earth fill. Exterior walls are 10-inch masonry cavity with vermiculite insulation. Steel beams encased in wood are used in the roof construction over the entry, lounge, and dining areas. Otherwise conventional wood framing is used. Roofing material is asphalt shingle.

Plywood paneling is used for walls in communal areas; partitions are 6-inch masonry, painted. Ceilings are acoustical tile in all areas except the

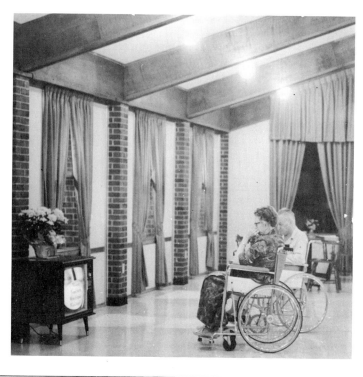

kitchen, laundry, and mechanical areas where gypsum wallboard is used. Floors are vinyl asbestos tile except for ceramic tile in bathing areas and quarry tile in the kitchen.

Convenience and safety features included in the interior design are built-in dresser-wardrobes and mirrors in patients' rooms, telephone shelves at wheelchair height, safety handrails in corridors, and grab bars in toilets, baths, and showers. All toilets are equipped with lugs for bed pans and modified bed pan cleaners. General

bathing equipment includes a shampoo lavatory and a high tub with hydraulic lift. The building uses gas-fired heating and electric cooling.

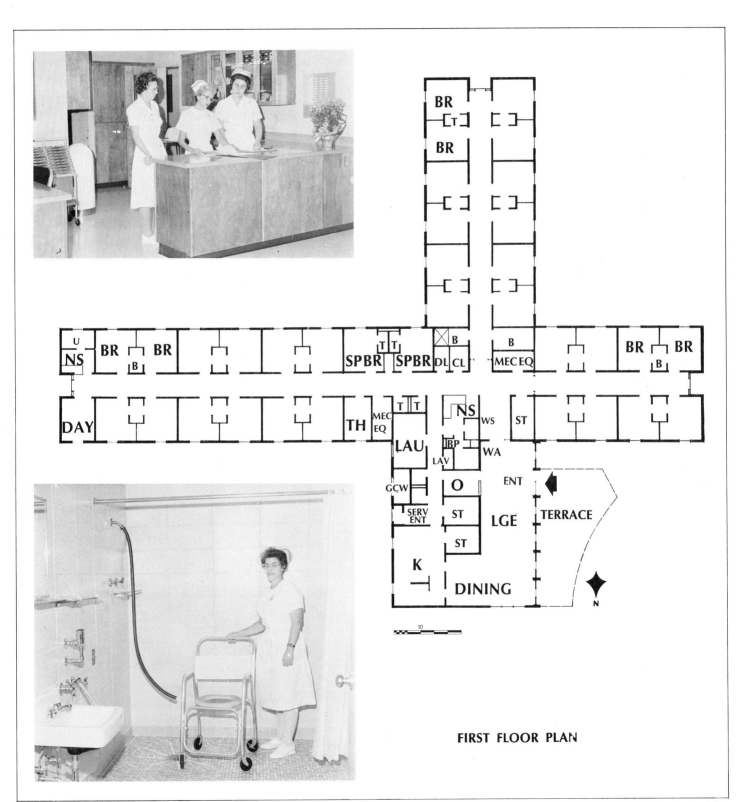

FIRST FLOOR PLAN

BRIARWOOD NURSING HOME
Atlanta, Georgia

ARCHITECT
Enloe, West & Granade, Inc.
Atlanta, Georgia

PURPOSE
Nursing

CAPACITY
94 beds

COST
$418,000 (excluding fees)

SPONSOR
Briarwood Nursing Home, Inc.
(proprietary)

The desire to avoid the tunnel effect of long narrow corridors—the dreaded "institutional look"—has led these designers to devise a floor plan which virtually eliminates the corridor.

They have so broadened the space separating the rooms in the patient wings of their lazy-H-shaped building that they have turned the hallways into day room activities areas. A walk "down the hall" for a patient can now mean nodding to fellow patients or stopping to chat with a neighbor or friend.

The nurses also benefit from this arrangement. They have complete sight control of rooms and they can watch the comings and goings of patients from their stations at the center of the inside wall. In addition to this main "living space" each wing also includes a TV lounge, reading room, and terrace.

The 1-story building (with a basement in the central portion) is of concrete construction. Floor is concrete slab on grade (except over basement), and is covered with vinyl

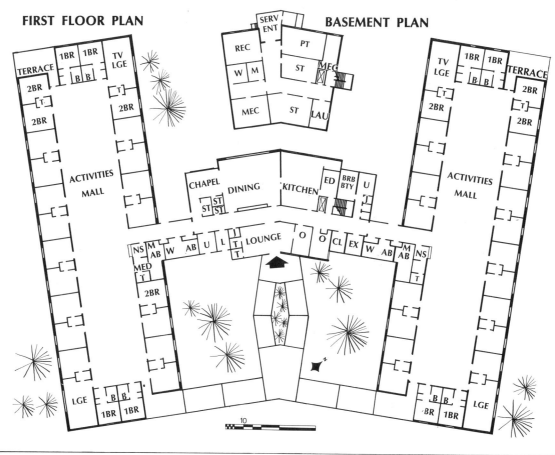

FIRST FLOOR PLAN

BASEMENT PLAN

asbestos tile. Exterior walls are brick and concrete block. Plastered partitions are used between patients' rooms, baths, etc. Ceilings are plastered and covered with acoustical tile in the commons areas of the building.

The broad V-shaped center section connecting the wings contains the kitchen, dining rooms for patients and staff, a beauty and barber shop, chapel, administrative and medical offices, treatment rooms, and central bathing facilities.

The basement houses a games room and physical therapy facilities in addition to mechanical equipment, laundry, lockers, and other service or maintenance areas.

CRITTENDON NURSING HOME
West Memphis, Arkansas

ARCHITECT
Eason Anthony Mckinnie and Cox
Memphis, Tennessee

PURPOSE
Nursing

CAPACITY
105 beds

COST
$328,360

SPONSOR
Crittendon Medihomes (proprietary)

A square notched into the corner of a second square enclosing still a third square describes the basic plan of this nursing home in Arkansas. The inner square is a landscaped courtyard. It is surrounded on all four sides by the patient wings of the home. The corner square is used for the home's general facilities: recreation, dining, crafts, and therapy rooms, beauty parlor, offices, and main entrance. A covered drive offers protection from the weather.

The simple 1-story design is executed in masonry with steel roof joists and

deck. The exterior is finished in red brick with green-painted gutter downspouts, with a mansard type of roof over the covered drive. The building is centrally heated and air-conditioned.

Most of the patients' rooms are semi-private but they may be used as private at the patient's option. Three walls of each room are painted sheetrock; one wall has a wood grain finish. The institution meets all local, state, and federal requirements and will be licensed to give skilled care to geriatric patients. There are nursing

TYPICAL NURSING CORE

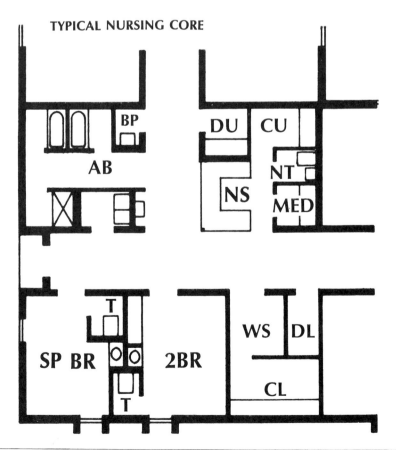

stations at the three outer corners of the patient "square." The home is within the city limits of West Memphis immediately adjacent to the Crittendon Memorial Hospital and several doctors' clinics.

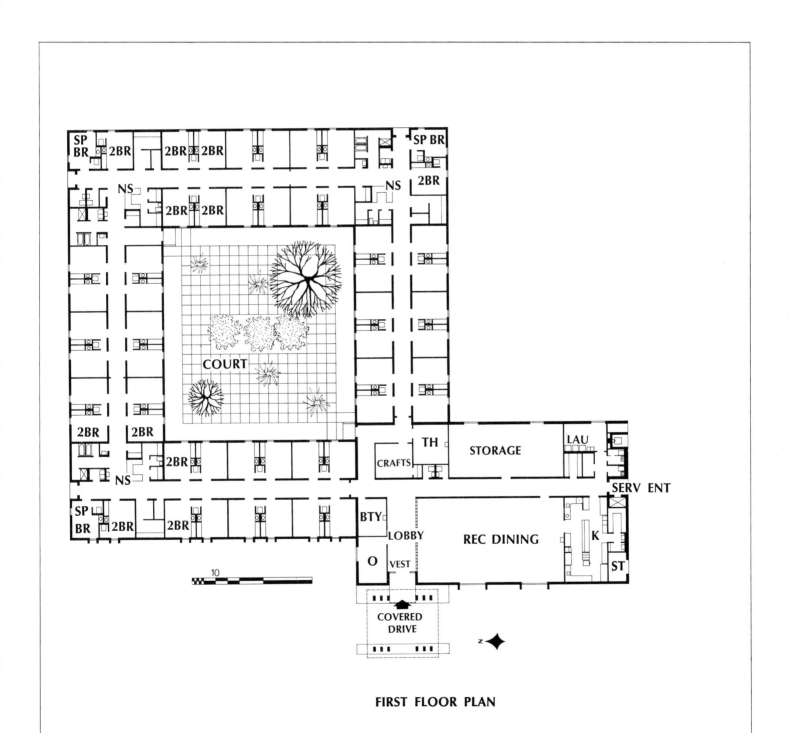

FIRST FLOOR PLAN

EATON COUNTY MEDICAL CARE FACILITY
Charlotte, Michigan

ARCHITECT
Clark R. Ackley, A.I.A.
Lansing, Michigan

PURPOSE
Nursing

CAPACITY
100 beds

COST
$970,000 (construction only)

SPONSOR
Eaton County

A broad V-shaped patient pavilion extends out to one side of the central administration building in this county nursing facility in Michigan. An 18-acre site, the bequest of a local citizen, will allow ample room for the future addition of a symmetrical wing on the other side. The 2-story structure provides convalescent care for geriatric patients who qualify for assistance by the County Department of Social Welfare. Since the building meets state and federal requirements it is eligible for matching funds for operating costs from the State

Department of Social Services. This plus the fact that the cost of care per patient in the recovery and rehabilitation stages is considerably less in an after-care institution than in a general hospital should effect extensive savings for the public in the long run.

The majority of patients' rooms are semi-private with toilets in each. Audio-visual equipment has been installed at bedsides and in bathrooms, dining rooms, and day rooms to provide immediate contact with the nurses' stations (at the base of the

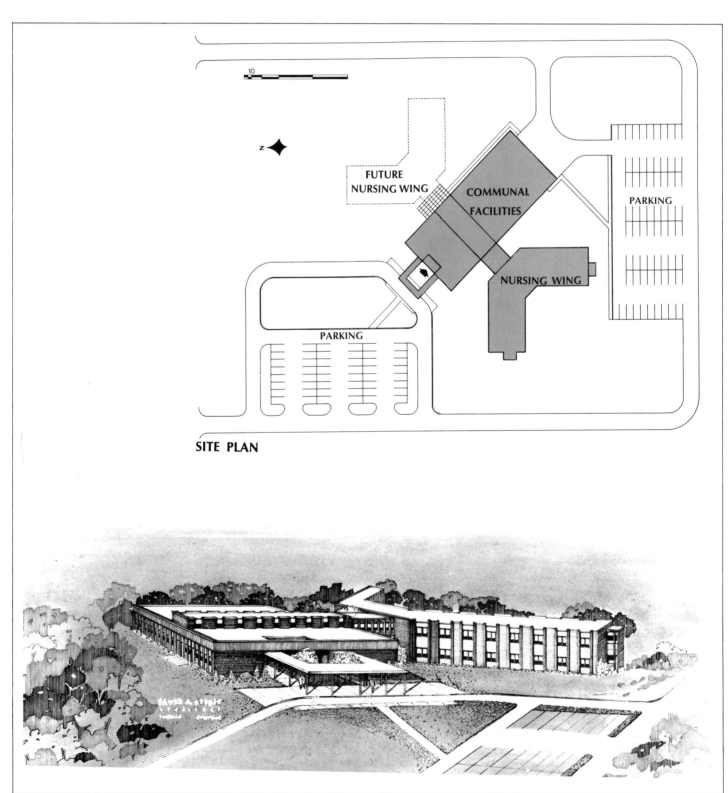

SITE PLAN

210

"V") on each floor. A hexagonally shaped day room lies opposite each station.

Patients who on special occasions may be receiving a large group can make use of an activities room with pantry facilities in the main building. In addition to offices and reception area, the building also houses a meditation room for patients or visitors, physical and occupational therapy rooms, and the laundry, boiler, and other utility or maintenance services. These facilities have all been designed with ample room for expansion.

Cellular precast concrete is used for the floor and roof slabs of the building. Exterior walls are brick with concrete block back-up, plastered, with lime-stone panels between the windows. Partitions are metal stud and plaster. Heating in patients' rooms is by fin-tube radiation. Heating and air-conditioning units are used in the lobby and office area.

continued

FIRST FLOOR PLAN

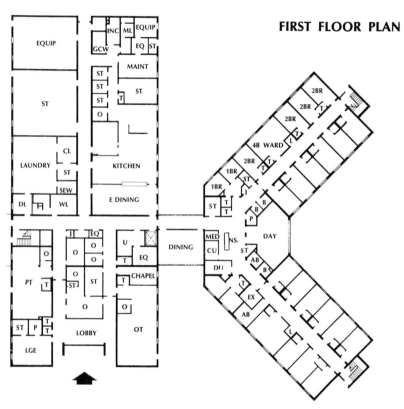

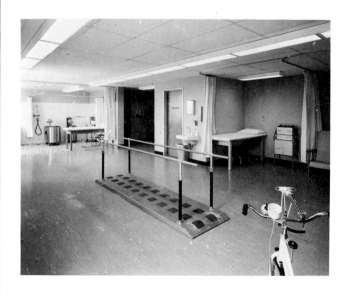

SECOND FLOOR PLAN

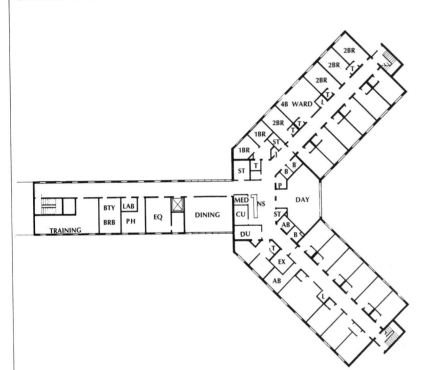

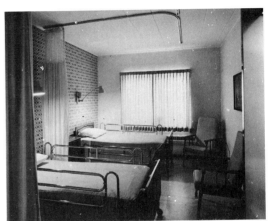

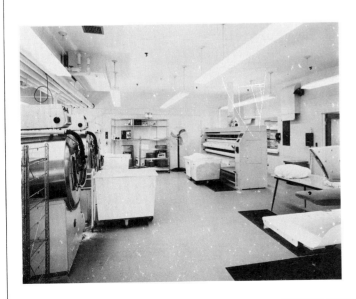

M. B. SYVERSON LUTHERAN HOME
Eau Claire, Wisconsin

ARCHITECT
Larson, Playter, Smith
Eau Claire, Wisconsin

PURPOSE
Nursing

CAPACITY
85-100 residents

COST
$925,520

SPONSOR
Grace Lutheran Foundation, Inc.

The designers of this medium-sized nursing home in a residential section of Eau Claire made the most of spatial illusions to achieve a proper balance of the building's bulk to its smallish site. On the street side the building appears to be a 2-storied structure in keeping with the property and the nature of the community. Along the river which borders the rear of the site, however, just the opposite effect was produced: The building was angled and fitted into the river bank so that it looms as a large and imposing 3-storied structure, highly visible across the water.

A large majority of the residents' bedrooms are singles with private toilets. Many rooms have balconies which overlook the river from the second and third floors. The rooms are disposed along the main axis of the building and on one half of the main floor. Nursing stations are centrally located on all three floors, while lounges, decks, and terraces are conveniently distributed at the ends as well as the center of each floor.

The main floor facilities include sewing

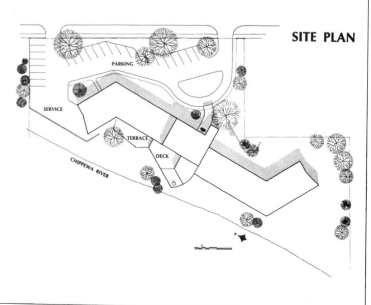

SITE PLAN

and crafts rooms, a barbershop, chapel, and the main dining room and kitchen, along with offices and service areas. A portion of the third floor houses a small infirmary, therapy, and examination rooms.

The exterior of the reinforced concrete frame building is exposed concrete and brick. A penthouse was chosen to house mechanical equipment in order to avoid flooding problems.

Interior finishing includes plaster walls, vinyl asbestos tile or carpeting for floors, and acoustical tile ceilings.

Windows and entrance doors are aluminum; interior doors are wood.

continued

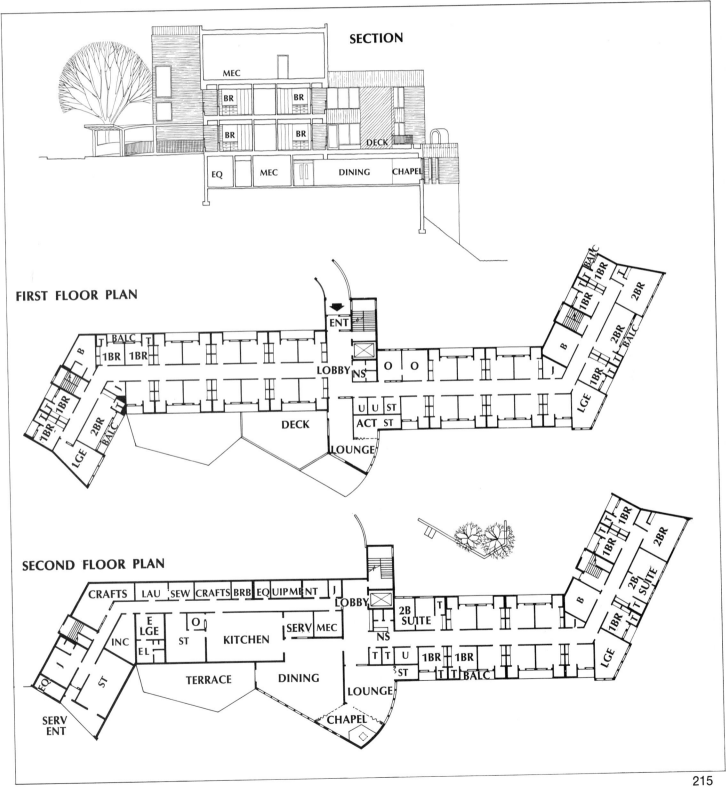

SECTION

FIRST FLOOR PLAN

SECOND FLOOR PLAN

TWO BED SUITE

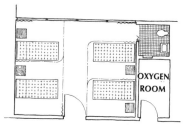

FOUR BED INFIRMARY

TWO BED ROOM

ONE BED ROOM

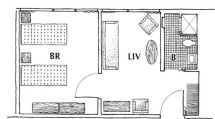

TWO BED SUITE

Lounge at north end

Nurses' station

CENTRAL ISLAND NURSING HOME
Plainview, New York

ARCHITECT
Neumann, Taylor and Schonwald
Stanley Dicker, P.E.
New York, New York

PURPOSE
Nursing

CAPACITY
200 beds

COST
not available

SPONSOR
(proprietary)

A long narrow site dictated the F-shaped plan of this 3-story nursing home on Long Island. The main entrance is in a corner of the building where the lower cross-bar of the F meets the stem. Patients' rooms, the majority semi-private, occupy most of the stem and the upper cross-bar on the first floor supervised by a nurses' station at the intersection. Other facilities on the main floor include a large lounge and recreation room, administrative and medical offices, and a library. There are separate dining and activities rooms on each patient floor, and for the home as a whole there are physical and occupational therapy facilities and a beauty and barber shop.

The exterior of the steel frame and concrete structure is beige brick contrasted with white window spandrels. Interior finishings were selected to create a home-like atmosphere. Floors are either resilient tile or carpeted, walls are gypsum board and/or plaster and ceilings are acoustical tile.

FIRST FLOOR PLAN

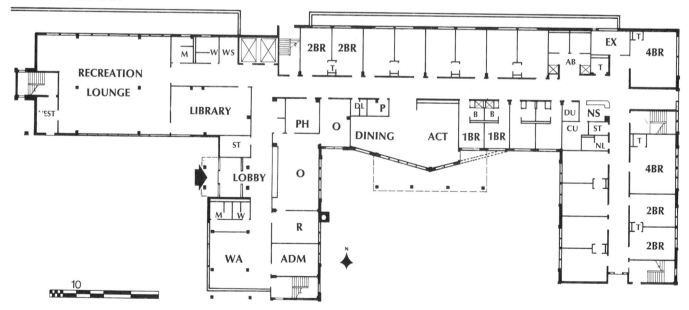

TOPEKA PRESBYTERIAN MANOR
Topeka, Kansas

ARCHITECT
Brown & Slemmons
Topeka, Kansas

PURPOSE
Nursing

CAPACITY
121 beds

COST
$1,558,000

SPONSOR
United Presbyterian Foundation of Kansas

A growing number of nursing homes are being planned in stages, with the expectation that at a later date more extensive nursing care or expanded facilities may be necessary. The 2-story Topeka home is a case in point.

The rectangular portion, completed in 1964, presently serves independent or self-care residents in single or double rooms. Four nursing stations provide the minimal supervision appropriate at this time, but stand ready to supply skilled care should the need arise.

In 1966 the circular building representing stage 2 was added. This was designed to be a special care unit with pairs of nursing stations situated at the central core of each floor. At present 36 patients may be cared for, but the building is designed to serve nearly twice that number. Concrete frame construction is used throughout, with brick exteriors and plastered interiors.

All patients' rooms are equipped for individual air-conditioning control and wired for a complete audio-visual intercommunication system. Day rooms

or parlors are located within walking distance of rooms in both buildings.

The first two floors of the main building house a large lounge, beauty and barber shops, dining, recreation, and physical therapy rooms. A triangular-shaped chapel seating 100 connects to the main building at an angle at the southeast corner of the site.

The view from the portico along the north side of the main building extends across a landscaped area toward the state Governor's mansion. The grounds include a pond approached from a gently sloping garden. Gardening facilities are available for interested patients, and there is a sun deck atop the second floor of the main building.

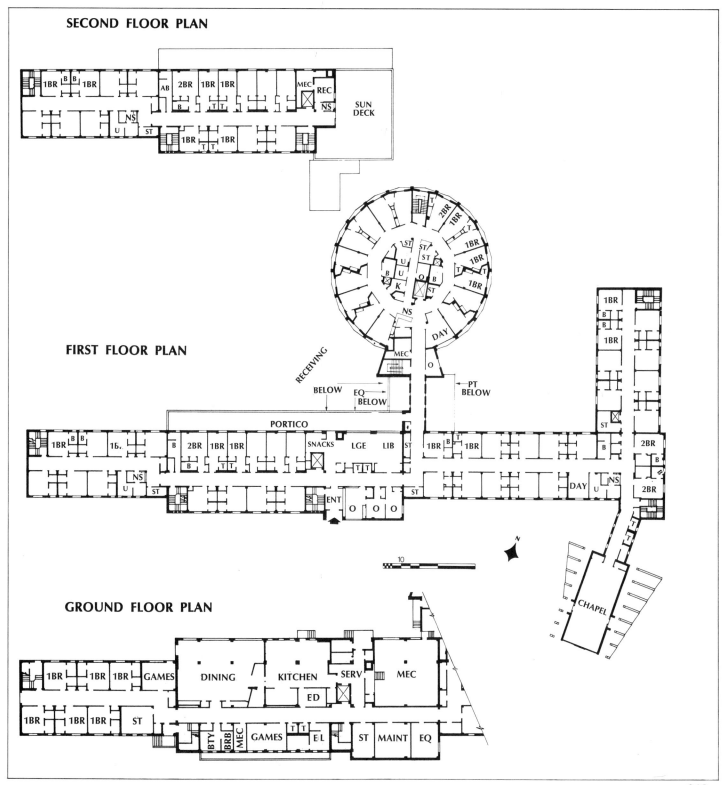

SECOND FLOOR PLAN

FIRST FLOOR PLAN

GROUND FLOOR PLAN

HARTWYCK WEST NURSING HOME
Cedar Grove, New Jersey

ARCHITECT
Eleanore Pettersen, A.I.A.
Saddle River, New Jersey

PURPOSE
Nursing

CAPACITY
113 beds

COST
$997,912 (excluding fees)

SPONSOR
(proprietary)

At first glance the contours of this 2-level nursing home suggest a jet aircraft with wings attached perpendicularly but swept back at their ends. These unusual lines were part of an overall plan to create a convalescent home which is as non-institutional as possible. The wings were bent back to shorten the length of corridors. The triangular spaces at the ends are used for lounges, each decorated in a different style such as Mediterranean or French or Italian Provincial. The corridors themselves have different colored handrails and carpeting to add interest and to aid patients in

identifying their wing.

The floor plan in detail is also unusually varied, allowing several room layouts. The majority of bedrooms are doubles, but some have the long wall on the window side, others follow the more conventional arrangement with long side walls. Toilet and bath facilities vary accordingly, with some double rooms provided with tub, toilet, and lavatory facilities to be shared by adjacent rooms; others with just toilet and lavatory arrangements. A number of rooms have private balconies. The plan also allows for a number of

outdoor sitting or activity areas to encourage patients to move outdoors and enjoy fresh air and sun.

The three nursing wings on the upper level are supervised by a pair of nursing stations at the central intersection. These are immediately adjacent to three intensive care units, and to utility and treatment rooms. A portion of the building jutting out at the back (the tail of the "fuselage") houses the lounge and dining area at this level.

One wing of the lower level is devoted to nursing for younger patients and is supervised by a single station near the center of the perpendicular part of the wing. The opposite wing houses the boiler room and service and maintenance areas. The central "fuselage" wing contains offices and such ancillary facilities as a pharmacy and gift shop, a beauty and barber shop, a meditation chapel (in the triangular-shaped end area), and occupational and physical therapy facilities which include a pool for hydrotherapy.

The site presented several problems: There was a 30-foot drop over the course of the property and a large part of the earth consisted of a fine sand and clay covering. This had to be removed and stabilized fill introduced. The footing design of the building was increased accordingly.

The building's frame is of structural steel with long span steel joists. The exterior walls are face brick with cinder block back-up. The mansard roof is built-up over steel decking with the sloped areas covered with asphalt shingles. Interior walls are gypsum wallboard on wood studs with 2-inch gypsum partitions.

continued

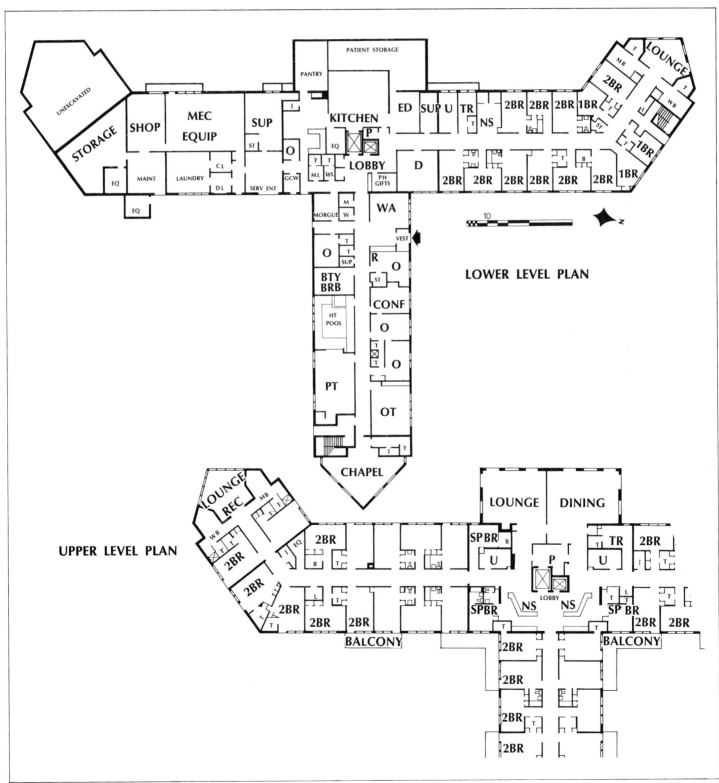

LOWER LEVEL PLAN

UPPER LEVEL PLAN

1

2

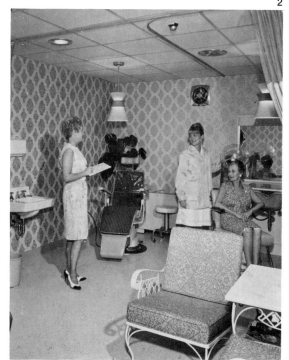

3

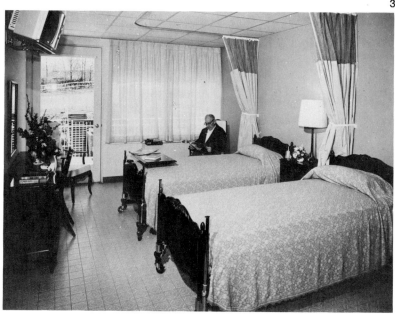

1 Reception area
2 Beauty shop
3 Typical 2-bed room
4 North end of the building with main
  lounge and dining room at right, other
  lounges in the foreground
5 Hubbard tank in hydrotherapy pool
6 French Provincial lounge

4

5

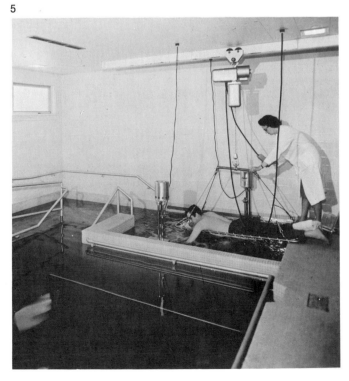

6

GIBSON COMMUNITY HOSPITAL ANNEX
Gibson City, Illinois

ARCHITECT
Coder Taylor Associates
Kenilworth, Illinois

PURPOSE
Nursing

CAPACITY
41 beds

COST
$501,152

SPONSOR
(non-profit)

The idea of building rest and rehabilitation centers in conjunction with a fully equipped hospital is gaining in popularity. Not only are there the economic advantages of lowered patient or room costs in the nursing facility, but there is also a psychological value for the patient. He can reside in a building with a more home-like atmosphere, one free of the hospital associations of acute or serious illness. A case in point is the Gibson Community Hospital Annex, a 2-level L-shaped building connected

to Gibson Community Hospital. Rates for care in the Annex are less than half those of the hospital. At the same time the equipment and facilities of the hospital are ready to serve a patient should the need arise. Both home and hospital benefit financially from the arrangement since some administrative functions and the food preparation service can be shared. Only a serving kitchen is needed in the nursing facility.

Most of the rooms on the patient floor of the Annex are doubles, divisible by

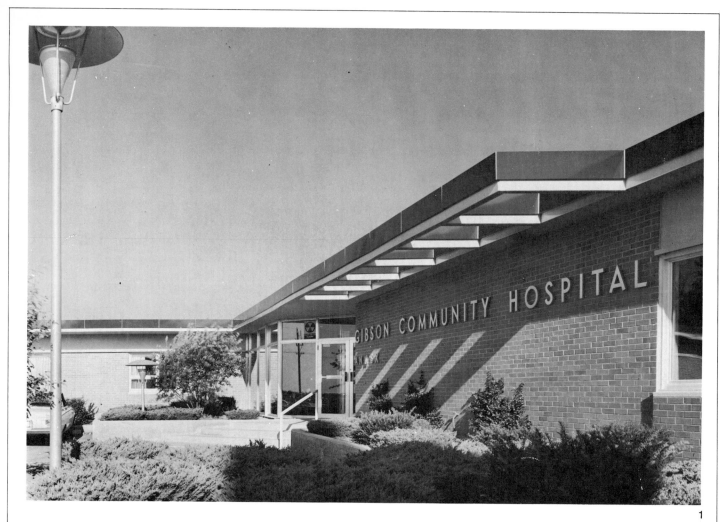

1

2

a curtain or folding partition. One toilet serves two patients and a bathtub serves four. Central bathing facilities are provided for patients needing assistance. The nurses' station is at the corner of the L overlooking the shorter corridor which is reserved for patients requiring greater care. The area between the nursing wings and the existing hospital houses a dining room and a lounge. This opens onto a large terrace overlooking landscaped grounds. On the lower level are rooms for physical and occupational therapy, group activities, and storage.

In keeping with the desire to give the building a residential look, a gabled roof was placed over the lounge and dining room. This permits clerestory day lighting at the north end of these central areas.

The exterior of the reinforced concrete building is brick with concrete block back-up. The roof is steel bar joist with precast gypsum plank deck, 4-ply tar-and-gravel roofing. Metal stud lath and plaster interior partitions extend to the roof decking to minimize sound transmission. Ceilings are acoustically treated. Flooring is vinyl tile on concrete. Patient rooms are provided with television and individual controls for fan coil heating, cooling, and ventilating units.

3

1 View of main entrance from hospital
2 Gabled roof lounge and terrace face south. Annex and hospital are connected by a passageway next to the lounge and dining area
3 Detail of entrance

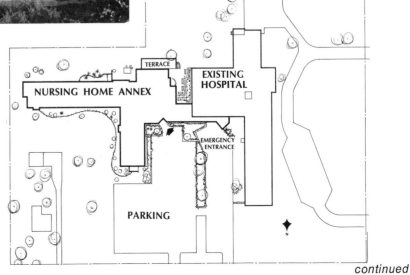

SITE PLAN

continued

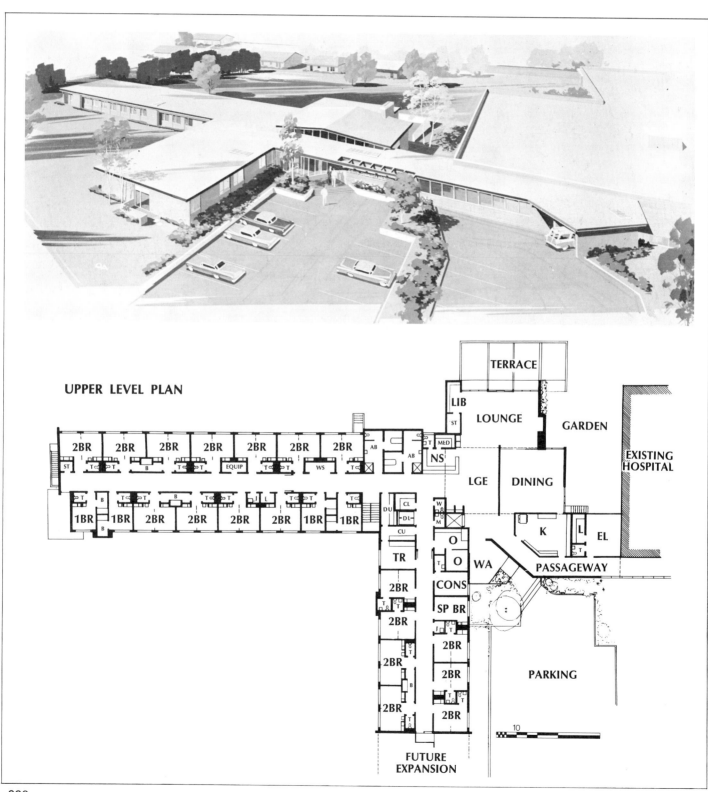

UPPER LEVEL PLAN

forced concrete with a 4-inch slab floor. The frame roof is sheathed with plywood and surfaced with built-up asphalt and gravel. The raised wood center section is a screen wall to conceal mechanical projections.

Exterior walls are frame, 4-inch wood siding. Cement asbestos panels with baked enamel finish are used under windows. Brick fins enhance the novel shape of the building at the same time concealing the downspouts.

Interior finishes are plasterboard with acoustical tile ceilings for sound insula-tion in the service and corridor areas. Floors are covered with sheet vinyl except for mosaic tile in bath and toilet areas.

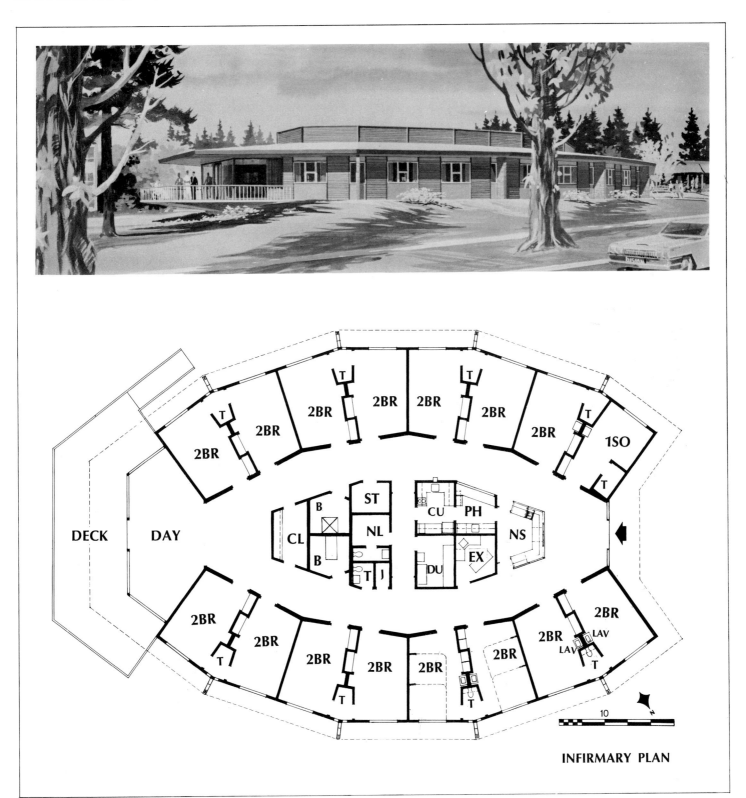

INFIRMARY PLAN

**VALLEY MANOR GERIATRICS CENTER
EXTENDED CARE FACILITIES**
Concord, California

ARCHITECT
*Ratcliff—Slama—Cadwalader
Berkeley, California*

PURPOSE
Nursing

CAPACITY
70 beds

COST
$710,000

SPONSOR
(proprietary)

With stucco walls and redwood sunshades, numerous small terraces, and variations in ceiling height, this 1-story L-shaped building looks more like a residential garden apartment than an extended care nursing facility. Indeed the emphasis in design was on patients' rooms. All are semi-private, 204 square feet in area (44 square feet more than the federal minimum requirement for this type of facility); all have small alcoves on the garden side of the room opening out onto sheltered terraces. The ceiling is higher over the middle of the room, lower in the portion fronting on the terrace.

The building is the first of two phases of construction. The second phase will add 135 more beds to the total capacity, at which time an existing 35-bed home will be demolished. The Phase I 70-bed facility will house a new kitchen, dining-recreation room, and administrative offices for the home, as well as physical and occupational therapy facilities. A number of smaller communal areas are also provided, one of which will feature a birdcage. A basement included in the plan will be used for electrical and mechanical equipment, a repair shop, and storage areas.

The building uses reinforced concrete footings with retaining walls at the basement. Floors are concrete slab on grade. Walls and roof are of wood frame construction.

Interior finishes include resilient tile floors, gypsum wallboard partitions and ceilings, and natural hardwood doors and trim. The lounge-dining area is carpeted and the ceiling wood-paneled. Packaged heating and air-conditioning units will be located on the roof.

SITE PLAN

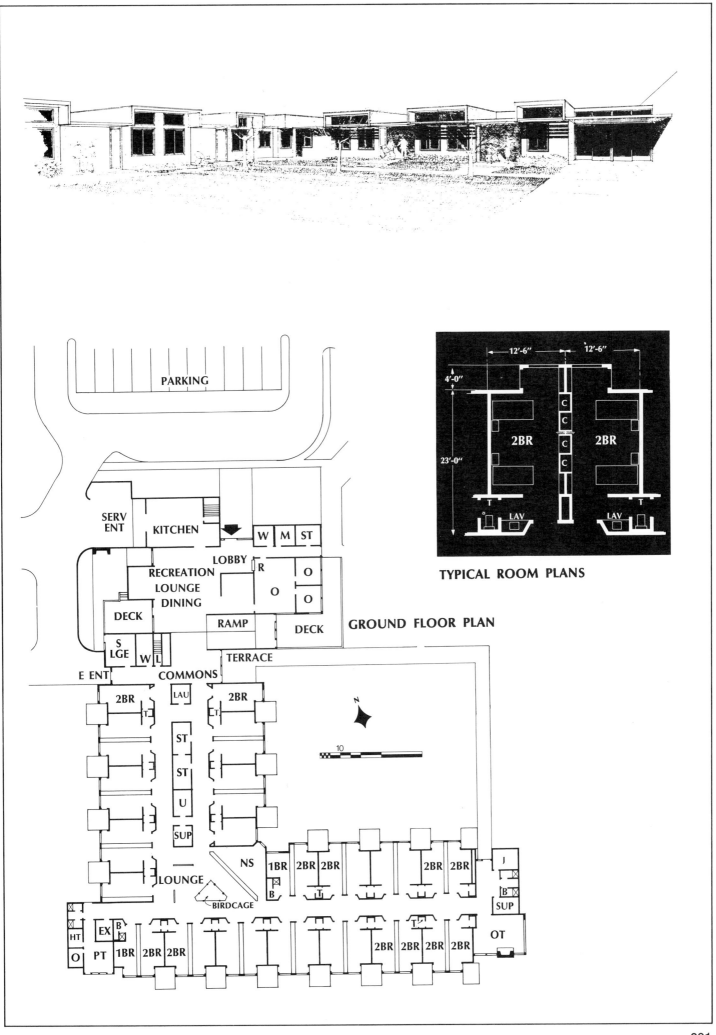

PARKING

TYPICAL ROOM PLANS

12'-6"   12'-6"

4'-0"

23'-0"

2BR   2BR

C C C C

T   LAV   LAV   T

SERV ENT

KITCHEN

W M ST

LOBBY

R

O O O

RECREATION
LOUNGE
DINING

DECK

RAMP

DECK

GROUND FLOOR PLAN

S LGE

W L

TERRACE

E ENT

COMMONS

2BR

LAU

2BR

T T

ST

N

ST

10

U

SUP

NS

1BR 2BR 2BR

2BR 2BR

J

B

LOUNGE

B

SUP

BIRDCAGE

HT

EX B

OT

O

PT

1BR 2BR 2BR

T

2BR 2BR 2BR 2BR

**SUNNYSIDE FARMS
NURSING HOME—ADDITION**
Manasquan, New Jersey

ARCHITECT
*Gordon Powers & Associates
New York, New York*

PURPOSE
Nursing

CAPACITY
40 beds

COST
$163,000

SPONSOR
Sunnyside Farms, Inc. (proprietary)

A single innovation in the plan for the extension to the Sunnyside Farms Nursing Home has been sufficient to distinguish the building from others on the contemporary scene and mark it for architectural honors. This was the use of 5-sided rooms for semi-private patients. Three of the walls form a conventional U-shape upon entering from the corridor. The remaining two walls point outward giving the room a feeling of openness. These walls end in windowed areas so that when they come together they form a triangular bay which projects from the facade.

The unusual window arrangement allows each patient to enjoy an individual view and sitting area, even when the room-dividing curtain is drawn.

By providing the rooms with double sliding doors, one adjacent to each bed, and adding individual closets and built-in dressers, the architect further enhanced the sense of privacy he feels is most important for nursing home residents. At the same time he was able to save space. The use of sliding doors has the additional advantage of convenience of operation for wheelchair

1

2

patients or for the movement of beds. The only shared facilities are the lavatories and toilets which have been built into the triangular spaces between the window walls of adjacent rooms.

What makes the plan outstanding from a practical point of view is that the architect was able to accomplish his aims of privacy in rooms-with-a-view and still keep spatial requirements minimal. The total room area is only 277 square feet—10% under the minimum recommended by the U.S. Public Health Service for a conventional rectangularly shaped semi-private room.

The addition contains a total of 20 pentagonal rooms. These have been incorporated into a Y-shaped 1-story building that is connected to the original home. The lobby, with reception area and offices, lies in the stem of the Y where the new building joins the old. Here, wide windows, and a side wall of turquoise, blue, and white glazed brick extending outdoors have been used, again to accent the view rather than the interior.

In order to keep the costs of the unique structure within narrow budgetary limits, stock materials were used as much as possible. The bay windows were formed of stock sash with conventional framing. Basic construction is block wall, wood joist and stud, with stucco exterior and dry-wall interiors.

In addition to the patient rooms, the plan calls for a centrally placed nurses' station, a cantilevered porch extending from the west end of the building, boiler

continued

1 West end showing cantilevered porch

2 Path leads to lobby entrance and connection to existing home at left

3 Lobby with glazed brick wall extending outside

3

FIRST FLOOR PLAN

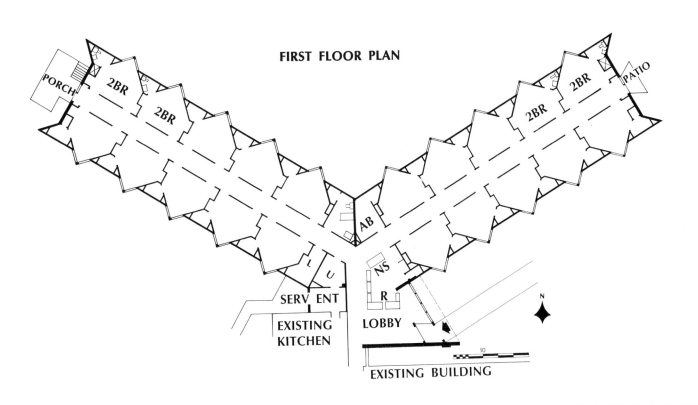

room and hot water supply, utility rooms, electrical service, and a septic system. Dining, recreation, and other ancillary facilities are provided in the older building.

The design earned the 1962 Award of Special Distinction in the Interior Awards Program of *Institutions Magazine.*

1

2

3

1 Typical patients' room. Note closet, built-in dresser, and door to toilet facilities

2 Projecting bays provide sunny sitting areas

3 Patients' room showing corridor wall with sliding doors

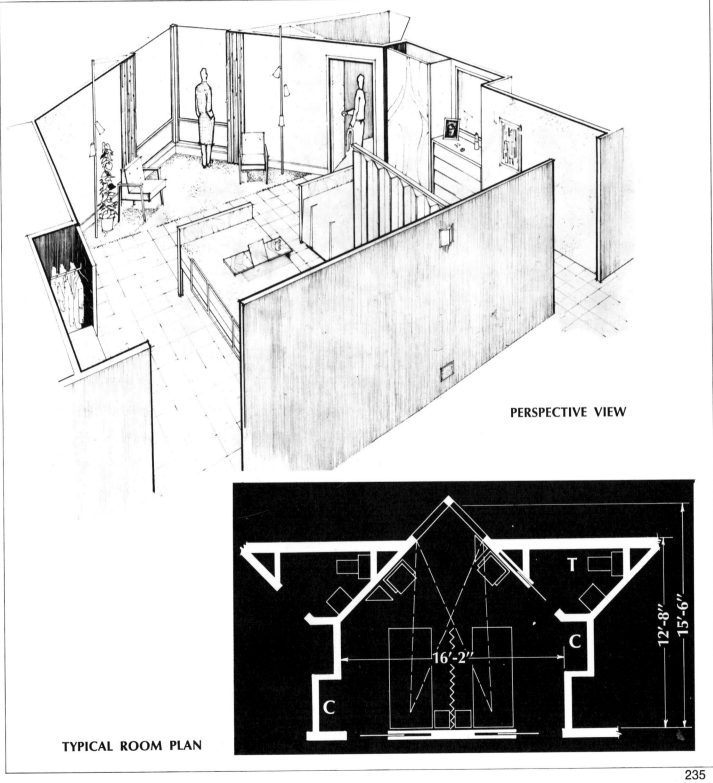

PERSPECTIVE VIEW

TYPICAL ROOM PLAN

12'-8"

15'-6"

16'-2"

T

C

C

AURORA BOREALIS
Aurora, Illinois

ARCHITECT
Daniel Comm Associates
Chicago, Illinois

PURPOSE
Nursing

CAPACITY
112 beds

COST
$630,000

SPONSOR
(proprietary)

Aurora, Illinois, a pleasant community near Chicago, now boasts a special housing complex for the elderly which includes apartments, a shopping center, and a motel in addition to a nursing home, the first building to be built. "Aurora Borealis" consists of four 1-story wings extending from a 2-story core. Designed with the well-to-do convalescent patient in mind, all rooms have private outdoor patios accessible through sliding glass doors. There are nursing stations at the intersection of each pair of 28-bed wings.

The core unit on the first floor houses a chapel, a dining and recreation room, and a beauty and barber shop, in addition to the lobby, executive offices, and medical facilities. At the second floor level the core contains occupational therapy facilities and a large terrace. The kitchen and laundry as well as the boiler room and storage areas are in the basement.

Composite steel columns and concrete were used in the core area. The wings have brick exterior bearing walls which carry precast concrete roof sections.

SITE PLAN

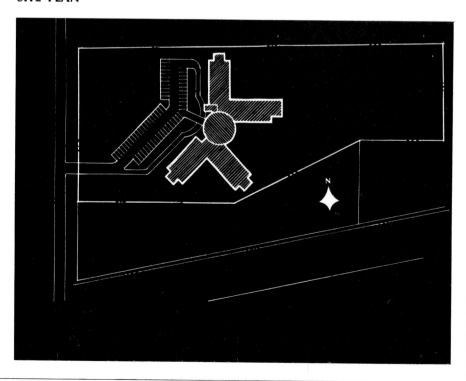

The sections also serve as branch ducts for the year-round air-conditioning system. Interior partitions are gypsum dry-wall with a high sound control rating.

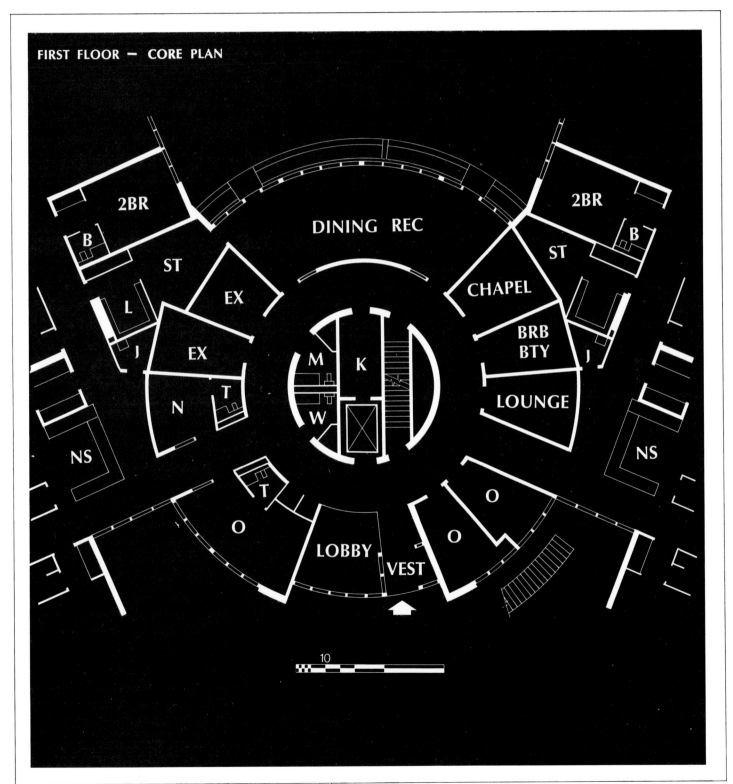

FIRST FLOOR — CORE PLAN

2BR · B · ST · L · J · EX · EX · N · T · NS · T · O · LOBBY · VEST · O · O · M · K · W · DINING REC · CHAPEL · BRB BTY · LOUNGE · ST · 2BR · B · J · NS

10

BIVINS MEMORIAL NURSING HOME
Amarillo, Texas

ARCHITECT
Hucker & Pargé
Amarillo, Texas

PURPOSE
Nursing

CAPACITY
64 beds

COST
$1,500,000

SPONSOR
Mary E. Bivins Foundation (non-profit)

This 1-story nursing home is one of a group of health care, medical education, and research facilities planned for the Amarillo Medical Center, a non-profit foundation-sponsored complex to be built on a 396-acre lake front site in Amarillo. The Bivins home was designed for chronic bed-ridden patients not requiring hospital care.

Patients will be housed in six wings radiating from a hexagonal hub containing a pair of nursing stations and dining and day rooms. Two wings are reserved for intensive care patients; a third will be used for private suites. A pair of passageways enclosing a courtyard leads from the nursing pavilion to a central service and administration unit with offices, chapel, treatment rooms, kitchen, laundry, and storage area. These facilities and the additional storage room and mechanical equipment housed in the partial basement will serve a duplicate nursing pavilion planned for the future.

The nursing unit does not have a basement, but the floors are built over a crawl space which carries

TYPICAL WALL SECTION

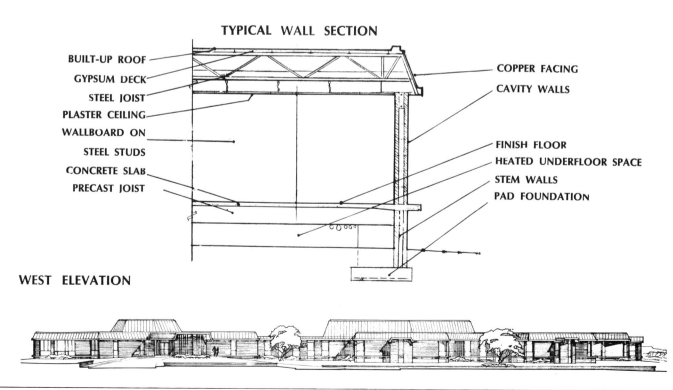

BUILT-UP ROOF
GYPSUM DECK
STEEL JOIST
PLASTER CEILING
WALLBOARD ON
STEEL STUDS
CONCRETE SLAB
PRECAST JOIST

COPPER FACING
CAVITY WALLS

FINISH FLOOR
HEATED UNDERFLOOR SPACE
STEM WALLS
PAD FOUNDATION

WEST ELEVATION

mechanical and electrical services. Not only will maintenance be facilitated but warm air returns from the year-round heating and air-conditioning systems will heat the floors comfortably.

The home has been placed at the southern end of an 8.7 acre site north of the lake so that good views are possible from the main day room areas.

The building's foundation is poured-in-place concrete. Bearing walls are brick cavity. Floors are concrete poured over pre-stressed concrete joists. Roof construction is steel long span joists bearing on steel beams carrying a poured gypsum deck with a built-up roof.

In keeping with the natural materials of the southwest, the exterior of the building is finished in adobe-colored brick. Bronze anodized aluminum is used around doors and windows. Glass is glare-resistant. Interior masonry walls are exposed brick of the same adobe color as the exterior. Corridor walls are faced with vinyl. Partitions are ⅝ inch gypsum wallboard with additional vinyl covering in toilets.

Ceilings are plastered and corridor and patient room floors are covered with a mastic-applied carpeting of tight weave.

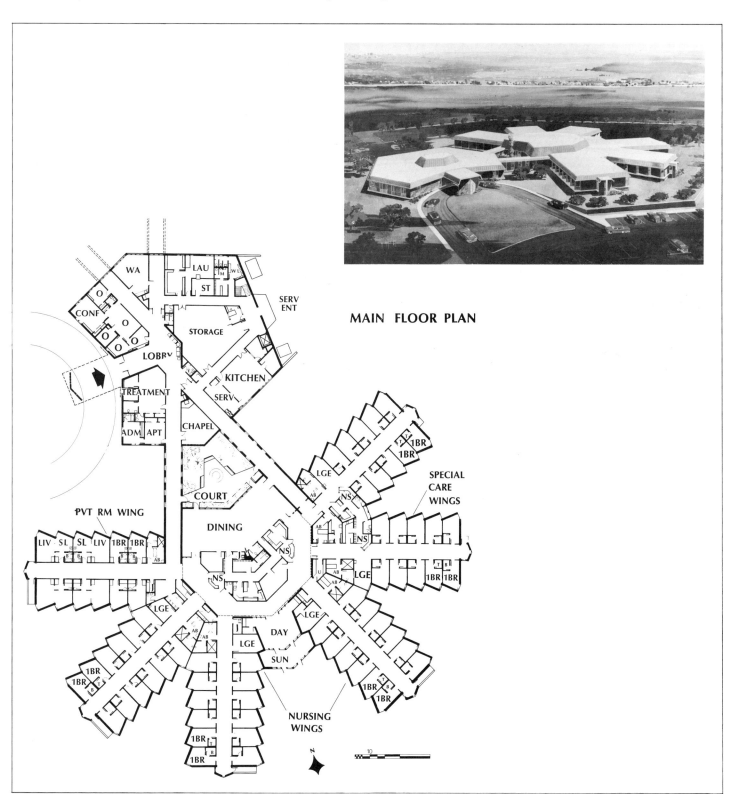

MAIN FLOOR PLAN

RIVERVIEW MODERNIZATION—EXTENSION
Philadelphia, Pennsylvania

ARCHITECT
Bellante and Clauss
Philadelphia, Pennsylvania

PURPOSE
Nursing

CAPACITY
466 light-care nursing patients
200 infirmary patients

COST
$13,185,000 (all buildings)
$8,300,000 (nursing and infirmary units only)

SPONSOR
The City of Philadelphia

In their master plan for modernizing this city facility, the architects stated that "the pleasure, comfort, individual dignity and initiative of Philadelphia senior citizens regardless of race, creed or walk of life has been the primary objective."

To accomplish this end the architects conceived of a series of cross-shaped cottage units for ambulatory aged persons. These would be paired or clustered around a commons building in self-contained complexes which would replace several large dormitories, institutional in character.

The City of Philadelphia approved the idea and the plan won a 1955 design award of *Progressive Architecture* in the public buildings category. In 1956 five cottages and one central "meeting house" were built.

Recently it was decided to extend the modernization. Again some of the older institutional buildings are to be replaced, but a consideration this time was the fact that as older people live longer their general health declines. So Riverview's second phase of modernization calls for the modification of several existing cottages to serve

1

self-reliant wheelchair patients and the addition of six new cottages with supporting facilities suitable for a less ambulatory population. For those requiring extensive nursing or medical supervision, a 200-bed infirmary complex is also planned.

The six new cottages (with a total capacity of 476 patients*) will be paired around three commons buildings. Like the existing meeting house, each commons building will

*Since the new units and infirmary replace older structures, the total capacity of Riverview will remain the same: 1,100 residents.

house a dining room and a pantry, a snack bar, gift shop, beauty and barber shops, visiting area, therapy center, and a medical office and examination room. The cottages themselves will follow layouts similar to the existing units. Three wings will be sleeping areas spacious enough to allow for wheelchair movement and storage.

These wings will be supervised from a raised nursing station. Toilet and bathing facilities, suitable for wheelchair patients, will be centered, and also supervised from the raised control center. One of the sleeping

wings will end in a solarium connecting to other parts of the complex. The fourth wing will serve as a day room.

The infirmary complex will be composed of a medical treatment building centered between two men's and two women's bed-patient buildings. Corridors overlooking garden courts will connect these buildings, (also cross-shaped), to the treatment center.

continued

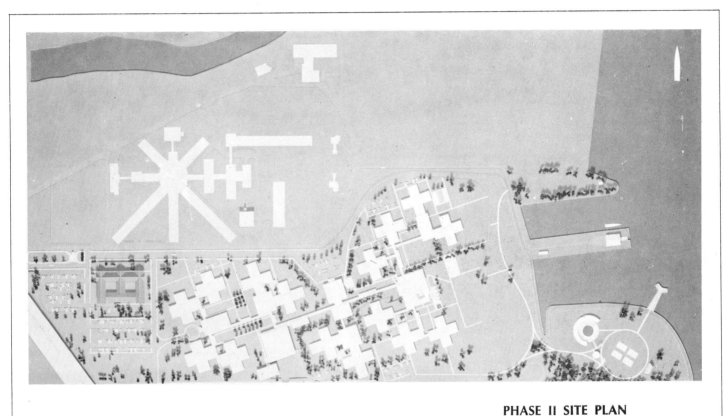

2

1 View along one side of a cottage looking toward another. Sunlight piercing the overhang creates a spotlight effect

2 Aerial view

PHASE II SITE PLAN

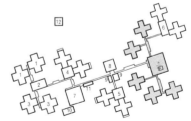

▦ 1956 Modernization
1 Men's infirmary cottages
2 Medical treatment center
3 Women's infirmary cottages
4 Men's cottage complex
5 Women's cottage complex
6 Women's cottage complex
7 Kitchen services
8 Administration
9 Chapels
10 Maintenance
11 Employees' dining
12 Boiler plant
13 Existing building

RIVERVIEW MODERNIZATION— EXTENSION

The new units will be reinforced concrete structures with brick exterior walls, built-up slag roofs, aluminum windows, and hollow metal doors. Interior walls are plaster or structural glazed tile and brick; floors are terrazzo, ceramic, or resilient tile. Ceilings are plaster, acoustically treated where sound control is important.

In addition to the patient complexes, the new plan incorporates a new administration building, chapels, boiler plant, maintenance facilities, and a kitchen and services building. Recreational facilities will be re-vamped to make better use of the natural charms of the Delaware River site. New walks and landscaped courts have been designed, and, at the waterfront, a wading pool, barbecue and picnic area, band shell, and fishing pier are planned.

1

1 View from a solarium toward the central
  meeting house
2 Tile "pinwheels" (see plan) are used
  as partitions to separate bed units

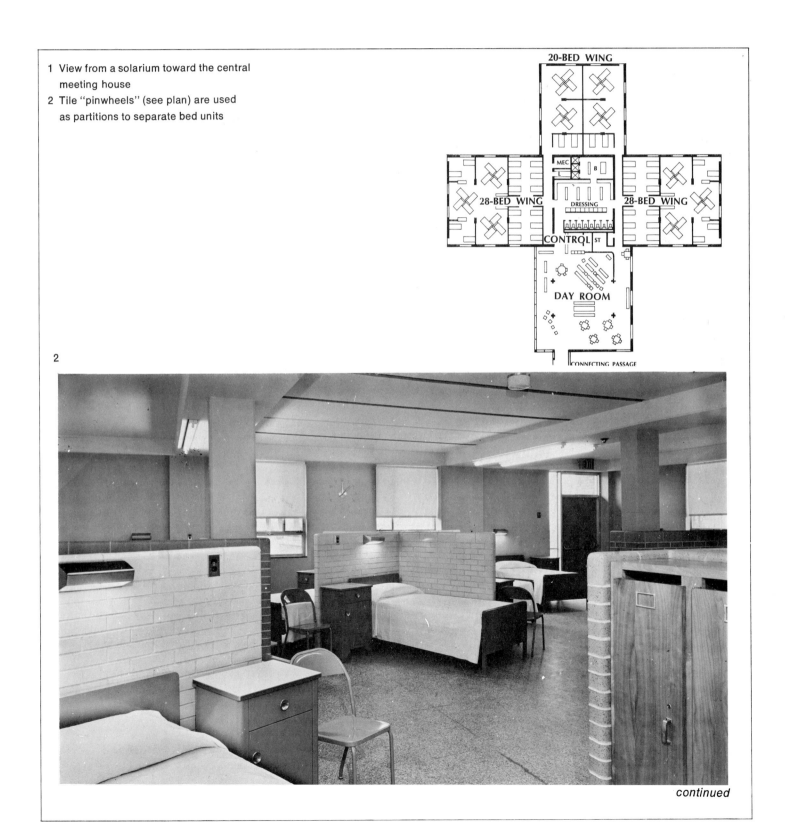

2

continued

1 A recreation day room in one of the
  men's cottages
2 Weaving is one of the activities offered
  in the occupational therapy workshop
  in the basement of the meeting house
  building
3 Meeting house recreation room
4 Ramp for use of wheelchair patients
5 The dining hall is convertible into an
  auditorium

SANFORD NURSING HOME
Farmington, Minnesota

ARCHITECT
S. C. Smiley & Associates
Minneapolis, Minnesota

PURPOSE
Nursing

CAPACITY
26 beds

COST
$291,816

SPONSOR
Sanford Hospital Corp. (non-profit)

Small towns are rarely provided with hospitals or major medical facilities, but generally must rely on those in larger cities miles away. Not so in the case of Farmington, a rural community about 30 miles southeast of Minneapolis. In 1964 the community built a 50-bed general hospital which was designated Hospital of the Month by *Modern Hospital* magazine. Now a nursing home addition has been designed as part of long-range plans for a medical complex.

The new 1-story building shares the hospital's laboratory, X-ray, and treatment rooms, food preparation, administration services, and heating plant. The nursing home has its own recreation areas, dining room-solarium, and occupational therapy facilities. Its design, a neat T-form with patients' rooms arranged in the cross-bar, allows a central nursing station for the supervision of patients.

The building's construction is essentially reinforced concrete over steel joists with a metal deck and built-up roof. Exterior is brick with concrete block back-up. Interiors are plastered. Floors are resilient or ceramic tile.

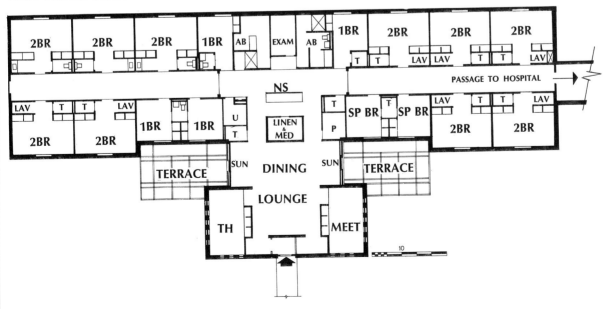

SITE PLAN

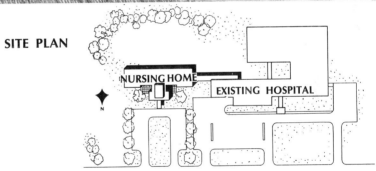

FIRST FLOOR PLAN

THE PRESBYTERIAN HOME—INFIRMARY ADDITION
Evanston, Illinois

ARCHITECT
*E. Todd Wheeler and
The Perkins and Will Partnership
Chicago, Illinois*

PURPOSE
Nursing

CAPACITY
100 beds

COST
$1,550,000 (construction only)

SPONSOR
The Presbyterian Home

An interesting therapeutic approach to nursing care for the aged is to group patients according to similar interests.

In the infirmary addition to the complex of buildings that make up the Presbyterian Home in Evanston, there are eight or nine patients each in such "family groups." Every patient has a private bedroom and toilet, but shares a day room or living area with the other members of the group. A cross-shaped floor plan permits placing individual groups in each of the four wings. One nursing station at the intersection serves the whole unit.

Its location permits direct vision into all four common rooms.

This arrangement is carried through on all three stories of the building. A full basement, aligned with the floor level of the existing structure and extending six feet above grade, is used for ancillary facilities. These include a clinic, an X-ray suite, examination rooms, offices, lockers, a laboratory, and a pharmacy. Since the infirmary is an addition to an existing plant which includes central dining areas, occupational and physical therapy rooms, recreational facilities,

1

and beauty and barber shops, it was not necessary to provide for these. A future 100-bed addition is also planned.

The foundations of the building are reinforced concrete on spread footings. The floors and roof are concrete slabs on shallow beams bearing on closely spaced concrete columns. A penthouse housing elevator equipment and ventilating fans, and a portion of the connection between the building and the older infirmary are steel-framed. Exterior walls are masonry, (matching existing buildings),

with limestone used for window sills and as decorative horizontal strips.

Interior walls are plaster over gypsum block, clay tile, or metal lath. Floors are vinyl asbestos except in the administrative area where carpeting is used. Patients' rooms have built-in wooden wardrobe cabinets.

The building is heated and cooled through a combination of individual fan coil units in patients' rooms and a central ventilating system.

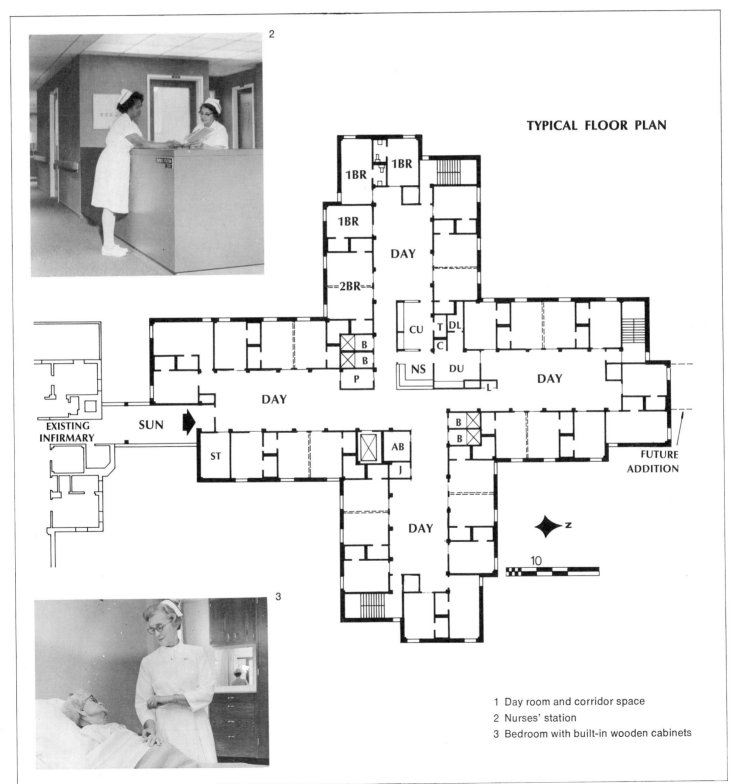

TYPICAL FLOOR PLAN

1 Day room and corridor space
2 Nurses' station
3 Bedroom with built-in wooden cabinets

HEBREW HOME FOR THE AGED
Rockville, Maryland

ARCHITECT
Cohen, Haft & Associates
Silver Spring, Maryland
Joseph Douglas Weiss, A.I.A., Consultant

PURPOSE
Nursing

CAPACITY
269 beds

COST
$3,900,000

SPONSOR
Greater Washington Jewish Community, Inc.

A 5-story nursing home to be built on the same site as a large community center is unusual even with today's progressive ideas for housing the aged. Moreover the Greater Washington Jewish Community Foundation wants the two buildings to be linked by an enclosed corridor. Ambulatory residents of the home can then walk under cover to the center to use the arts and crafts studios, auditorium, art lounge, and indoor swimming pool. The large suburban site includes a small lake and a boat dock is also planned.

In keeping with this philosophy of participation, the architects have tried to give the nursing home as residential an atmosphere as possible. Approximately 90 percent of the rooms are to be singles arranged in a pair of obliquely angled wings of varying widths. Where the wings are widest the floor plan calls for a central island flanked by a double corridor and patients' rooms. The islands will house nursing stations, examining rooms, bathing facilities, and service and utility areas. The narrower parts of the building will be served by a single corridor with rooms on either side. The net result of the variations in the width

BEAUTY SHOP

MEN'S SHOP

COFFEE SHOP

of the wings is to create exterior interest by means of prominences and recessed areas along the length of building. Dining rooms, lounges, and elevators will be placed at the intersection of the wings. The dining room on each floor was designed to function as a single unit although it appears to be two small dining areas each seating 25 persons.

The first floor of the home will offer extensive clinical and service facilities including a psychiatric unit, physical and occupational therapy facilities, a dental clinic, pharmacy, laboratory,

library, offices for staff and volunteers, and a music room. There is a hexagonally shaped extension of the building which houses the chapel.

Of interest on the first floor is a row of shops planned along an arcade to give the residents the feeling of being outside. There are men's and women's clothing shops as well as a beauty salon, barber shop, and coffee and gift shops.

The basement of the building will house a sewing room, a sheltered workshop, and a day center room

(under the chapel) in addition to utility, service, and maintenance areas.

The concrete frame building will have masonry exterior walls with terne metal at the bay windows. Floors are to be concrete slab; roof, steel frame with poured gypsum deck and terne metal. Interior partitions will be steel stud with dry-wall. The interiors have been designed by Barbara Dorn Associates to accent the residential quality.

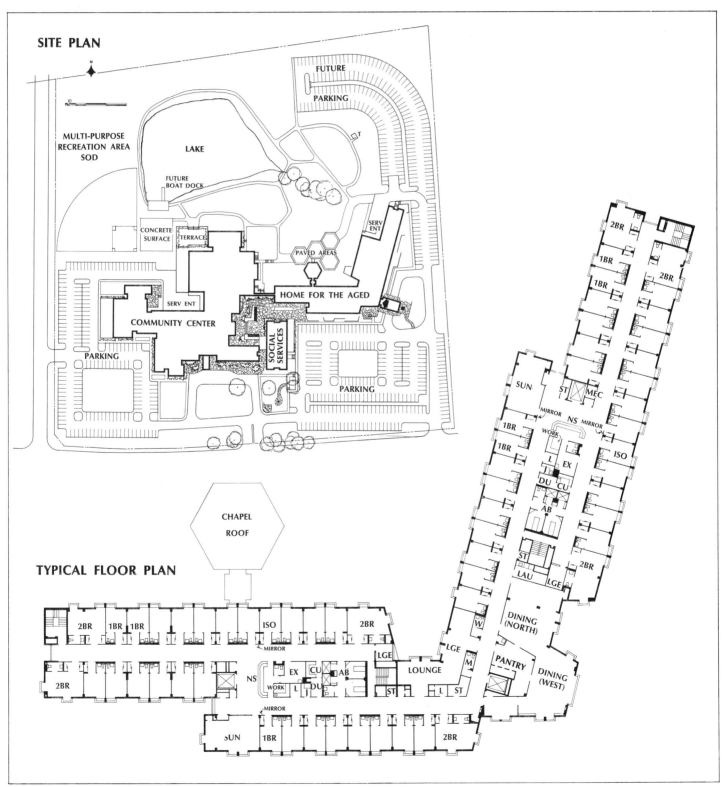

WILLIAMS COUNTY NURSING HOME (HILLSIDE)
Bryan, Ohio

ARCHITECT
*Sanzenbacher, Miller, Brigham & Scott
Toledo, Ohio*

PURPOSE
Nursing

CAPACITY
66 beds

COST
$718,075

SPONSOR
Williams County

In designing a county nursing home the criteria are likely to be to maximize the use of space while at the same time keeping overall costs modest. The Williams County 3-story nursing home accomplishes this by means of a simple rectangular design with patients' rooms lining the windowed lengths of the building. The nursing station and service facilities are centrally placed and flanked by a double corridor which is convenient both for patients and staff. Day rooms and physical therapy facilities are provided on each of the two nursing floors.

The ground floor of the building houses the central dining room and lounge, (extending out at the northwest corner of the building), and also a chapel, recreation and occupational therapy rooms, a beauty parlor, a barber shop, and kitchen, storage, equipment, maintenance, and staff facilities.

A corridor at the northeast end of the building connects it to an existing nursing home now used for ambulatory male patients and living quarters for the superintendant.

TYPICAL FLOOR PLAN

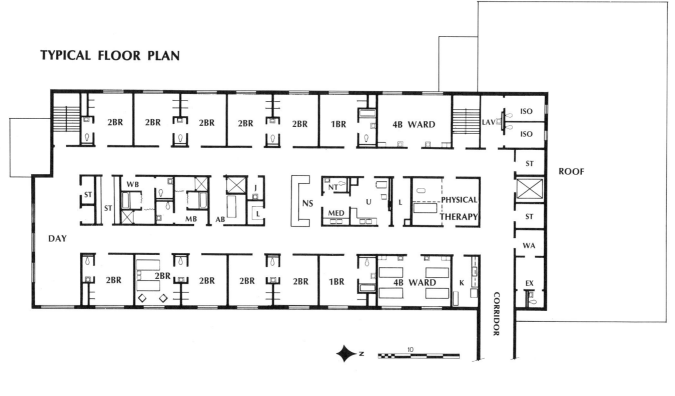

The exterior walls of the home are
load-bearing; brick with concrete block
back-up. The interior core is structural
steel. Floors are steel joist and
concrete and interior partitions are
dry-wall on steel studs.

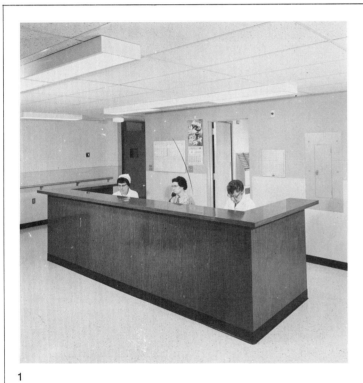

1

2

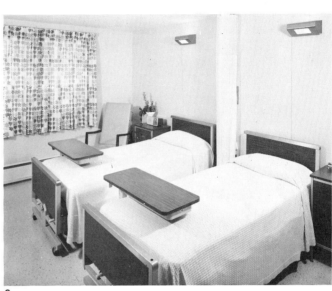

3

1 Nurses' station
2 Typical 2-bed room
3 Dining room
4 Main lounge

4

HEMPSTEAD PARK NURSING HOME
Hempstead, New York

ARCHITECT
Alan L. Aaron, A.I.A.

PURPOSE
Nursing

CAPACITY
240 beds

COST
$1,750,000 (excluding fees)

SPONSOR
(proprietary)

This 4-story nursing home attached to Hempstead General Hospital was the first nursing facility to be approved under the New York State Metcalf-McKlusky Law, which requires a certificate to show the need for beds. Each of the three upper floors of the X-shaped building can house 80 patients in 36 double rooms and 8 singles. Two nursing stations placed diagonally in the central core area supervise 40 beds each, but either one could control the whole floor if necessary. There is a lounge in each patient wing and a pair of dining rooms

near the core on all three floors. Patients' rooms have been individually decorated to create a hotel-like atmosphere.

Administrative and doctors' offices, (including podiatry, psychiatry, and dental specialties), physical therapy, and recreation rooms have been reserved for the first floor which connects to the hospital through a passageway. The cellar, in addition to containing the boiler room and other building service facilities, also houses X-ray and cobalt therapy rooms, and a

kitchen which serves both the home and the hospital.

The steel frame building is finished in face brick with decorative quartz chip panels between the windows. The entryway is tiled. Interior finishing includes acoustical tile ceilings, plaster walls, and carpeted or tiled floors. The building is air-conditioned and provided with an emergency generator service, master television antenna, and oxygen outlets for every patient room.

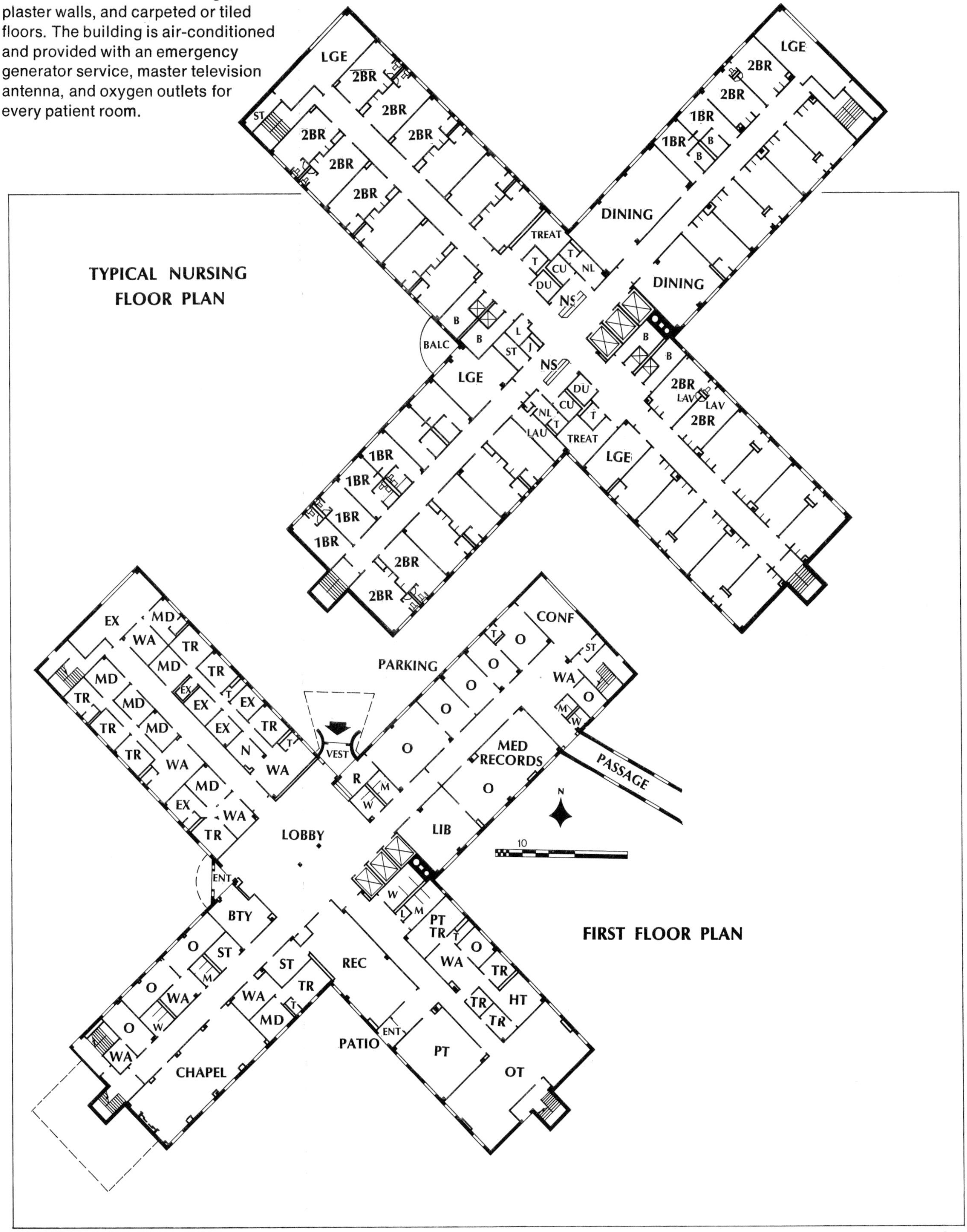

TYPICAL NURSING FLOOR PLAN

LGE · 2BR · 2BR · 2BR · 2BR · 2BR · ST · TREAT · T · CU · NL · DU · NS · B · BALC · B · L · ST · LGE · NS · DU · CU · NL · T · T · LAU · TREAT · LGE · 1BR · 1BR · 1BR · 1BR · 2BR · 2BR

LGE · 2BR · 2BR · 1BR · 1BR · B · B · DINING · DINING · B · B · 2BR · LAV · LAV · 2BR

FIRST FLOOR PLAN

EX · MD · WA · TR · MD · TR · TR · MD · EX · T · EX · TR · MD · EX · EX · TR · N · T · WA · TR · WA · MD · EX · WA · TR

VEST · R · M · W · PARKING · T · O · O · CONF · ST · O · WA · O · M · W · MED RECORDS · O · PASSAGE · N · LIB · W · M · PT TR · T · O · WA · TR · TR · HT · TR · TR

LOBBY · ENT · BTY · O · ST · M · O · WA · O · W · O · WA · CHAPEL · ST · WA · MD · T · TR · REC · ENT · PATIO · PT · OT

10

WARTBURG LUTHERAN HOME FOR THE AGING—INFIRMARY

Brooklyn, New York

ARCHITECT
Eggers and Higgins
Robert H. Welz, A.I.A., Project Director
New York, New York

PURPOSE
Nursing

CAPACITY
90 beds

COST
$2,100,000 (including furniture)

SPONSOR
Wartburg Lutheran Home

The infirmary addition to a building complex that dates back to the nineteenth century is the first of three structures to be built in a major modernization and replacement plan. The two others will be residences. Care has been taken that the new buildings will preserve the residential character of the older ones, some of which had been private dwellings. A new garden has been planned, and an enclosed garden in the center of the site will be left intact.

The new infirmary is a 4-story concrete frame building with a brick and concrete exterior. A tunnel at the boiler room level and passageways at the upper three floors of the building will link it with the old infirmary, leaving a covered terrace area at the main floor level. Another tunnel will connect the infirmary to the existing main building.

The infirmary follows a T-shaped plan, with a long cross-bar housing the patient wings. The facade of this part of the building consists of a series of projecting bays which the architects felt would harmonize well with the bay

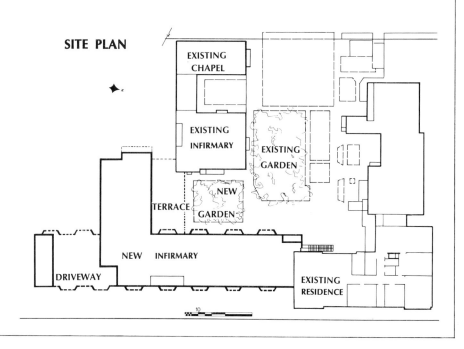

SITE PLAN

EXISTING CHAPEL

EXISTING INFIRMARY

EXISTING GARDEN

NEW GARDEN

TERRACE

NEW INFIRMARY

DRIVEWAY

EXISTING RESIDENCE

window construction typical of many Brooklyn residences. More practically, the bays will house the toilet and lavatory facilities of the single rooms, leaving the corridor side of the room uncluttered.

The stem of the T on each of the patient floors is used for the dining room and pantry, several double bedrooms, and bathing and service facilities. The nurses' station is at the intersection of the stem and cross-bar. A 6-bed intensive care unit has been placed on the top floor.

Main floor facilities include an assembly room and lounge, medical and dental offices, a library and conference room, a gift shop, and offices for the staff, which includes caseworkers and a recreational director. In keeping with the residential atmosphere, floors are generally carpeted throughout the building, ceilings are acoustically tiled, and walls are plastered.

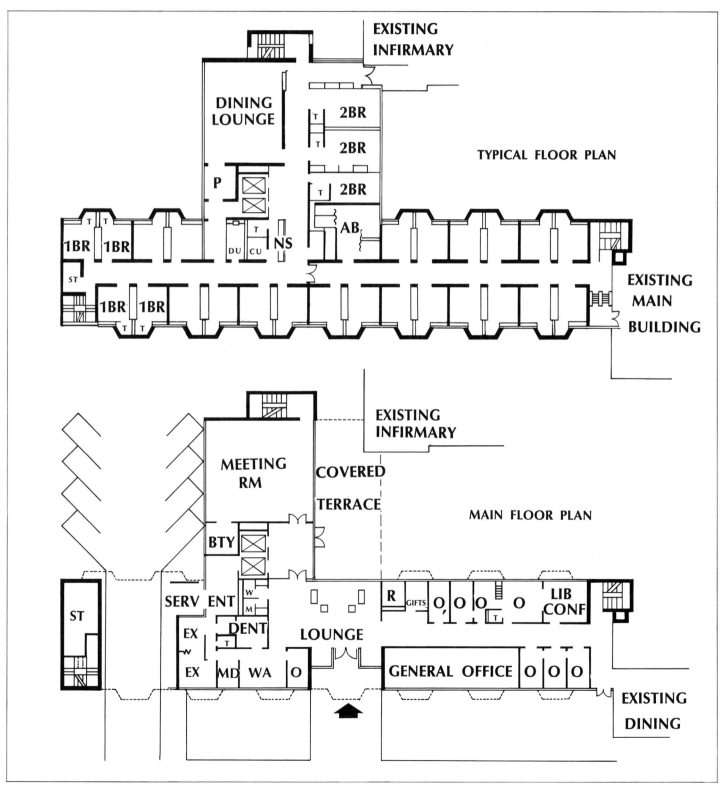

**ST. JOSEPH ON THE FLAMBEAU
NURSING HOME**
Ladysmith, Wisconsin

ARCHITECT
*Mark F. Pfaller Associates, Inc.
Milwaukee, Wisconsin*

PURPOSE
Nursing

CAPACITY
160 beds

COST
$1,553,498

SPONSOR
Servants of Mary, Inc. (non-profit)

When a nursing home addition was proposed for St. Mary's Hospital in Ladysmith, the architects were faced with the problem of a limited site, but one with a beautiful view of the Flambeau River. Their 3-story serpentine-curved building is a practical and esthetic solution to the problem. The 160-bed addition is linked to the hospital to the north, but a majority of patients' rooms are placed at the opposite side of the building to take advantage of the southern exposure and river view.

The connection to the hospital eliminates the need for many of the ancillary services that a nursing facility would normally provide. A laundry for the entire complex and a large physical medicine department are the only major services installed in the new building.

The slope of the land down to the river edge made it possible to grade the lower level and provide outdoor patios and activities areas. The outdoor theme is further enhanced by balconies along the river and side facades,

built in between projections from the
patient rooms which house toilet
facilities.

A small almond-shaped chapel projects
from the north side of the building
at the right of the main entrance.

Exposed concrete and face brick have
been used for the exterior of the
concrete frame building. Interior
finishing includes suspended
acoustical ceilings, painted concrete
block walls, vinyl asbestos tile floors,
and wood cabinetwork.

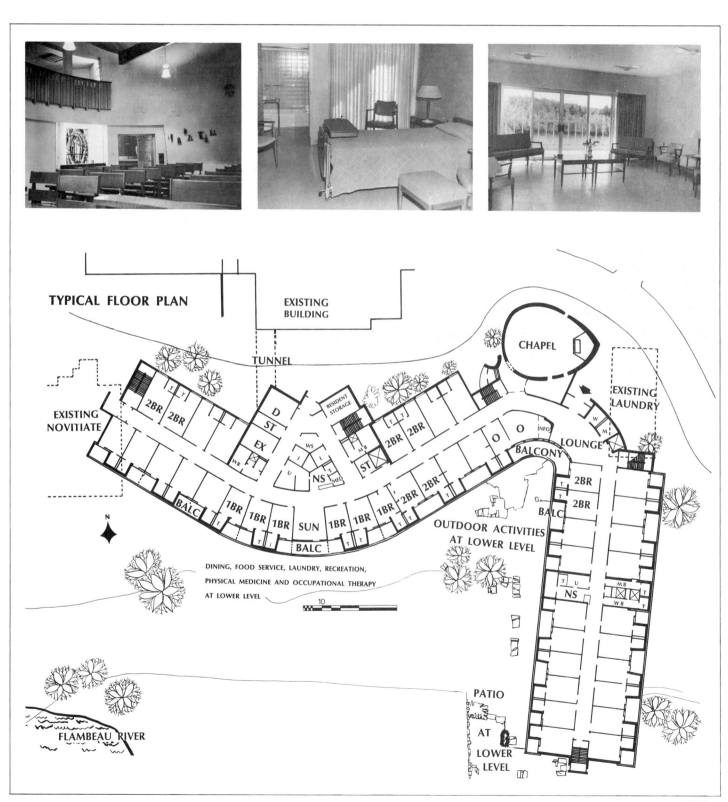

TYPICAL FLOOR PLAN

EXISTING
BUILDING

TUNNEL

CHAPEL

EXISTING
LAUNDRY

EXISTING
NOVITIATE

RESIDENT
STORAGE

2BR 2BR

D
ST
EX
WB

WS

NS
MED

MB
ST

2BR 2BR

O O O
INFO

LOUNGE

BALCONY

2BR
2BR

BALC

BALC
1BR 1BR 1BR SUN 1BR 1BR 1BR 2BR 2BR

T

OUTDOOR ACTIVITIES
AT LOWER LEVEL

N

BALC

DINING, FOOD SERVICE, LAUNDRY, RECREATION,
PHYSICAL MEDICINE AND OCCUPATIONAL THERAPY
AT LOWER LEVEL

10

T U

NS

MB

WB T

FLAMBEAU RIVER

PATIO

AT

LOWER

LEVEL

THE HEBREW HOME FOR THE AGED AT RIVERDALE—ADDITION
Riverdale, New York

ARCHITECT
Gruzen & Partners
New York, New York

PURPOSE
Nursing

CAPACITY
140 beds

COST
$3,000,000 (construction only)

SPONSOR
Hebrew Home for the Aged

Designed to take maximum advantage of sun and site—a hill overlooking the Hudson River and the Jersey Palisades—this 5-story nursing home is a handsome example of contemporary design and materials. The facade of the reinforced concrete building is of board-formed concrete with red brick and solar glass infill panels. These textures combined with ingenious projections of balconies alternating with windowed areas from floor to floor on all four sides of the building give it a highly modeled appearance. This arrangement allows

a large amount of natural light to enter the building. Even interior corridors were designed to exit onto balconies so that sunlight could penetrate the core of the building and create a warm residential feeling.

The first two floors of the building are given over to administrative offices and reception areas, a board room, an occupational therapy suite, and a 2-story-high sheltered workshop. The workshop will be visible from the lobby so that it will serve as a focal point of interest and activity for visitors

1

1 Main entrance, east side of building
2 Vertical lines of board-formed concrete accent modeling at a corner of the building

and residents both. The entry will become the new main entrance for the home which consists of several buildings dating back to World War I. There is a 3-story red brick building, (the brick in the addition was chosen to match), a dining hall, an infirmary, and six cottages.

The new building was not planned to add capacity to the home. It is part of an overall program to relieve crowded conditions and update the older structures. The upper three floors of the new building contain 60 single and 40 double rooms all placed at the perimeter. Every room has a private bath. The center core on each nursing floor contains a nurses' station, medical offices, treatment rooms, service and utility areas, and the patients' dining area, laundry, and bath and shower facilities.

The building has been set slightly below the crest of the hill so that its roof is at the same height as the 3-story building and in such a way that the three floors open out onto grade. Aged patients who dislike climbing can take the elevator and then walk out to other levels.

A 1-story wing set above grade on the north side of the addition connects it to the older building. In addition to facilitating traffic, the wing houses meeting rooms, sitting areas, and a large fireplace. The roof will also serve as a meeting and recreation area for residents and guests. Plans call for a sunken garden, a barbecue pit, and raised planting boxes set around a seating area.

2

continued

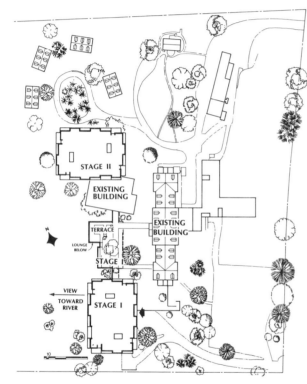

SITE PLAN

2

1 West side of building with connecting
   wing at left
2 Southeast view with river in background
3 Typical double room

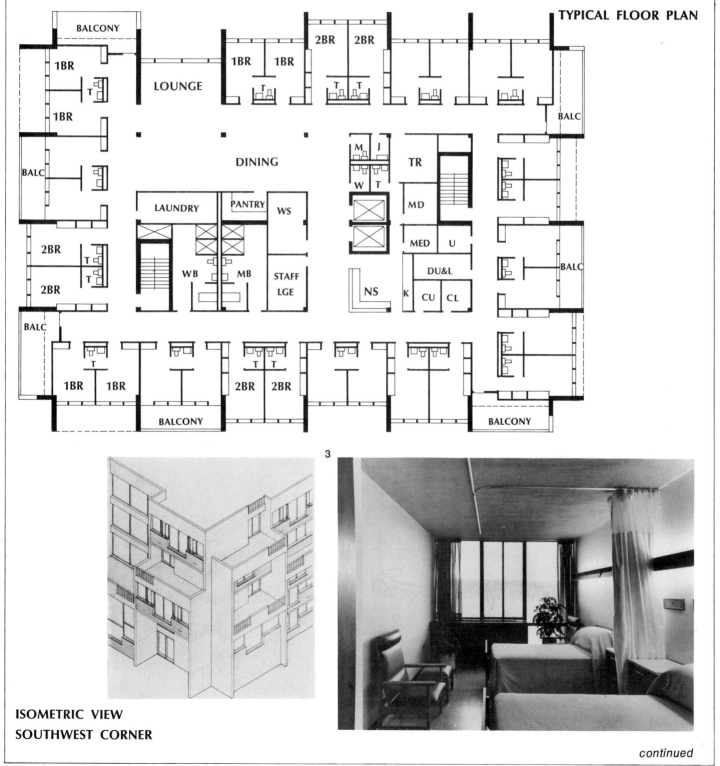

TYPICAL FLOOR PLAN

BALCONY

1BR

T

1BR

BALC

2BR

T
T

2BR

BALC

LOUNGE

1BR | 1BR

2BR | 2BR

T

T | T

DINING

LAUNDRY | PANTRY | WS

WB | MB | STAFF LGE

M | J

W | T

TR

MD

MED | U

DU&L

K | CU | CL

NS

BALC

BALC

1BR | 1BR

T

2BR | 2BR

T | T

BALCONY

BALCONY

3

ISOMETRIC VIEW
SOUTHWEST CORNER

continued

1

2

1 Main lounge in first floor wing connects
  addition to older building
2 Shop near main entrance
3 A view of the river from a typical balcony

3

THE FRIEDMAN BUILDING of the Jewish Home & Hospital for Aged
New York, New York

ARCHITECT
Joseph Douglas Weiss and Associates
New York, New York

PURPOSE
Nursing

CAPACITY
228 beds

COST
$5,500,000 (excluding fees)

SPONSOR
Jewish Home & Hospital for Aged

The 8-story Friedman Building is the most recent addition to one of the oldest and largest facilities for the aged in the world. The Jewish Home and Hospital, founded in 1870 "to help the aged live out their lives in security," consists of a hospital and a number of apartment houses and nursing homes at various locations in New York City. Additions currently planned will bring the total number of residents served to some 1,400.

In addition to providing residential and health care, the Home has pioneered in research and education on the care of the aged, and has extensive clinical, chemical, and research laboratories. The Friedman Building will augment these facilities by adding classrooms for lectures and demonstrations. With these additions the training unit will be the largest ever built as part of an institution.

The home's essential purpose, course, is to care for the elderly. Each of the patient floors in the Friedman Building contains 10 single and 14 double rooms, each with lavatory and toilet facilities. A voice communication system connects each room with the

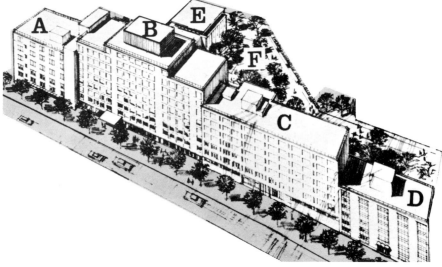

Key
A Sutro Building
B Friedman Building
C Frank Pavilion
D Stern Residence (proposed)
E Goldsmith Building
F "Esther's" Garden

nursing station at the center of the corridor. This part of the building is wider to accommodate a large day and dining room, bathing facilities, a treatment room, and service or utility areas.

On the first floor this wider part has been further extended to connect the Friedman Building to the Goldsmith Building in back. A large 250-seat auditorium, smaller recreation and family rooms, a chapel, library, conference room, and gift shop are found in this area, which also opens out onto "Esther's Garden" with a variety of plantings, walks, and sitting areas.

Other first floor facilities of the Friedman Building include a large social service department, administrative and staff offices, occupational therapy and rehabilitation medicine facilities, a canteen, and an office and lounge for volunteers.

There is a large medical department on the ground floor of the Friedman Building which extends into the Sutro Building next door. The Frank Pavilion, for private patients, lies on the other side. The three interconnected buildings constitute Central House with a total capacity of 517 patients.

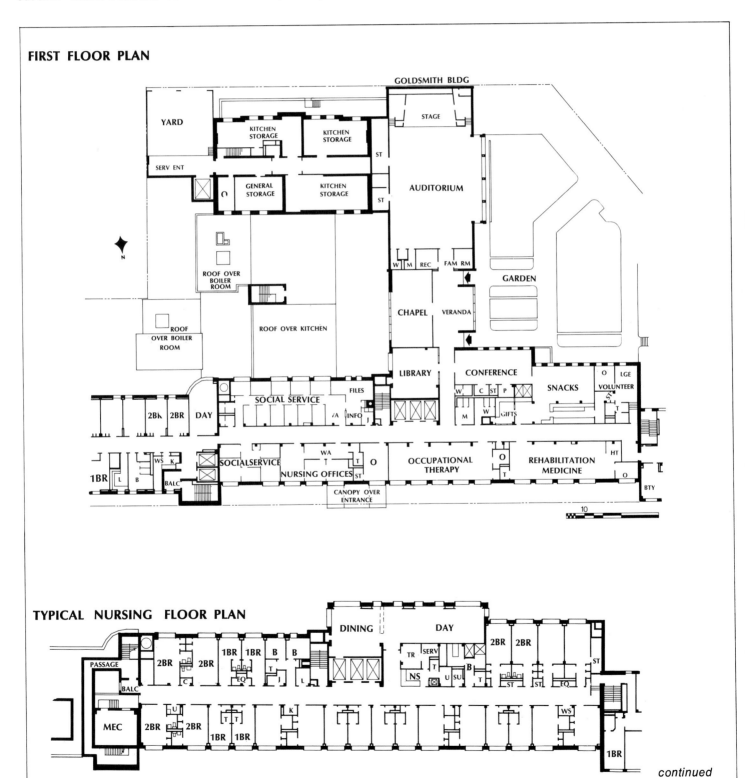

FIRST FLOOR PLAN

TYPICAL NURSING FLOOR PLAN

continued

1

1

2

SITE PLAN

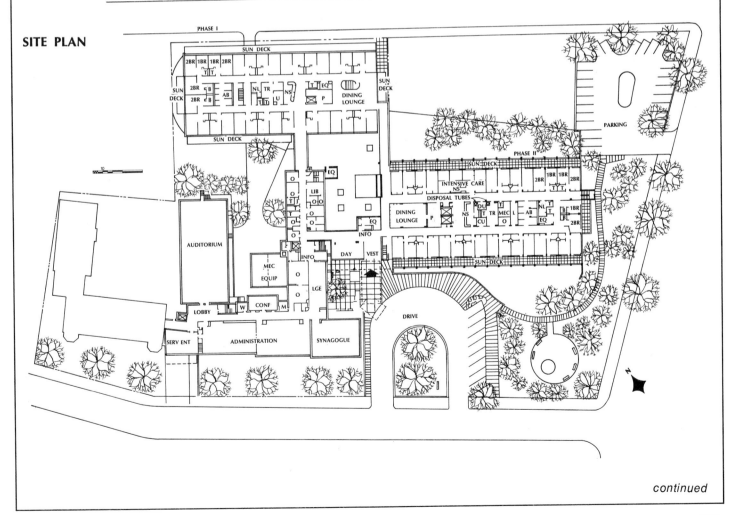

continued

ing a foyer. A toilet room which opens
from the foyer is spacious enough to
allow maneuvering by a person in a
wheelchair. One part of the top floor is
reserved as a private pavilion. Here the
rooms have full bathrooms and are
large enough to permit occupancy by
couples as well as single persons.
Several rooms with interconnecting
soundproof doors may be used as
double room suites.

All rooms open onto a sun deck wide
enough to accommodate a bed. In the
private wing the deck is broken up
by the projections of bathrooms.
Elsewhere the deck forms a continuous
walkway for patients to use for strolling
and socializing, sunning, or cultivating
flowers. Another socializing area is
the roof of the Phase II building which
contains an open garden terrace and a
sheltered lounge for games, cocktails,
and refreshments.

There is a large day room-visiting
area and a pair of dining room-lounges
on each nursing floor. The lounges are
situated in "islands" that run the
length of the buildings. Nurses'
stations, treatment rooms, offices,
supply areas, and central bathing
facilities have also been placed here.
There is a small electronically
monitored intensive care unit with
a separate nursing station on the
first floor.

The doors leading from corridors to
patients' rooms are recessed in alcoves
to avoid an institutional feeling, and
color-coded to aid in identification.
Color-coding is also used on corridor
floors and walls and on the doors
leading to the balconies.

The use of color is one of many
features designed to facilitate patient
movement. Other convenience or
safety features include the use of
levers rather than round knobs on
doors, light switch toggles which
glow in the dark, and doors glazed with
oblong panels to permit visibility from
standing or wheelchair positions.
Bathing facilities have been planned
for the handicapped person. There are
large shower stalls without curbs and
special free-standing tubs raised four
inches from the floor and fitted with
removable front sections. These are at
heights appropriate for use by
wheelchair patients.

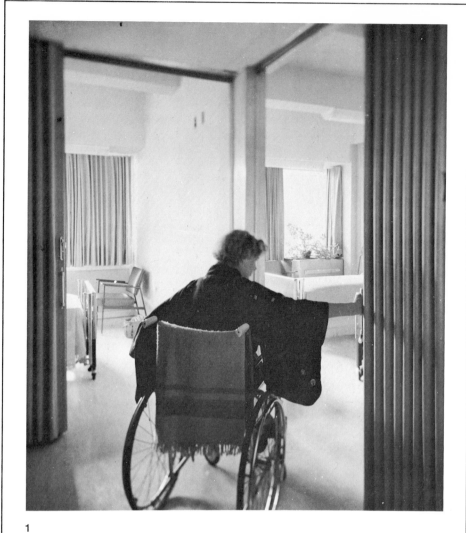

1

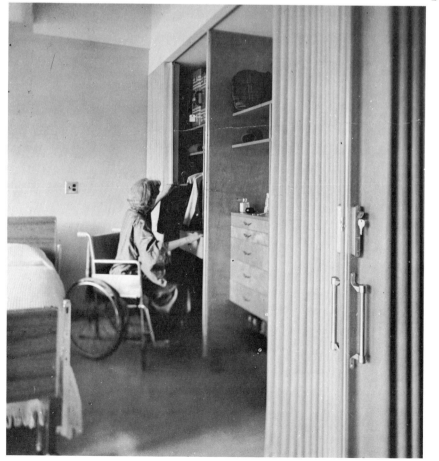

2

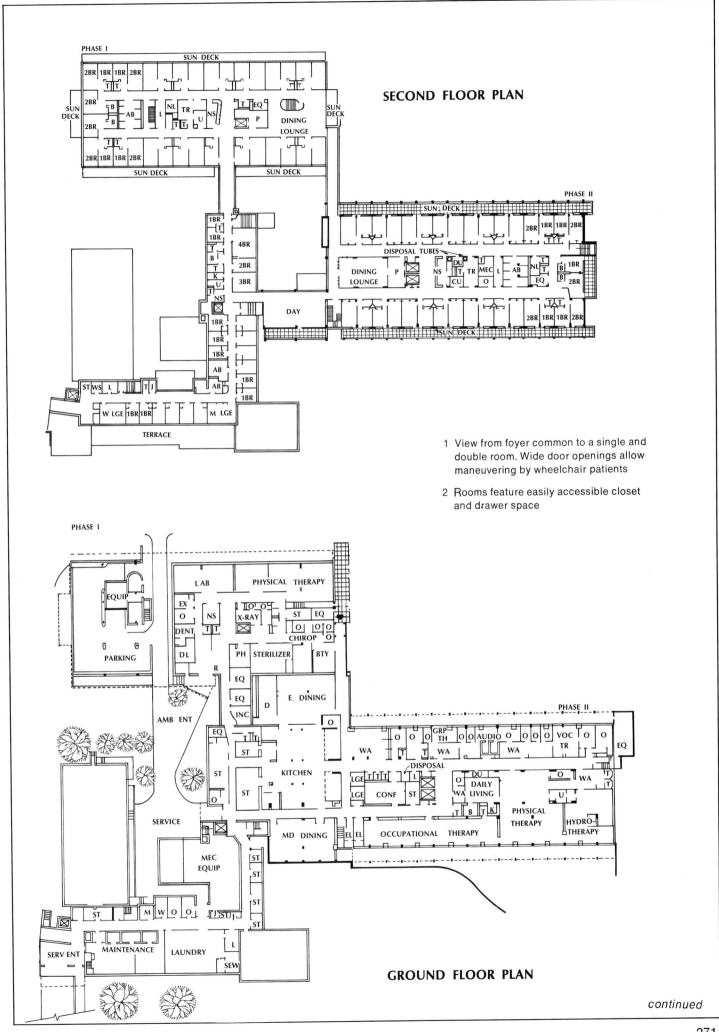

SECOND FLOOR PLAN

PHASE I

SUN DECK

2BR 1BR 1BR 2BR

2BR
SUN DECK
2BR
2BR 1BR 1BR 2BR

SUN DECK

B B AB L NL TR U NS EQ P DINING LOUNGE
T T

SUN DECK

SUN DECK

PHASE II

SUN DECK

2BR 1BR 1BR 2BR

DISPOSAL TUBES

DINING LOUNGE P NS DU CU TR MEC L AB NL EQ B B 1BR 2BR

1BR
1BR
B
K
U
T
NS

4BR
2BR
3BR

DAY

1BR
1BR
1BR
AB
AB
1BR
1BR

ST WS L T J

W LGE 1BR 1BR M LGE

TERRACE

SUN DECK

2BR 1BR 1BR 2BR

1 View from foyer common to a single and double room. Wide door openings allow maneuvering by wheelchair patients

2 Rooms feature easily accessible closet and drawer space

PHASE I

EQUIP
PARKING

LAB
EX O
NS
DENT
DL
R

PHYSICAL THERAPY
X-RAY ST EQ
CHIROP
PH STERILIZER BTY

AMB ENT

EQ
EQ
INC

EQ
ST
ST
O
ST

D E. DINING

KITCHEN

SERVICE

MEC EQUIP

ST
ST
ST
ST
ST

PHASE II

GRP TH AUDIO VOC EQ
WA WA WA TR
DISPOSAL
LGE DU WA
LGE CONF ST WA DAILY LIVING
T B K PHYSICAL THERAPY
U HYDRO-THERAPY
MD DINING EL EL OCCUPATIONAL THERAPY

SERV ENT
MAINTENANCE
LAUNDRY
M W O O J ST
SEW

GROUND FLOOR PLAN

continued

Rooms are equipped with central
oxygen and suction systems, an audio-
visual call and intercommunication
system, and alarm signals in toilets
and baths. Corridors and bath areas
are fitted with handrails or grab bars.

Of interest is a waste disposal system
designed to minimize the chance of
infection. There are two 16-inch
pneumatic tubes, one for waste, the
other for soiled items.

The Phase I building is steel encased
in a concrete frame. Floors and
balconies are reinforced concrete
slab. Exterior walls are brick masonry.
Windows and exterior doors are
aluminum; stairways are steel and
concrete. Floors are finished in sheet
rubber except in bath, cleaning, and
pantry areas where ceramic tile
is used.

The Phase II building has a reinforced
concrete frame with exposed exterior
concrete columns and brick masonry
walls. Partitions are steel stud faced
with a double layer of gypsum board
on each side. Epoxy terrazzo flooring
is used in the physical medicine,
rehabilitation, sanitation, and food
service areas. All ceilings are
acoustically treated. The facility is
centrally air-conditioned with
individual thermostatic controls in
every room.

1

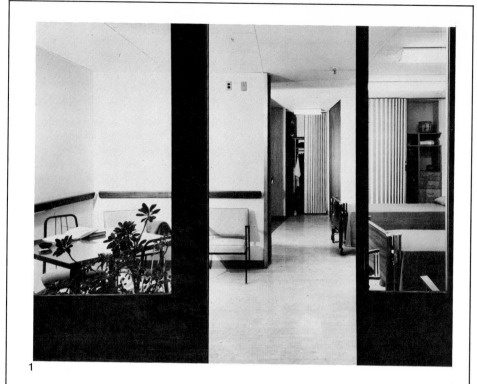

2

1 View from balcony into a suite for couples
  in Phase I building. It consists of a sitting
  area, bed area, full bath, and two
  wardrobe units

2 Typical lounge and balcony on a
  patient floor

ST. JOHN'S HOME OF MILWAUKEE—ADDITION
Milwaukee, Wisconsin

ARCHITECT
Losch & Haeuser
Milwaukee, Wisconsin

PURPOSE
Nursing

CAPACITY
54 beds

COST
$763,000

SPONSOR
Episcopal Church

What is the optimal way to expand a nursing home in a crowded downtown area where space is both limited and expensive? The architects of the Saint John's addition drew two plans; one rectangular, the other circular. When they compared the two it was clear that the circular scheme would be more practical. Not only would such a plan take up less ground space, but if the patients' rooms were placed around the rim there would be a high ratio of room to corridor area, the rooms would be easily accessible from an inner circular hallway, and all patients could be provided with large windowed views.

So the novel 3-story structure was built, with the modification that the drum-shaped patient floors are cantilevered out over a rectangular-shaped ground floor. The setback at the lower level provides space for parking and landscaping, and creates a platform for the circular part. The architects felt that this would have the esthetic advantage of making the building appear lighter and more graceful than if the whole structure were round, sitting on the ground like a fat silo.

A part of the first floor of the new structure extends beyond the circular overhang to connect the new and old buildings. The dining room, kitchen, and administrative offices have been placed here, while above this there is a roof garden and a circular solarium/chapel. The solarium is directly accessible from the second floor of the adjacent buildings.

The 50 residents of the original home represent a well population. The extension was designed for semi-ambulatory or bedfast patients. The second and third floors each contain four semi-private and 14 single rooms. The third floor constitutes a hospital floor, with a treatment room, dentist's and chiropodist's offices, a laboratory, and diet kitchen in the center ring. Five rooms on the first floor can be converted for nursing care use.

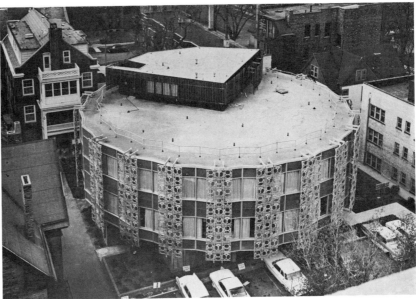

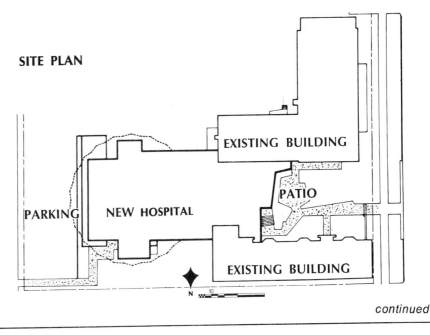

SITE PLAN

EXISTING BUILDING

PATIO

PARKING   NEW HOSPITAL

N   10

EXISTING BUILDING

continued

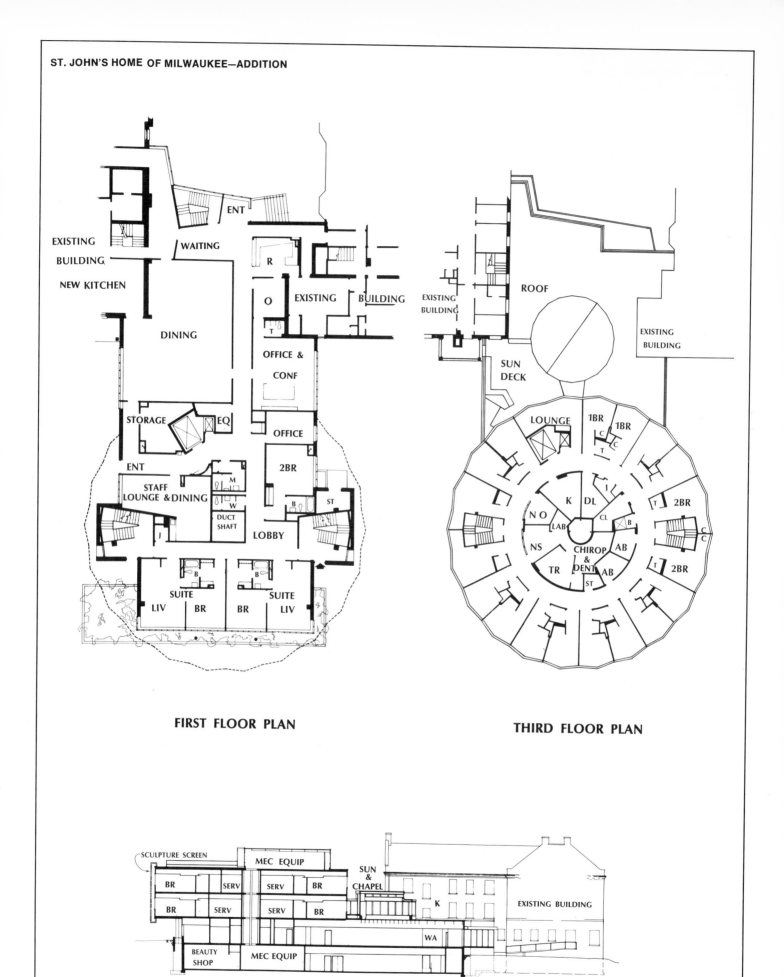

FIRST FLOOR PLAN

THIRD FLOOR PLAN

SECTION

All patient rooms have wide glass window walls with cast aluminum sculptural projections. These decorative accents were added primarily for esthetic reasons, but they also give patients a sense of privacy and security, and offer some protection from the sun. The rooms are heated by hot water circulating through coils above radiant metal ceiling panels. The perforated panels provide ventilation as well. A 9-foot diameter shaft running through the central core of the building carries the bulk of mechanical services to a penthouse unit on the roof. This also conceals all the roof equipment except the cooling tower.

When the architects considered the structural framework for the unusual building they again compared two different approaches. Given a choice of a traditional steel framing or concrete flat lift slab, they chose the slab. Not only were there inherent economies in using concrete, but the lower total height would serve the circular form well.

After footings and foundations were poured, the columns were erected and the first floor slab was poured. A combination curing and separating compound was then sprayed on the surface. Next, forms were made for the circular second, third, and roof slabs, and steel collars were welded to the slabs' reinforcing bars. The collars slip up around the columns, and the slabs are lifted up into position.

In specifying the interior finishing of the building, the architects stressed both the psychological and functional use of color. Bright colors were to be used in areas not likely to be seen for long periods of time; neutral ones would suit places like the walls opposite the beds in patient rooms. Patient room doors were to be individualized through a variety of stencil patterns. But general purpose entryways were to be color-coded. Thus elevator doors, dumbwaiters, and stair entries are all painted red; nurses' stations are blue-gray; toilet doors are natural birch.

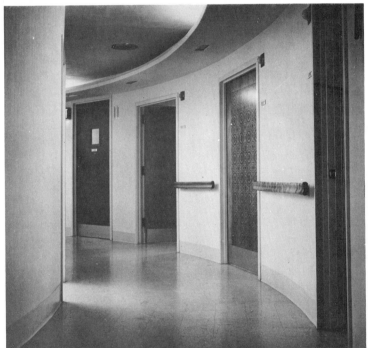

Room furnishings and lighting were chosen to simulate residential décor. Where possible, antique furnishings from the original home were incorporated.

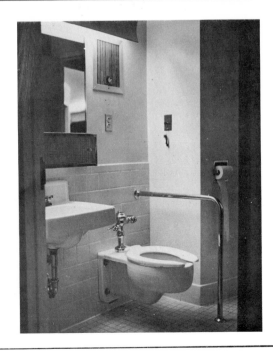

KAHL HOME FOR THE AGED AND INFIRM
Davenport, Iowa

ARCHITECT
Stewart, Robison, Laffan
Davenport, Iowa

PURPOSE
Nursing

CAPACITY
112 beds

COST
$1,388,524

SPONSOR
Catholic Diocese of Davenport
Operated by The Carmelite Sisters

Situated high on a bluff overlooking the Mississippi River, this 5-story extension to a 30-bed nursing home was designed to tie into the existing structure lower on the slope. Both buildings will share the new kitchen, dining and recreation area at the ground level of the addition. Seating capacity for the dining room is 230, anticipating future expansion. The canopied main entrance is on the first floor.

The three stories above the main entrance as well as part of the first floor are devoted to patients' bedrooms, 43 double rooms and 26 singles. There is a nursing station and a parlor on each floor.

A modern chapel with angled side walls and curved sanctuary lies directly in line with the main entrance and extends into the garden at the rear. Highlighting the west wall of the sanctuary are abstractly patterned stained glass windows. The chapel will seat 150, including 20 wheelchair patients at the rear.

The building's beams and joists are concrete and the exterior is finished in brick. Ceilings and steel stud partitions are plastered. The building is air-conditioned and patients' rooms are equipped with fan coil units adjustable for heating and·cooling.

1

1 View of the administration wing (first floor rear) showing part of the side of the chapel

2 Main entrance

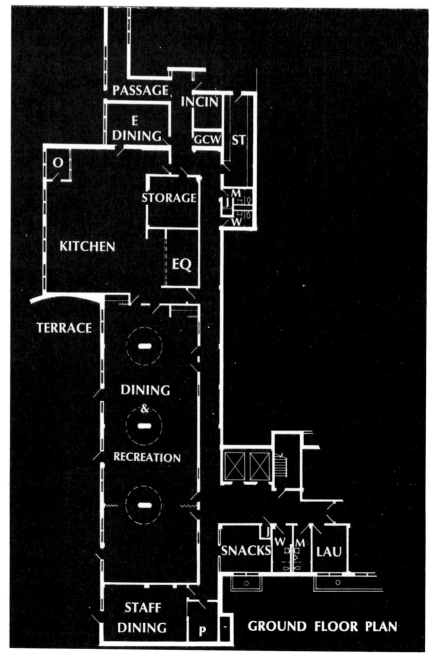

PASSAGE

INCIN

E DINING

GCW ST

O

STORAGE

M
W

KITCHEN

EQ

TERRACE

DINING
&
RECREATION

SNACKS W M LAU

STAFF
DINING P

GROUND FLOOR PLAN

2

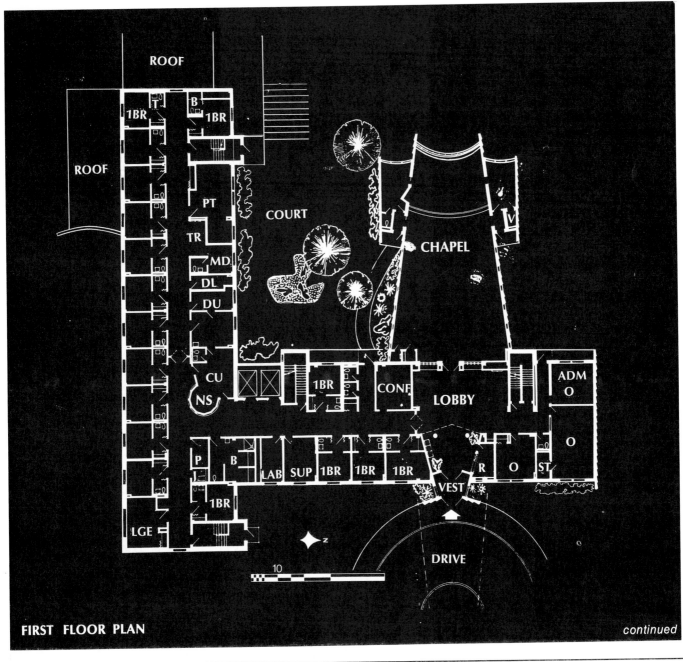

ROOF

ROOF

1BR · T · B · 1BR

PT

TR

MD

DL

DU

CU

NS

P · B

1BR

LGE

COURT

LAB · SUP · 1BR · 1BR · 1BR

CHAPEL

CONF

LOBBY

VEST

R · O · ST

ADM
O

O

DRIVE

10

FIRST FLOOR PLAN

continued

1

2

1 Curved west wall of sanctuary and
  sacristy
2 The sanctuary of the chapel
3 Main lobby

3

Federal Prototypes for Nursing Homes

The Federal government's increasing interest in the housing and health care of the aged is reflected in the architectural prototype plans shown on the following pages. In addition to recommended floor plans, typical room layouts are shown along with descriptions of the equipment and furnishings recommended.

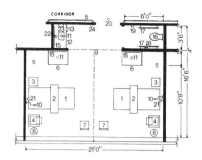

TWO BED ROOM PLAN

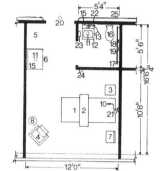

ONE BED ROOM PLAN

EQUIPMENT LEGEND

1. Adjustable height bed
2. Overbed table
3. Bedside cabinet
4. Easy chair with ottoman
5. Built-in locker
6. Built-in dresser
7. Straight chair
8. Floor lamp
9. Cubicle curtain
10. Nurses' calling station
11. Wall bracket light
12. Lavatory
13. Receptacle, waste, foot-operated closed top
14. Shelf
15. Mirror
16. Water closet
17. Grab rail
18. Toilet paper fixture
19. Nurses' calling station
20. Corridor signal light
21. Bed light
22. Soap dispenser
23. Paper towel dispenser
24. Night light
25. Hand rail

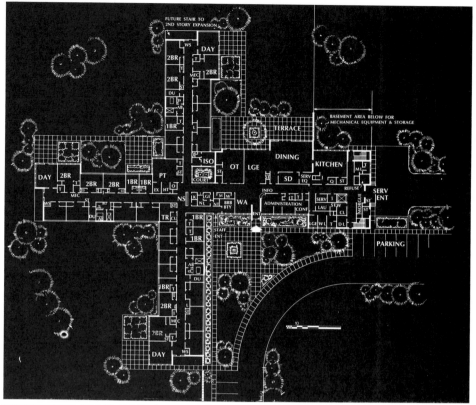

PROTOTYPE PLAN FOR A 50-BED NURSING FACILITY

Designing a nursing home is like solving a mathematical problem in game theory. You have certain rules—health standards, building codes, government regulations—and certain parameters—the number of patients, the type of facility, location, budget. You want to come up with a winning solution: a successful design, esthetically pleasing, economical to build and service, psychologically satisfying to both patients and staff. Obviously there is no unique strategy for winning this game, but certain techniques are more flexible. They can be applied under a variety of conditions of climate, site, purpose, and the like, and they lend themselves readily to expansion and extension of services.

Such "strategies" describe the prototype plans for a 50-bed nursing home and a larger 164-to-248 bed facility designed by the Architectural, Engineering and Equipment Branch of the Division of Hospitals and Medical Facilities of the United States Public Health Service.

Variations of these strategies have appeared throughout this volume in what have been called "cross-shaped," "X-shaped," or "cruciform" plans. In the case of the larger facility, the plan is the satellite type in which a cluster of cross-shaped pavilions surround a central communal activities building. These designs are popular because they are sound architectural ideas which have proven their effectiveness in use.

In the 50-bed cruciform plan the patient rooms are distributed in three wings which extend from a central core area. The core is both the control center, with a nurses' station at the intersection of the patient wings, and the focal region for group activities or services for patients and visitors. Here are found occupational and physical therapy rooms, a beauty and barber shop, the entrance lobby, the main lounge, and offices. The fourth wing provides additional group facilities—it contains the dining room and kitchen—and also incorporates the employees' lockers and areas for general storage, mechanical equipment, and other supporting or service facilities.

The size of the home—50 beds—was chosen on the basis of a survey by the American Nursing Home Association which showed that the average number of beds in existing homes was 41.5. The size is also considered ideal in terms of maintaining a residential or home-like atmosphere and keeping within an efficient operating budget.

The larger satellite facility is a natural development of the 50-bed plan. Instead of patient wings extending from a common core, separate 1-story cross-shaped buildings are connected to a large central core building.

PROTOTYPE PLAN FOR CORE & SATELLITE TYPE OF NURSING FACILITY

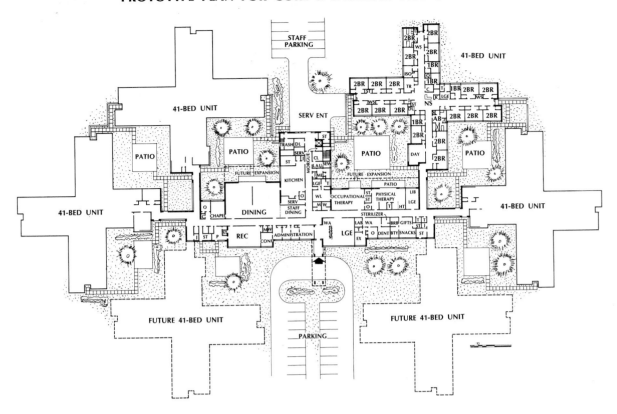

All wings of the patient pavilions are used for patient rooms, (capacity is 41 beds), with a nurses' station, a treatment room, and assisted bathing facilities at the central intersection. The dining room and kitchen are placed in the core building along with other ancillary facilities.

The value and variety of such ancillary facilities, the amount of space which should be allotted to them as well as to patient rooms, and the detailed description of equipment, materials, safety, and convenience features which are recommended for nursing homes are described at length in the introduction and will not be dealt with here. We may, however, take note of a few highlights in the Federal prototype plans which exemplify the careful human engineering which has contributed to the success of these designs:

- The cruciform layout cuts down on corridor length, creating a more residential atmosphere and providing more efficient nursing control.

- Small, separate wings permit the distribution of patients according to sex, severity of illness, common interests, or other criteria.

- The majority of rooms are doubles, with dimensions permitting the placement of beds so that each occupant has a window view. (Several single-bed rooms are provided for isolation of infectious patients or for the seriously ill.)

- Depending on variables in construction materials and methods, there may be inherent economies in placing the long dimensions of patient rooms parallel to the long dimension of the wing.

- The physical therapy room opens onto a patio which may be used for outdoor exercise.

- Exterior space, (especially in the satellite arrangement), falls naturally into a variety of areas which may be used for gardens, recreational activity, sitting, or strolling. Some of these courts may be enclosed on all four sides affording wind protection; some may be covered with a sunshade or more permanent cover for year-round use.

- Additions to a satellite facility can take place with a minimum amount of discomfort to the patients since the buildings are individual self-contained units. On the other hand if the site is limited, patient units may be stacked: The plan lends itself to use in a multi-story building as well as in horizontal extensions.

BIBLIOGRAPHY Banfield, Edward C. and Grodzins, Morton. *Government and Housing in Metropolitan Areas.* New York: McGraw-Hill Book Co., 1958.

Barker, Michael B. *California Retirement Communities.* Berkeley: Center for Real Estate and Urban Economics, Institute of Urban and Regional Development, University of California, 1966.

Berezin, Martin and Stanley, C. *Geriatric Psychiatry: Grief, loss and emotional disorders in the aging process.* New York: International Universities Press, 1965.

Beyer, Glenn H. *Housing and Society.* New York: Macmillan Co., 1965.

Beyer, Glenn H. and Nierstrasz, F.H.J. *Housing the Aged in Western Countries.* New York: Elsevier Publishing Co., 1967.

Burgess, Ernest W., ed. *Aging in Western Societies.* Chicago: University of Chicago Press, 1960. ————. *Retirement Villages.* Ann Arbor: University of Michigan, 1961.

Cicero, Marcus Tullius. *De Senectute.* ("On Old Age.") Edited by Leonard Huxley. Oxford: Oxford University Press, 1923.

Clark, Margaret, Ph.D., and Anderson, Barbara G., Ph.D. *Culture and Aging, An Anthropological Study of Older Americans.* Springfield: Charles C. Thomas, 1967.

Cooley, Frederick Leland, and Cooley, Lee Morrison. *The Retirement Trap.* New York: Doubleday & Co., 1965.

Cornell University. *Housing Requirements of the Aged; A Study of Design Criteria.* Ithaca: Cornell University Housing Research Center, 1958.

de Ropp, Robert S. *Man Against Aging.* New York: St. Martin's Press, 1960.

Donahue, Wilma, *et al. Management of Public Housing for the Elderly; Background Readings: A Collection of Papers.* publ. no. 487. Washington, D.C.: National Association of Housing and Redevelopment Officials, 1965.

Field, Minna. *Aging With Honor and Dignity.* Springfield: Charles C. Thomas, 1968.

Finzi, Bruno, M.D. *Contributo Alla Storia della Geriátrica a Venezia.* Venice: Ospedale Geriátrica Guistinian, 1964.

Frush, James. *The Retirement Residence; An Analysis of the Architecture and Management of Life-care Housing.* Springfield: Charles C. Thomas, 1968.

Frush, James, and Eshenbach, Benson. *Housing—Costs and Financing.* Springfield: Charles C. Thomas, 1968.

Geist, Harold. *The Psychological Aspect of Retirement.* Springfield: Charles C. Thomas, 1968.

Good, Lawrence R., Siegel, Jane W., and Bay, Alfred P., eds. *Therapy by Design; Implications of Architecture for Human Behavior.* Springfield: Charles C. Thomas, 1965.

Hansen, P. From, ed. *Age With a Future: Proceedings of the Sixth International Congress of Gerontology, Copenhagen, 1963.* Philadelphia: F. A. Davis Company, 1964.

Kurtz, Russell H., ed. *Manual for Homes for the Aged.* New York: Federation of Protestant Welfare Agencies, Inc., 1965.

Leeds, Morton, and Shore, Herbert, eds. *Geriatric Institutional Management.* New York: G. P. Putnam & Sons, 1964.

McQuillan, Florence L. *Fundamentals of Nursing Home Administration.* Philadelphia: W. B. Saunders, 1967.

Musson, Noverre, and Hensinkveld, Helen. *Buildings for the Elderly.* New York: Reinhold Publishing Corporation, 1963.

National Council of Social Services. *The Elderly; Handbook on Care and Services.* London: National Old Peoples Welfare Council, 1968.

National Council on the Aging. *Buildings for Older People.* New York: National Council on the Aging, 1961.

Nicholson, Edna E. *Planning New Institutional Facilities for Long-Term Care.* New York: G. P. Putnam & Sons, 1956.

Paul, Samuel. *Apartments, Their Design and Development.* New York: Reinhold Publishing Co., 1967.

Roth, Julius A., and Eddy, Elizabeth M. *Rehabilitation for the Unwanted.* New York: Atherton Press, 1967.

Rutherford, Robert B., M.D., and Holst, Arthur J. eds. *Architectural Designs: Homes for the Aged; the European Approach.* Peoria: Howard Company, 1963.

Shanas, Ethel; Townsend, Peter; Wedderburn, Dorothy; Friis, Henning; Milhøj; and Stehouwer, Jan. *Old People in Three Industrial Societies.* New York: Atherton Press, 1968.

Simon, Anne W. *The New Years, a New Middle Age.* New York: Alfred A. Knopf, 1968.

Tibbitts, Clark, and Donahue, Wilma. *Aging in the Modern World; A Guidebook for Leaders; A Series of Adult Study Discussion Programs.* Ann Arbor: University of Michigan Institute for Human Adjustment, 1957.

United States Department of Health, Education and Welfare. *Human Aging: A Biological and Behavioral Study.* Edited by James E. Birren, *et al.* Public Health Service Publication No. 986. Bethesda: National Institute of Mental Health, 1963.

Vivrett, Walter K. "Housing and Community Settings for Older People." *Handbook of Social Gerontology: Societal Aspects of Aging.* Edited by Clark Tibbitts. Chicago: University of Chicago Press, 1960.

Pamphlets

Beyer, Glenn H. *Economic Aspects of Housing for the Aged.* Research Report No. 46. Ithaca: Cornell University, 1961.

Beyer, Glenn H., and Woods, Margaret E. *Living and Activity Patterns of the Aged.* Cornell Research Program on Housing for the Aged; Report No. 6. Ithaca: Cornell University, 1963.

Brown, Albert M. *The Story of Council Gardens, A Design for Elderly Living.* Ohio: Council Gardens, 1967.

Caravaty, Raymond D., and Haviland, D. S. *Life Safety From Fire, A Guide for Housing the Elderly.* Troy: Center for Architectural Research, Rensselaer Polytechnic Institute, 1967.

Diamond, Beverly, ed. *Furniture Requirements for Older People.* New York: National Council on the Aging, 1963.

Douglas Fir Plywood Ass'n. *Builders Guide to the Retirement Home Market.* Tacoma, Washington.

Eltz, Sylvia. *Housing for the Aged and Disabled in Sweden.* Stockholm: Swedish Institute for Cultural Relations With Foreign Countries, 1965.

Joint Commission of Accreditation of Hospitals. *Standards for Accreditation of Extended Care Facilities: Nursing Care Facilities and Resident Care Facilities.* Chicago: JCAH, 1968.

Kälvesten, Anna-Lisa. *Social Benefits in Sweden.* Stockholm: Swedish Institute for Cultural Relations With Foreign Countries, 1965.

Laroque, Pierre. *Politigue De La Vieillesse: Rapport de la Commission d'Étude des Problémes de la Vieillesse.* Paris: La Documentation Française, 1962.

Levine, Myra A. *Proxemics and Patient Care.* Chicago: Loyola University School of Nursing, 1967.

Liebowitz, Bernard. *An Experiment in Environmental Change and Proxemics; Implications for Homes For the Aged.* Philadelphia: Philadelphia Geriatric Center, 1967.

Lowman, Edward W., M.D., and Rusk, Howard A., M.D. *Self-Help Devices.* Monograph 21. New York: New York Medical Center Institute of Physical Medicine and Rehabilitation, 1963.

Michanek, Ernst. *Housing Standards and Housing Construction in Sweden, Facts and Views Compiled.* Stockholm, Swedish Institute for Cultural Relations With Foreign Countries, 1964.

National Swedish Institute for Building Research. *Study of Dimensions of Equipment in Housing for Old Persons.* Stockholm: National Swedish Institute for Building Research, 1965.

New York University Graduate School of Public Administration. *Bibliography: Management of Housing for the Elderly. New York: New York University, 1962.*

Rudfield, Kursten. *Welfare of the Aged in Denmark.* Copenhagen: Det Danske Selskab, 1963.

The Retirement Hotel. Cornell Hotel and Administration Quarterly Reprint, Ithaca: Cornell University. February, 1961.

U.S. Bureau of Family Services. *Foster Family Care for the Aged.* Report No. 56 P. A. Washington, D.C.: U.S. Government Printing Office, 1965.

U.S. Department of Housing and Urban Development. *Minimum Property Standards; Housing for the Elderly With Special Consideration for the Handicapped.* Publication No. 46. Washington, D.C.: U.S. Government Printing Office, 1967. (Ask for latest bulletins.)

U.S. Department of Housing and Urban Development. *Minimum Property Standards for Nursing Homes.* Washington, D.C.: U.S. Government Printing Office, 1967.

U.S. Federal Housing Administration. *Intensity of Development and Livability of Multi-Family Housing Projects.* Washington, D.C.: U.S. Government Printing Office, 1963.

U.S. Public Health Service. *Nursing Homes: Environmental Health Factors; A Syllabus.* P. H. S. Publication No. 1009. Washington, D.C.: U.S. Government Printing Office, 1967.

U.S. Public Health Service. *Nursing Homes: Environmental Health Factors.* (21 Pamphlets.) P. H. S. Publication Nos. 1009 - 1030. Washington, D.C.: U.S. Government Printing Office, 1963.

U.S. Congress, Senate, Committee on Aging. *Long Range Programs and Research Needs in Aging and Related Fields.* Survey, 90th Cong., 1st sess., Part I. Washington, D.C.; U.S. Government Printing Office, 1968.

Winkler, Revy, and Savage, Peg. *Sex and The Senior Citizen.* New York: Frederick Fell, Inc., 1968.

Articles

Frillin, Calvin. "Wake Up and Live." *The New Yorker,* XL (April 4, 1964), 120-177.

Kassabaum, George E. "Housing For The Elderly: Technical Standards of Design." *Journal of American Institute of Architects,* vol. 38 (Sept., 1962), 61-65.

"Normal and Abnormal Sex Behavior in Aging." *Geriatric Focus,* vol. 7 (July-August, 1968), 1, 5-6.

The Gerontologist. Gerontological Society. vol. 8, no. 2, 1968.

Zelditch, Morris. "The Home for Aged—A Community." *Journal of Jewish Communal Service,* October, 1961.

Zelditch, Morris, and Bram, Howard. "The Modern Home for the Aged." *The Gerontologist,* vol. 5 (June, 1965), 67-73.

ILLUSTRATION CREDITS

Pgs. 39, 40, 41—Marvin Lyons, Los Angeles, Calif.; 42, 49 (bottom)—Lindemuth Photo, Columbia, O.; 44 (top)—Dambrans Photo, Columbus, O.; 48 (top)—Squire Haskins, Dallas, Tex.; 48 (bottom), 50—Bleeker Green, John Rogers & Herschel Fisher, Dallas, Texas; 51—Louis Checkman, Jersey City, N. J.; 52 (bottom), 54—Amir Farr, Los Angeles, Calif.; 56, 57 (upper right & bottom)—Watkins Associates, St. Louis, Mo.; 60 (top)—Coda, Englewood, N. J.; 60 (bottom), 61 (right)—Chilton—Butler, Ridgewood, N. J.; 64, 65—Harvey Patteson, San Antonio, Tex.; 66 (bottom two), 67—Joel Strasser, Sioux Falls, S. D.; 73 (top), 74, 75—Clyde May, Atlanta, Ga.; 80 (rendering)—Dale Fisher Associates, Ann Arbor, Mich.; 80, 82, 83—General Electric; 84—Ken Kuwahara, Honolulu, Hawaii; 85—Herbert Bauer, Honolulu, Hawaii; 86, 87—James Y. Young, Honolulu, Hawaii; 88, 89—Darrell Thompson, Atlanta, Ga.; 90, 91, 92—Orlando R. Cabanban, Oak Park, Ill.; 95, 96, 97—Rondal Partridge, Cambridge, Mass.; 100 (bottom two), 104 (top left), 105—Ed Unterman, Tropical Graphic Arts, Miami, Fla.; 101—Creative Direction for Advertising, Miami, Fla.; 104 (bottom)—Spot News, Perrine, Fla.; 108—Max Gruzen, New York, N. Y.; 114, 116—Ezra Stoller Associates, Rye, N. Y.; 117, 118, 119—Bill Harris, St. Louis, Mo.; 120—H. Bernstein, Yonkers, N. Y.; 121 (top left)—Mal Gurian Assoc., New York, N. Y.; 121 (top right), 123—Irene B. Bayer, New York, N. Y.; 124, 125, 126, 127, 128—St. Joseph's Hospital, Houston, Tex.; 130, 131, 132—Sundahl, Stockholm, Sweden; 133, 134, 135, 136, 137—Marianne Gotz, Stuttgart, West Germany; 146, 147, 148—Lennart Olson, Bandhagen, Sweden; 154, 155, 156, 157, 158—Chris F. Payne, Montreal, Canada; 164—Fotografia Ferruzzi, Venice, Italy; 166 (top two), 167 (top two)—Foto Mattiazzo, Venice, Italy; 167 (bottom right)—R. Barascuitti, Fotoreportage, Venice, Italy; 177, 178—William Wollin Studio, Madison, Wis.; 180—J. Alexander, Wheaton, Md.; 181—E. Cross, Washington, D.C.; 184, 186—Cliff E. Lohs, Elgin, Ill.; 185, 187—Elgin Daily Courier-News, Elgin, Ill.; 194—Fairly Chandler, Magnolia Springs, Ala.; 196, 197—Douglas Lyttle, Kalamazoo, Mich.; 198, 201 (top left)—Fairfax Nursing Home, Fairfax, Minn.; 204 (bottom), 205—Greenbough Nursing Center, Clarksdale, Miss.; 204 (rendering)—QA Architectural Arts, Los Angeles, Calif.; 206, 207—Clyde May, Atlanta, Ga.; 211, 212, 213—Architectural Art, Lansing, Mich.; 220 (rendering)—QA Architectural Arts, Los Angeles, Calif.; 224, 225, 227—Philip A. Turner, Chicago, Ill.; 226, 227 (rendering)—QA Architectural Arts, Los Angeles, Calif.; 232, 233, 234, (top two)—Alexandre Georges, New City, N. Y.; 234 (bottom)—George Cserna, New York, N. Y.; 240, 242, 243, 244—Lawrence S. Williams, Upper Darby, Pa.; 246 (bottom), 247—Chicago Photographers, Chicago, Ill.; 248 (renderings)—Barbara Dorn and Associates, San Francisco, Calif.; 250, 251—John Davidson, Bryan, O.; 258, 259, 260, 261, 262, 263—Maxon Gruzen, John Hill, Peter Samton, New York, N. Y.; 264, 266—H. Bernstein, Yonkers, N. Y.; 267—Paulus Leeser, New York, N. Y.; 268, 270, 272—Kay Harris, New York, N. Y.; 273 (top), 275—Walter Sheffer, Milwaukee, Wis.; 276, 277, 278—Tony Kelly, Davenport, Ia.